Oh Brother, where art thou?

✝

St Luke's is an independent, acute surgical hospital. 255 honorary consultants give their time for free and every year we carry out hundreds of operations and provide life-saving treatment for your brothers and sisters in the clergy. This is only made possible by the generosity of your parishioners and we ask that you remember us in your weekly collection. One day it may be you that needs our help.

Tel 020 7388 4954 fax 020 7383 4812
email stluke@stlukeshospital.org.uk
www.stlukeshospital.org.uk Registered Charity No. 209236

THE

CHURCH PULPIT

YEAR BOOK

2005

*Sermons for Sundays, Holy Days,
Festivals and Special Occasions
Year A*

edited by Dr J. Critchlow

CANTERBURY
PRESS
Norwich

© Canterbury Press 2004

First published in 2004 by the Canterbury Press Norwich
(a publishing imprint of Hymns Ancient & Modern Limited,
a registered charity)
St Mary's Works, St Mary's Plain,
Norwich, Norfolk, NR3 3BH

www.scm-canterburypress.co.uk

British Library Cataloguing in Publication data

A catalogue record for this book is available
from the British Library

ISBN 1-85311-583-5

Typeset by Rowland Phototypesetting Limited,
Bury St Edmunds, Suffolk
Printed in Great Britain by
St Edmundsbury Press Limited, Bury St Edmunds, Suffolk

Editor's Preface

In a world where increasingly short-term, immediate gratification seems only a credit-card transaction away, I am often given a rather blank stare when I ask someone: 'What is your long-term expectation?'

'The Second Coming of Christ' is definitely not the answer that springs to most people's lips. Yet surely this is the highest and best expectation one can have! Doesn't Jesus not only assure us that it will come, but also imply that we have the challenge of helping it to come sooner rather than later (Matt. 24.14; Mark 13.10)?

As we use the sermons in this, the 102nd *Church Pulpit Year Book*, can we not pray with renewed expectation that the words will fall on receptive ears, on good ground, and that the fruitfullest of harvests will ensue? I am writing this Preface as news has come through of the discovery of many new dialects in India, a country that already holds the record for the greatest number and variety of dialects and languages. 'Minority' tongues these may be – but together they represent many millions of people who still do not have even a part of the Bible in translation.

Do we really want to colonize the moon, before reaching all the nations on earth with God's Good News? Is it more important to even out the GDP or National Debts, than to share the message of Christian salvation? 'Listening out' for Jesus earned Mary the highest praise anyone could wish for (Luke 10.42). May every Christian of 2005 follow in her steps.

Matt. 24.14 and Mark 13.10 may seem too great an expectation, in purely human terms; but with the God who kicks the 'im' from 'impossible' on our side, we already have the victory in faith!

J.C.
Advent 2003

CONTENTS

Unless otherwise stated, the readings are taken from *The Christian Year: Calendar, Lectionary and Collects* (London: Church House Publishing, 2000) and are for Year A.

2004

Nov. 28   **First Sunday of Advent**
Principal Service: Isa. 2.5; Matt. 24.44 Walking in the Light of the Lord 1
Second Service: Isa. 52.9 Sing It Loud! 3

Dec. 5   **Second Sunday of Advent**
Principal Service: Matt. 3.12 Wheat – and Chaff 5
Second Service: 1 Kings 18.21 On the Lord's Side. 7

Dec. 12   **Third Sunday of Advent**
Principal Service: Matt. 11.4–5 Proof – If You Need It 10
Second Service: Acts 13.36 Serving God's Purpose 12

Dec. 19   **Fourth Sunday of Advent**
Principal Service: Matt. 1.20 A Gift from God. 14
Second Service: Rev. 22.16 The Bright Morning Star. 16

Dec. 24   **Christmas Eve**
Morning Eucharist: Luke 1.72 God Has Remembered. 18

Dec. 25   **Christmas Day**
Midnight or early Eucharist: Luke 2.20 And It Is True! 20
In the day: Principal Service: John 1.12–13 Born Again 22
Second Service: Isa. 65.24; Phil. 2.5 Supreme Encouragement. ... 25

Dec. 26   **First Sunday of Christmas**
Principal Service: Matt. 2.14–15 This Was to Fulfil 27
Second Service: Phil. 2.1–2 Christ the Encourager 29

2005

Jan. 2   **Second Sunday of Christmas**
Principal Service: John 1.18 The Unseen God?. 31
Second Service: Col. 1.11–12a Divine Provision. 33

Jan. 9   **Baptism of Christ** (First Sunday of Epiphany)
Principal Service: Isa. 42.4; Matt. 3.16 Until. 35
Second Service: Heb. 1.3 Word of Power 37

Jan. 16   **Second Sunday of Epiphany**
Principal Service: John 1.35–36 God's at Work 39
Second Service: Ezek. 3.4; Gal. 1.11–12 Our Gospel 41

Jan. 23   **Third Sunday of Epiphany**
Principal Service: Matt. 4.16–17 From Darkness to Light 43
Second Service: 1 Peter 1.8–9 For What We Receive 45

Jan. 30   **Fourth Sunday of Epiphany**
Principal Service: John 2.11 Glory Revealed 47
Second Service: Philemon 6–7 Refreshed by Love 49

Feb. 6   **Sunday next before Lent**
Principal Service: Matt. 17.6–8 Bowled Over 51
Second Service: Ecclus. 48.4a, 9 Assumptions of Old 53

Feb. 9   **Ash Wednesday**
        Principal Service: 2 Cor. 5.21 For Our Sake 55
        Second Service: Isa. 1.17 Practical Christianity 57
Feb. 13   **First Sunday of Lent**
        Principal Service: Rom. 5.18–19 A Difference of One 59
        Second Service: Ps. 50.14–15 Calling on God 61
Feb. 20   **Second Sunday of Lent**
        Principal Service: John 3.17 No Condemnation. 63
        Second Service: Num. 21.5 The Penalty for Ingratitude 66
Feb. 27   **Third Sunday of Lent**
        Principal Service: Rom. 5.2b–5 Christian Character. 68
        Second Service: Josh. 1.9; Eph. 6.19–20 Be Bold! 70
Mar. 6   **Fourth Sunday of Lent (Mothering Sunday)**
        Principal Service: Col. 3.15–16 Inner Peace 72
        Second Service: Eph. 5.86–9 Walking in the Light 74
Mar. 13   **Fifth Sunday of Lent (Passion Sunday)**
        Principal Service: John 11.14–15 For Your Sake. 76
        Second Service: Lam. 3.21–23 Great is the Lord's Faithfulness 78
Mar. 4   **Palm Sunday**
        Principal Service: Matt. 26.14–15 For a Price 80
        Second Service: Isa. 5.3–4 What More Was There to Do? 82
Mar. 21   **Monday of Holy Week**
        Heb. 9.13–14 Through the Eternal Spirit 84
Mar. 22   **Tuesday of Holy Week**
        John 12.20–21 We Wish to See Jesus 85
Mar. 23   **Wednesday of Holy Week**
        Heb. 12.1–2a With Perseverance 87
Mar. 24   **Maundy Thursday**
        1 Cor. 11.23–24 Special Revelation 89
Mar. 25   **Good Friday**
        Principal Service: John 19.28–30 Giving Up the Spirit. 91
        Second Service: Col. 1.22–23 Reconciliation 93
Mar. 26   **Easter Eve**
        (not the Easter Vigil) John 19.41; Matt. 27.59 The Peace of the Garden . . 95
Mar. 26–27 Easter Vigil
        Matt. 28.1–2 Heaven and Earth Are Moved 97
Mar. 27   **Easter Day**
        Principal Service: John 20.15, 17 The First News 99
        Second Service: Rev. 1. 13–14, 17–18 Easter Glory. 101
Apr. 3   **Second Sunday of Easter**
        Principal Service: John 2.30–31 Jesus Is the Messiah 102
        Second Service: Dan. 6.10 Prayer Comes First 105
Apr. 10   **Third Sunday of Easter**
        Principal Service: Luke 24.32 Spiritual Heartwarming 107
        Second Service: 1 Cor. 3.12–13 Every Piece Counts 109
Apr. 17   **Fourth Sunday of Easter**
        Principal Service: John 10.4–5 Discernment 111
        Second Service: Eph. 2.17–18 One in Christ 113
Apr. 24   **Fifth Sunday of Easter**
        Principal Service: John 14.10–11 God in Christ 115
        Second Service: Rev. 21.9–10 Come not to Sojourn, but Abide 117

May 1	**Sixth Sunday of Easter**	
	Principal Service: John 14.21 Loving Revelation	119
	Second Service: Rev. 22.2 Tree(s) of Life.	121
May 5	**Ascension Day**	
	Acts 1.7–8 My Witnesses	123
May 8	**Seventh Sunday of Easter** (Sunday after Ascension Day)	
	Principal Service: John 17.3 This Is Eternal Life.	125
	Second Service: Eph. 1.17–18 Enlightened Hearts.	127
May 15	**Day of Pentecost** (Whit Sunday)	
	Principal Service: Acts 2.3–4 Gift of the Spirit	129
	Second Service: Acts 2.19–21 The Invitation Is to All	131
May 22	**Trinity Sunday**	
	Principal Service: Matt. 28.19–20 Remember!	133
	Second Service: Isa. 6.4–5 Woe Is Me?	135
May 26	**Corpus Christi** (Day of Thanksgiving for Holy Communion)	
	Principal Service: John 6.57–58 True Living.	137
	Evening Prayer: Luke 9.13 For Our Part	140
May 29	**First Sunday after Trinity** (Proper 4)	
	Principal Service: Matt. 7.24–25 How Firm a Foundation?	142
	Second Service: Luke 8.15 Patient Endurance	144
June 5	**Second Sunday after Trinity** (Proper 5)	
	Principal Service: Matt. 9.21–22 Faith for Healing	146
	Second Service: 1 Sam. 18.14–16 The Common Touch	148
June 12	**Third Sunday after Trinity** (Proper 6)	
	Principal Service: Matt. 10.8 Giving Freely.	150
	Second Service: 1 Sam. 21.6 When the Need Arises	152
June 19	**Fourth Sunday after Trinity** (Proper 7)	
	Principal Service: Matt. 10.26–31 For the Third Time	154
	Second Service: 1 Sam. 24.11 Magnanimity	156
June 26	**Fifth Sunday after Trinity** (Proper 8)	
	Principal Service: Gen. 22.2 Beyond Endurance?	158
	Second Service: 1 Sam. 28.6–7 Back from the Dead.	160
July 3	**Sixth Sunday after Trinity** (Proper 9)	
	Principal Service: Rom. 7.19–20; Matt. 11.17 Jesus' Yoke, Our Yoke	162
	Second Service: 2 Sam. 2.4–5 Loyalty Is Rewarded	164
July 10	**Seventh Sunday after Trinity** (Proper 10)	
	Principal Service: Rom. 8.1–2 Absolution.	166
	Second Service: 2 Sam. 7.20–21 Keeping Faith.	168
July 17	**Eighth Sunday after Trinity** (Proper 11)	
	Principal Service: Matt. 13.24, 38–39 An Unwanted Takeover	170
	Second Service: Acts 4.13 Boldness in Faith	172
July 24	**Ninth Sunday after Trinity** (Proper 12)	
	Principal Service: Matt. 13.52 Old and New	174
	Second Service: Acts 12.5, 12 Prayer Marathon	176
July 31	**Tenth Sunday after Trinity** (Proper 13)	
	Principal Service: Matt. 14.13–14 Antidote to Grief	178
	Second Service: 1 Kings 10.1; The Problem of Pride.	180
Aug. 7	**Eleventh Sunday after Trinity** (Proper 14)	
	Principal Service: Matt. 14.31–33 Little Faith	182
	Second Service: Acts 14.9–10 One Man's Faith	184

Aug. 14	**Twelfth Sunday after Trinity** (Proper 15)	
	Principal Service: Matt. 15.27–28 Humble Determination	186
	Second Service: Acts 16.10 Directed by the Spirit	188
Aug. 21	**Thirteenth Sunday after Trinity** (Proper 16)	
	Principal Service: Matt. 16.16–17 Divine Revelation	189
	Second Service: Acts 17.18, 29 Resurrection Doctrine	192
Aug. 28	**Fourteenth Sunday after Trinity** (Proper 17)	
	Principal Service: Matt. 16.27–28 God Will Repay	193
	Second Service: Acts 18.9–11 Green Light for Ministry	195
Sept. 4	**Fifteenth Sunday after Trinity** (Proper 18)	
	Principal Service: Matt. 18.18–20 Agreeing as Best We Can	197
	Second Service: Acts 19.11, 19–20 Extraordinary Miracles	199
Sept. 11	**Sixteenth Sunday after Trinity** (Proper 19)	
	Principal Service: Matt. 18.21–22 Ad Infinitum.	201
	Second Service: Acts 20.32 Message of Grace.	203
Sept. 18	**Seventeenth Sunday after Trinity** (Proper 20)	
	Principal Service: Matt. 20.13–15 God's Generosity	205
	Second Service: Acts 26.24–25 Out of Mind?	207
Sept. 25	**Eighteenth Sunday after Trinity** (Proper 21)	
	Principal Service: Matt. 21.32 Ungodly Intransigence	209
	Second Service: 1 John 2.22–23 Only through Jesus	211
Oct. 2	**Nineteenth Sunday after Trinity** (Proper 22)	
	Principal Service: Matt. 21.43–46 Arresting Fear	213
	Second Service: 1 John 2.7–8 Old and New	215
Oct. 9	**Twentieth Sunday after Trinity** (Proper 23)	
	Principal Service: Matt. 22.7–9 Divine Expediency	217
	Second Service: 1 John 3.11 No Half Measures.	219
Oct. 16	**Twenty-First Sunday after Trinity** (Proper 24)	
	Principal Service: Matt. 22.18, 21 Fair Division.	220
	Second Service: 1 John 4.2, 4 Infallible Test	223
Oct. 23	**Last Sunday after Trinity** (Bible Sunday)	
	Principal Service: Col. 3.15–17 People of the Book	224
	Second Service: Isa. 55.10–11 Word of Trust.	227
Oct. 30	**Fourth Sunday before Advent**	
	Principal Service: Matt. 24.12–14 Enduring with Joy	229
	Second Service: Dan. 7.13–14 World Service.	231
Nov. 6	**Third Sunday before Advent**	
	Principal Service: Matt. 25.11–13; 1 Thess. 4.16 The Day Will Come	233
	Second Service: Judg. 7.19 Every One Counts	235
Nov. 13	**Second Sunday before Advent**	
	Principal Service: 1 Thess. 5.4–6 You Should Be Prepared	237
	Second Service: Rev. 1.9–10a I, John.	239
Nov. 20	**Christ the King** (Sunday next before Advent)	
	Principal Service: Matt. 25.40 Head of the Family.	240
	Second Service: 2 Sam. 23.3–4 Ruling in the Light	243

SERMONS FOR SAINTS' DAYS AND SPECIAL OCCASIONS

The readings in this section are taken from Brother Tristam SSF, *Exciting Holiness* (Canterbury Press, 1997); Robert Atwell, *Celebrating the Saints* (Canterbury Press, 1998).

The Mission to Seafarers
A world mission agency of the Church of England

Earning a living at sea, bringing food to our tables and resources for our industry, is one of the most dangerous jobs in the world. On average 10 ships and 25 seafarers are lost at sea every month. Pirate attacks on merchant ships are on the increase with hundreds of assaults each year – sometimes resulting in loss of life.

Through a network of chaplains, lay staff and volunteers, the Mission has a presence in 300 ports around the world, caring for the spiritual and practical welfare of seafarers and their families.

If you would like to share in God's work among seafarers by joining our worldwide team of chaplains or our voluntary service scheme for young people, by supporting us in prayer, or by inviting a preacher or speaker to your parish, please contact us at:

**The Mission to Seafarers
St Michael Paternoster Royal,
College Hill, London EC4R 2RL
Tel: 020 7248 5202
Fax: 020 7248 4761
Email: general@missiontoseafarers.org
Website: www.missiontoseafarers.org**
Registered charity no: 212432

**Caring for seafarers
around the world**

2004

Nov. 30	St Andrew, Apostle.	245
Dec. 7	St Ambrose, Bishop of Milan, Teacher of the Faith	247
Dec. 14	St John of the Cross, Poet, Teacher of the Faith.	249
Dec. 26	St Stephen, Deacon, First Martyr.	250
Dec. 27	St John, Apostle and Evangelist	252
Dec. 28	Holy Innocents.	254

2005

Jan. 1	Naming and Circumcision of Jesus	256
Jan. 6	Epiphany.	257
Jan. 21	St Agnes, Child-Martyr at Rome	259
Jan. 25	Conversion of Paul	261
Feb. 2	Presentation of Christ in the Temple	263
Feb. 14	SS Cyril and Methodius, Missionaries to the Slavs	264
Feb. 27	George Herbert, Priest and Poet	266
Mar. 1	St David, Bishop of Menevia, Patron of Wales	268
Mar. 17	St Patrick, Bishop, Missionary, Patron of Ireland.	269
Mar. 19	St Joseph of Nazareth	271
Apr. 4	Annunciation of our Lord to the Blessed Virgin Mary	273
Apr. 23	St George, Martyr, Patron of England	275
Apr. 25	St Mark the Evangelist	277
May 2	SS Philip and James, Apostles	278
May 14	St Matthias the Apostle.	280
May 26	St Augustine, First Archbishop of Canterbury.	282
May 31	Visit of the Blessed Virgin Mary to Elizabeth	283
June 8	Thomas Ken, Bishop of Bath and Wells, Hymn-writer	285
June 9	St Columba, Abbot of Iona, Missionary	286
June 11	St Barnabas the Apostle.	288
June 22	St Alban, First Martyr of Britain	290
June 24	Birth of John the Baptist	292
June 28	St Irenaeus, Bishop of Lyons, Teacher of the Faith.	293
June 29	SS Peter and Paul, Apostles.	295
July 3	St Thomas the Apostle	297
July 11	St Benedict of Nursia, Abbot of Monte Cassino, Father of Western Monasticism	298
July 22	St Mary Magdalene.	300
July 25	St James the Apostle.	301
July 26	SS Anne and Joachim, Parents of the Blessed Virgin Mary	303
July 29	Mary, Martha and Lazarus, Companions of our Lord	304
Aug. 6	Transfiguration of our Lord	306
Aug. 11	St Clare of Assisi, Founder of the Minoresses (Poor Clares)	308
Aug. 15	The Blessed Virgin Mary (Feast of the Assumption).	309
Aug. 24	St Bartholomew the Apostle.	311
Sept. 3	St Gregory the Great, Bishop of Rome, Teacher of the Faith	312
Sept. 14	Holy Cross Day	314
Sept. 21	St Matthew, Apostle and Evangelist	315
Sept. 29	St Michael and All Angels	317
Oct. 4	St Francis of Assisi, Friar, Deacon, Founder of the Friars Minor.	319
Oct. 18	St Luke the Evangelist.	320

Oct. 28	SS Simon and Jude, Apostles	322
Nov. 1	All Saints' Day	323
Nov. 2	Commemoration of the Faithful Departed (All Souls' Day)	325
	A Sermon for Harvest Thanksgiving	327
Nov. 11	A Sermon for Remembrance Day	328
	Scripture Index	332
	Subject Index	335

First Sunday of Advent 28 November 2004
Principal Service Walking in the Light of the Lord
Isa. 2.1–5; Ps. 122; Rom. 13.11–14; Matt. 24.36–44

'Come, let us walk in the light of the Lord!' Isaiah 2.5
'You . . . must be ready, for the Son of Man is coming at an unexpected hour.' Mathew 24.44

Expecting the unexpected
Would we have it any other way? History has shown that when the Second Coming of Jesus has been given a specific date, time and place, chaos has ensued. God tells us especially at the start of a new Church year, when time is more than usually in our thoughts, that it is not for us to know when Jesus will come: we need to be in a state of continual preparedness.

But how do we keep our spiritual kettle on the boil? How do we stop readiness-fatigue creeping in? Only by keeping our eyes on God, and expecting the unexpected. God will continue to surprise us in many ways – perhaps mainly in giving us not merely the answers to our prayers, but in exceeding our requests. Many of the Jews were expecting a Messiah for their nation: God sent the Saviour of the world.

Living above expectations
Walking 'in the light of the Lord' means living above the world's expectations. Those outside the Church observe how Christians meet difficulties and disasters – how situations which naturally point one way are turned inside out and round about for God. Ever since the time of Christ, the Church has been 'turning the world upside down' (Acts 17.6) – and, even against its inclination, the world sits up and takes notice. If more Christians did more turning, the world would notice even more. Those who walk in God's light stand out from the crowd, though not necessarily by criteria recognized by the world. When Mother Teresa went home to be with the Lord, she had only a couple of blue-and-white saris and a bucket for washing – yet she was known to millions the world over.

God's light
Do we fully realize what God's light is? No, certainly we don't – for it is 'the light that shines in the darkness, and the darkness

1

did not overcome it' (John 1.5). It's a light, therefore, to which Satan, the Prince of Darkness, has no answer. It's a light that blazes the darkness out of a situation so that God can deal with it: the same light that shone in a world that was careening around in the darkness that people had brought upon themselves. God's light is not only a state to be anticipated; because Jesus lives, we can walk in it now. Without it, there is little mileage in anticipation.

Drawing aside

Advent is essentially a time of expectation. If we use it well, we can expect the best Christmas yet. But if we allow the world of commerce and hype to dictate the terms, we may expect an anti-climax. Draw aside, if you can, to search God's will for your Advent. Taking stock of one's spiritual progress is good, as long as retrospection doesn't become the raison d'être of the season. With the census looming large, Mary and Joseph would not have had much time for quiet reflection in the weeks before Christ's nativity. But we need to make a space; and to make, if we can, our spiritual new year resolutions, primarily to continue growing towards what God wants us to be, what he created us to be and what he knows we can be.

Are we ready?

We are probably willing to be moulded into God's design – but are we ready? It's possible to stop short of full commitment until we've accepted a lower-geared life as the norm. 'Do you love me more than these?' our Lord is still challenging (John 21.15).

The dearest idol I have known,
Whate'er that idol be;
Help me to tear it from thy throne,
And worship only thee.

William Cowper

Often we have become so conditioned to the idol that we take it for granted. God's light lights up God's way, and no other. Would anyone really opt for less than 20/20 vision? If God's light is to mean anything at all, it has to mean everything. Either Jesus came to save the world, or he did not. If he did not come, there is no meaning to life. If he came, then what are we doing about it? Who are we telling? How are we showing that his coming has made a difference?

These are just *some* of the challenges of Advent!

Family service input
Using either a solid or helium-filled globe, site it in a prominent place in the church, with a different area spotlighted for each service in Advent. Encourage the young people to work on projects, art, links and/or campaigns for the various countries spotlighted.

Suggested hymns
Hark! a thrilling voice is sounding; O come, O come, Emmanuel; The advent of our King; We are walking in the light.

First Sunday of Advent *Second Service*
Sing It Loud!   Ps. 9; Isa. 52.1–12; Matt. 24.15–28
'Break forth together into singing, you ruins of Jerusalem; for the Lord has comforted his people, he has redeemed Jerusalem.' Isaiah 52.9

The Advent carols
Thank God for Advent carol services, and the uplift they give to worship at this season. The days are short, the nights long, dark and often cold; parties and feasting are still some way ahead. But the Advent readings and carols do much to restore our spiritual equilibrium. There must be times when God wonders if we have forgotten how to be joyful; and the more we sing out our faith, the more the Lord will be reassured – for no one with gloom in their heart can sing. Even though our lives may be in ruins, as was Jerusalem in the time of Isaiah, God encourages us to sing.

One important word
There is one word this Advent standing between our spiritual progress and its stagnation; one word that made a great difference in the apostolic Church; one word which can often make or break a situation; one word which every one of us can and should put into practice. And the word is ENCOURAGEMENT.

3

Barnabas (whose name meant 'son of encouragement') was an encourager of the early Church, selling his land and giving the money 'into the common purse' (Acts 4.36–37). Later, he was to have a big impact on the ministry of Paul. When the disciples (understandably) were cautious about accepting Paul's conversion, Barnabas spoke up for him (Acts 9.27) and later accompanied him on a mission (Acts 13.2ff.).

We can all be Barnabases, affirming others in their mission and ministry, taking heart also that no one called by God has ever been left to soldier on without the help, companionship or encouragement of another. Jesus had his mission team and a back-up team led by Mary; Paul had Barnabas, Silas, Mark, Timothy and Luke; William Tyndale, hounded to the Continent in a terrible wave of clerical opposition, had the services of a printer who risked torture and death for helping him; William Carey, translating the Bible in India, was similarly helped, as was Robert Morison in China.

Valued help

Do we value the help we are given, or take it for granted? Advent is a good time to lift our helpers and encouragers to God – in prayer, if not in songs of thankfulness. Surely each of us can review our lives and see, time and again, how a word or two of encouragement made the difference between success and failure.

But Advent is primarily the time when God encourages us with the coming of Christ, and the difference that this made to the world, and continues to make in so many lives. And the more we can sing the news of Advent, the more people will be attracted to sing with us. Joy is infectious, and the world is not so full of it that it can't cope with a lot more. That much of the world allowed Christ's coming to pass unnoticed two thousand years ago is in itself a good reason for seeking to reverse the situation today. We have become well versed in wallowing in the despair of stock-market collapses, terrorist attacks, epidemics, 'natural' disasters, and the rest of the world's persecution. But Jesus followed up his forecast of these by commanding, 'Take courage; I have conquered the world!' (John 16.33).

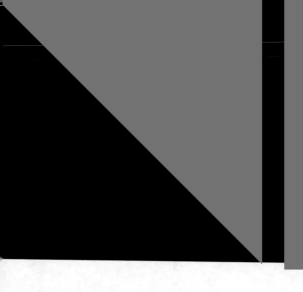

Because of Christ

Because of Christ's conquest, we can walk tall, we can be joyful, we can be bold. We can open our hearts in praise and song this Advent, because we are another year closer to the time when those swords shall be beaten into ploughshares, and spears into pruning-hooks (Isa. 2.4). After the gospel has been published in all nations, the End will come (Matt. 24.14; Mark 13.10). Among our number may be the Tyndales, Careys and Morisons of 2005; or perhaps the *encouragers* of these modern-day missionaries and Bible translators.

Perhaps we have not realized how full the Old Testament is of music. All those songs were once new. Then, because of Christ, men, women and angels in New Testament times composed new songs. This Advent, because of Christ, can we not follow in their steps? God the Music-Maker has already given us songs in our hearts. Surely, if Jerusalem in ruins could sing, we can too – amid the blessings God has given.

Suggested hymns

Hark! the glad sound; How lovely on the mountains; I will sing of my Redeemer; Ye holy angels bright.

Second Sunday of Advent   5 December 2004
Principal Service   **Wheat – and Chaff**   Isa. 11.1–10; Ps. 72.1–7, 18–19; Rom. 15.4–13; Matt. 3.1–12

'His winnowing-fork is in his hand, and he will clear his threshing-floor and will gather his wheat into the granary, but the chaff he will burn with unquenchable fire.' Matthew 3.12

Powerful preaching

The message of John the Baptist was uncompromising, yet many managed to ignore it; and today Satan has become so proficient in dulling the message even further that it is much easier to focus on Christmas and all it brings than on the Baptist's warning that the Day of Reckoning will come. We are not to worry over that day, but we are to bear it in mind. And we are in Christian duty bound to care about those whom we may help towards being separated then as wheat instead of chaff. God is not willing that

...ld perish (2 Peter 3.9), and we should be like-minded. ...ent all his energies into preaching the message. He would not be held to account for those who deliberately shut their ears and turned away.

Good grains of wheat

In the parable of the sower, Jesus described a 25 per cent success rate. For every four seeds that were sown, one fell prey to birds, one was trampled out of recognition, one was smothered to death – and one made good. The same is often true at conventions or crusades. For one reason or another, around one-quarter of the conversions are 'for real'. Are we to concentrate on nurturing these good grains of wheat and leave the rest to their fate? So it may indeed seem from the instructions of Jesus when he sent out the first missionaries: 'But whenever you enter a town and they do not welcome you, go out into its streets and say, "Even the dust of your town that clings to our feet, we wipe off in protest against you"' (Luke 10.10–11). Even the less-than-total success rate of the inexperienced preachers was enough to topple Satan 'from heaven like a flash of lightning' (v. 18). A few grains of good wheat can yield a very rich harvest.

The chaff – abandoned?

Yet don't we all know of those who have been nominal Christians, or rank unbelievers for years, who have come to a real and lasting faith after long-continued nurturing? Suppose we (or others) had given up on these precious grains of wheat? Remember the barren fig tree in the vineyard, and how the gardener pleaded for a stay of execution (Luke 13.6–9)! God would rather have love than sacrifice (Hos. 6.6). There will doubtless be no shortage of chaff on the Day of Reckoning; but anything we can do in the meantime to lessen this is surely time well spent. Besides, it is not for us to judge what is wheat and what is chaff. In the final analysis, we may be surprised at the definition of some who have passed as good wheat and others who seemingly have had no faith. Our Lord himself warned: 'Not everyone who says to me, "Lord, Lord", will enter the kingdom of heaven, but only one who does the will of my Father in heaven' (Matt. 7.21).

The ever-burning fire
Were anyone to assume that John's language was over-strong, and
more akin to Old Testament than New Testament theology, they
would be advised to read Mark 9.42ff., where Jesus also teaches
about the unquenchable fire. We are dealing with serious matters
here, matters of ongoing life and ongoing death. God is a merciful
God – but he is also our judge, and God is provoked every day.

These verses are a real challenge, as we go through the assessment period of Advent; are we making the most of God's opportunities? Or, if he seems not to be working us hard enough, is it
because we have got our attention off him? God is no waster of
time; he is its master. And he knows, better than anyone and
certainly better than ourselves, how to fill our time for him.

Among all the frenetic preparations for Christmas, we need to
make time for God. Since he has given us the reason for the season,
it is surely not right that we should allow his voice to be drowned
out by the noise of the world.

Even some of the good seed only brought in a 30 per cent
harvest, or a 60 per cent one. May we pray the Lord to let us be
100 per cent-ers (Matt. 13.8, 23)!

Family service input
Encourage the young people to discuss/compile types of good
spiritual wheat grains, and to talk about how this seed-sowing
can be increased in the parish.

Suggested hymns
Let saints on earth in concert sing; Lord of all hopefulness; On
Jordan's bank the Baptist's cry; The earth, O Lord, is one wide
field.

Second Sunday of Advent   *Second Service*
On the Lord's Side   Ps. 11 [28]; 1 Kings 18.17–39;
John 1.19–28

*'Elijah then came near to all the people, and said, "How long will you
go limping with two different opinions? If the Lord is God, follow him;
but if Baal, then follow him." The people did not answer him a word.'*
1 Kings 18.21

Deciding for God
There are many today who want to run with the hares and the hounds – or who are either antipathetic towards God or want to 'have their fling' and leave full commitment until later. They are hung up between two opinions, and cannot be relied upon to show loyalty to any person or cause.

We know how the contest on Carmel ended. Some of the people who had sullenly and silently faced Elijah fade out of the picture. Others, instantly changing sides, declare the sovereignty of God. Elijah did not linger with either group.

An elderly man, who was practically stone-deaf, was to be found in church every Sunday morning. One Sunday, a member of the congregation asked him why he came so regularly when surely he could hear nothing of the service. 'I want to show who's side I'm on,' he replied, simply. Just standing up and standing out for God mattered. We may never know the value of the message that our presence at Sunday worship sends to others. But God will know.

They who hesitate
Spurgeon once observed: 'Doubting, like toothache, is more distracting than dangerous. I never heard of its proving fatal to anyone yet.' We know that the Lord only kept Thomas waiting in doubt for one week; and, if the tradition that he afterwards went as a missionary to India is correct, Thomas obviously learnt his lesson in the upper room that night. But halting between two opinions where God is concerned is not good. 'He who is not with me is against me,' said Jesus – perhaps on more than one occasion.

Why are we sometimes so wary of casting our vote? The electioneering saying has a lot of truth in it:

> God is voting for us all the time.
> The devil is voting against us all the time.
> The way we vote carries the election.

Yet many still waver, wanting still more assurance that they will end up on the winning side. 'Even though someone rises from the dead, they will not believe,' remarked Jesus, in his parable of Dives and Lazarus.

So, what will it take to convince?

8

Bravery for God

Who would doubt Elijah's bravery in so openly challenging the prophets of Baal? It was sheer, naked faith in God, and the Lord responded magnificently and convincingly. Yet would some not say that he was putting out a fleece? Well, the timorous might – but Elijah was surely anything but timorous.

There are occasions today when we hang back – say, in the ministry of healing – because we wonder what we shall do, or how we shall look, if nothing happens. Elijah might have had such qualms on Carmel, but if so he didn't let them get in the way of his stand for God.

God will safeguard his own reputation, and surely we need not worry about ours. If we acknowledge God before others, he will do his part. It may not be according to our timing or desires, but he will be true for he cannot be any other.

After the climax

We know that, being human, reaction set in with Elijah after the excitement of the contest, and he let the threat of a woman throw his spiritual equilibrium out of kilter. We, too, are sometimes magnificent in a crisis and then allow our guard to drop when the pressure is off. Satan never sleeps, and we are always but a thought away from destruction; equally, one prayer away from divine help.

If God did not love us so much life would not be so exciting. Those who halt between two opinions, perching uncomfortably on the fence between good and evil, life and death, faith and unbelief, may have the relatively unexciting existence of mediocrity. But surely only a fool would settle for that.

Suggested hymns

Fight the good fight; Soldiers of Christ, arise; Stand up, stand up for Jesus; Who is on the Lord's side?

Third Sunday of Advent   12 December 2004
Principal Service   **Proof – If You Need It**
Isa. 35.1–10; Ps. 146.5–10, or Canticle: Magnificat;
James 5.7–10; Matt. 11.2–11

'Jesus answered them, "Go and tell John what you hear and see: the blind receive their sight, the lame walk, the lepers are cleansed, the deaf hear, the dead are raised, and the poor have good news brought to them."'
Matthew 11.4–5

Love in action
This was love – God's love – in action. The messengers could return to John with eyewitness testimony. We do not know why this question from John was aired: it may have been allowed, so that news of what was happening could be broadcast in the gloomy fortress of Machaerus. Who knows? Such news could have fuelled the flames of Herodias' venom to the point where she demanded John's head. The praise that Jesus immediately gave John (Matt. 11.9ff.) would suggest that there had been a deeper reason for John's question: it had not been occasioned merely to show a chink in the Baptist's armour, but for the greater glory of God.

This is not to say that John, with time on his hands and a dark prison cell for company, did not have doubts – did not wonder why God had allowed him such a short, fraught ministry before incarceration; did not, in fact, question whether Jesus, whom he had seen so briefly at the Jordan, was continuing the good work – and, if so, how. It would have taken an angel not to entertain such thoughts – and John was very, very human.

The understanding of Jesus
Yet Jesus knew John better than John knew himself, and the doubting did not alter our Lord's regard for his cousin. It is a lesson for us not to judge ourselves too harshly. God did not create automatons: he would rather have our questions – yes, and our doubts – than stoical indifference. We are human, though one day we shall be something else. But for the time being, warts and all, we struggle after the impossible ideal of Matthew 5.48: that it is all but impossible this side of the grave, is a poor reason for discontinuing the struggle.

10

Take myself, Lord, and all that you've made me,
For you've given a bounty to me;
Give me work evermore in your service,
Make me just what you want me to be.

And he will – but not overnight. John the Baptist was not perfected until the executioner's axe met up with the skin of his neck.

Our work and testimony

Suppose a delegation were to approach us, as John's disciples came to Jesus, and asked: 'How are you justifying your title of "Christian"?' What would be our reply, our defence, our justification? Are we living out the commission of Christ – in part or wholly? Are we healing the blind, making the lame walk, cleansing infections, curing the deaf, raising the dead, and preaching the gospel to the poor? Or do we leave much of that to the medical profession? Do we leave the poor to get poorer, and spend our time on elaborate liturgy and grandiose schemes of church synodical development? The gospel for today poses challenging questions. If it seems the wrong time of year to address them, it could be because we'd rather put them on the back-burner.

It has been said that 'Christians are the world's Bible of today'. If that is true (and no doubt we can think up a few caveats), the world is entitled to ask about the efficacy of Christ's commission today.

Gospel for the poor

Why did Jesus emphasize the gospel's targetting of the poor? Was it because they were less inhibited with the trappings and encumbrances of wealth and possessions, and would accept it with simplicity in faith? The poor, and the young, would appear to have been more fertile ground for the reception of God's word, while the likes of Nicodemus and Joseph of Arimathaea were far less numerous. And didn't Jesus tell his friends, at the dinner party when Mary anointed his feet, 'You always have the poor with you' (Mark 14.7)?

It is one of the mysteries of Christ's teaching that he would address all sickness and disease by curing it, while poverty he addressed by giving the gospel.

11

Family service input
Organize Christmas card outreach to every home in the parish.
Encourage the young people to make parish service cards for use
in the new year.

Suggested hymns
Give me oil in my lamp; Sleepers, wake! the watch-cry pealeth;
The Advent of our King; The Lord will come, and not be slow.

Third Sunday of Advent   *Second Service*
Serving God's Purpose   Ps. 12 [14]; Isa. 5.8–30; Acts 13.13–41 [or John 5.31–40]

'For David, after he had served the purpose of God in his own generation, died, was laid beside his ancestors, and experienced corruption.' Acts 13.36

The great difference
Perhaps a strange verse to choose for today's text? But it points
up the great difference that the coming of Jesus made, to life and
death, to faith, hope and the hereafter. Paul, preaching with great
fervour, eloquence and precision at Pisidian Antioch, has encapsu-
lated the whole of Jewish history prior to Christ in a few short
verses, before going on to teach about the new scheme of things
brought about by his Lord.

A descendant, in earthly terms, of David, Jesus' mission had
put the rest of Jewish history into a perspective that was new to
Jewish minds. David had lived – and died. Jesus had lived, died
– and risen. David had served the purpose of God in his own
generation; Jesus had changed the course of history for eternity.
We could go on: David had concentrated on living, fighting and
acquiring for his own nation; Jesus had come as the Saviour of
the world. David's body, being all-human, had perished in the
grave. Jesus, with a power that makes a nuclear warhead seem
harmless by comparison, had burst in True Life out of his tomb.

Yet there was one common denominator: Jesus had fulfilled his
mission. David, according to his lights, had also served the purpose of God – even though there was such a great difference in
the two missions, the two purposes.

Our purpose – God's purpose

We are still working out God's purpose for our lives: if it were otherwise, we should already be in heaven. Every day, in a trillion-trillion different ways at his disposal, God shows us something more of himself. Every day we are one day closer to knowing more.

> One more day's work for Jesus;
> How glorious is my King!
> 'Tis joy, not duty,
> To speak his beauty;
> My soul mounts on the wing,
> At the mere thought
> How Christ my life has brought.
> One more day's work for Jesus,
> One more day's work for Jesus,
> One more day's work for Jesus,
> One less of earth for me.
>
> *Miss A. Warner*

Although God deals with us as individuals, and each is unique in his sight, his purpose is worldwide (and perhaps larger). In his will and wisdom he causes us to meet some of those influenced by our lives; but many others we may perhaps never know. This great thought brings with it a great responsibility. David, despite his greatness and estimable worth, is remembered also for the Bathsheba episode. We need not point the finger, for we too are not perfect; but for the times we fall as well as for our successes, we shall be remembered.

Our gospel

> We are writing a gospel,
> A chapter each day,
> By the acts that we do
> And the words that we say.

Who will remember us as having led them to Jesus? That is the critical question relating to our serving the purpose of God. If Christians don't show Jesus to the world, consider how many

13

people may die without ever having heard of him? Consider how many may die even while we debate with ourselves as to how best we can tell them. God is calling us NOW, to stand up and stand out for Jesus. It does not matter whether we live for many years or only for a few. The question is: have we used all the time that God has given us, for serving his purpose? We have not been created to make money, amass possessions, to have a good time, or even to make a virtue out of suffering. We are here to proclaim Christ. It is as simple as that: to serve the purpose of God in living to his glory.

It also happens to be the greatest calling on record, with the longest-term benefits.

Suggested hymns
God is working his purpose out; O come, O come, Emmanuel; Oh, the love of my Lord is the essence; Thy kingdom come, O God.

Fourth Sunday of Advent 19 December 2004
Principal Service **A Gift from God** Isa. 7.10–16; Ps. 80.1–7, 17–19; Rom. 1.1–7; Matt. 1.18–25

'An angel of the Lord appeared to [Joseph] in a dream, and said, "Joseph, son of David, do not be afraid to take Mary as your wife, for the child conceived in her is from the Holy Spirit."' Matthew 1.20

From the Holy Spirit
We sometimes say, in delight at the birth of a child, that '(S)he is a gift from God'. No matter how much medical science discovers about the physical aspects of human life, any birth is still wonderful and far from being fully understood in practical terms.

Yet Jesus' birth is so much more mysterious, unknowable, unexplainable and indefinable. We can relate as children to God the Father; we can understand Jesus as Brother, Friend, even Saviour; but the Third Person of the Trinity defies explanation.

Why so much cogitation, with Christmas a few short days away? Because Joseph, startled by the angel's news, must have thought (even worried) deeply over the question of Mary's conception. Did he doubt it? Well, conceptions being what they are, he could see what was evident: the condition of his betrothed which had occasioned the angel's visit, to prevent a break-up of the couple whom God had chosen to rear his Son. Did he doubt the purity of Mary? Did he love her less, or more? We are so good at celebrating Christmas, we scarcely consider the man near the centre of the event: the stalwart, silent (for we never hear a word from him!) carpenter, who trekked the length and breadth of Bethlehem to find a bed for his young mother-to-be.

Behind every life there is at least one factor that we do not know; and this Sunday before Christmas is a good time to reflect on the courage and faith that must have sustained both 'parents' as Mary's time drew near. She, who had never borne a child before, would ask others – including Elizabeth – whether each new development was 'normal'. He, meditating on the angel's words, would wonder what a 'Holy Spirit child' may be like. And Mary, too, of course, had been told, at the annunciation, that her child would be 'holy', would be called 'Son of God' (Luke 1.35). He would not be *adam* ('mankind'), but God's Son. 'What does "God's Son" look like? What child shall I give birth to?' These must have been questions racing through Mary's mind time and again as the nine months of her pregnancy advanced.

Lord, what are you doing?
Did she ever ask, 'Lord, what are you doing?' She would have been only human if she had. It's a question very often asked today, when God leads us into new situations – especially if we feel he has then left us to get on with whatever he's brought us to. 'Lord, are you *sure* this is where you want me, what you want of me?' We may even get around to telling him where *else* we think we should be, something *else* we're sure we could be doing for him. Did Mary really preserve the impassive serenity we give her in stained glass and oil paintings? Or were there times when she had to fight panic, fear and feelings of helplessness or insecurity? Don't we love both Mary and Joseph for staying in God's will, despite poverty and uncertainty, in a country suffering insurrections and an oppressive, unsympathetic army of occupation?

The indwelling Spirit
In a wonderful way, since that great Pentecost following Christ's ascension, we can empathize with Mary, for we too have the Holy Spirit in us: not as the embryonic Christ who was to grow as a man

in Galilee, but as love, joy, peace, patience, kindness, generosity, faithfulness, gentleness and self-control (Gal. 5.22–23) – Christ, if you like, but in another form. We come to celebrate his birth at Christmas – but we bring him with us. We share his gospel with others, but the sharing does not deprive us of his presence. We can show him to the world, or we can hide him and try to pretend that his Spirit is not a part of us. Or we can use and increase his fruits with interest, until one day we are all Spirit – all love, joy, peace and the rest.

By then we shall be celebrating somewhere else. Before then let us make this Christmas one which others will remember for the right reason.

Family service input
Encourage the young people to write/draw/carve/compose something to bring to the altar on Christmas Day, as a thanks-giving for Christmas – for the good of the parish at large, or to present to their parents, friends or to patients in hospitals.

Suggested hymns
Come, thou long-expected Jesus; Hark! a thrilling voice is sound-ing; The Lord will come, and not be slow; Sleepers, wake! the watch-cry pealeth.

Fourth Sunday of Advent   *Second Service*
The Bright Morning Star   Ps. 113 [126];
1 Sam. 1.1–20; Rev. 22.6–21 [or Luke 1.39–45]

'It is I, Jesus, who sent my angel to you with this testimony for the churches. I am the root and the descendant of David, the bright morning star.' Revelation 22.16

This same Jesus
The heavenly being in John's vision is the same Jesus whose birth in a cattle shed at Bethlehem we are gearing ourselves to celebrate on Saturday; the same Jesus who is of the Spirit living inside us. Shall we focus on the little child Jesus, for we feel close to a baby? No, says John in our lesson: lift your spirits, set your sights higher, for Jesus has been glorified, and we are now closer to him by two

millennia. Celebrate his birth, but don't anchor him to Bethlehem. Don't try to limit the limitless Christ.

Angels figure prominently in the Christmas story, and John's visions tell us of their prominence in the spirit world. These same angels are active in our lives today, and we'd do well to reflect on how they have already worked to bring us to where we are.

We may never know more than a fraction of the disasters averted by our supporting angels – the times we were led to safety, the occasions when a word, a hug or a kiss brought peace to an awkward situation, the strangers who came to us with gifts and help when we most needed them, the comfort we received when the outlook was bleak ... God's angels take no days off, and are in God's service to help, guide, protect and sustain us. If that thought makes us feel important, knock it on the head. God is not willing for any of us to get lost – but he knows we'd never make it to heaven without angelic back-up.

The Christmas angels
The angels who appeared to Mary, Joseph and the shepherds were there to see that God's plans for the salvation of the world went ahead smoothly: otherwise, Mary *could* have said 'No', Joseph *could* have broken off the engagement, no one else in Bethlehem might have known of the birth, Herod's soldiers could have found the Child they were looking for. But as we acknowledge the Christmas angels, consistency demands that we also acknowledge those in the early Church, the visions of John, Christian history and the Church of today.

God's ongoing concern
A couple holidaying on the Continent heard of the death of their friend in England. His funeral was arranged for the day before their return. They decided to take a walk along the beach rather than go shopping or on an excursion. The sands were deserted, except for a man walking a dog. As he drew near, they were amazed to see how like their friend he was. They stopped to talk, and the man even sounded like their friend (cf. John 21.12). It was a good talk, and they felt somehow reassured. Then he left them, and after walking on a few paces, they looked back: the man and his dog had vanished. The time was 1.15 p.m. Back at the hotel, they rang home to ask how the funeral had gone. 'What time was

it exactly?' they asked. 'One-fifteen,' came the answer. It was as if God was saying, 'The hundreds of miles of sea and land between you and the funeral *are of no account.*'

No explanation needed
There are many dealings of God which we cannot explain by logic, reason or common sense. It was not any of these that planted Jesus in Mary's womb, or that caused him to burst from the tomb on Easter Day. If we try to find a rational explanation for everything, we shall miss out on a lot in life.

The nearest we can come to an explanation of Christmas, is to look into the eyes of a child – which is exactly what Mary and Joseph would do on that first Christmas morning. And what they saw must have convinced them that the Christmas angels had been right.

Suggested hymns
Angels from the realms of glory; Hark, the glad sound, the Saviour comes; Praise to the Holiest in the height; Ye holy angels bright.

Christmas Eve   24 December 2004
Morning Eucharist   God Has Remembered
2 Sam. 7.1–5, 8–11, 16; Ps. 89.2, 21–27; Acts 13.16–26; Luke 1.67–79

' "Thus [the Lord God of Israel] has shown the mercy promised to our ancestors, and has remembered his holy covenant." ' Luke 1.72

The Lord's data-bank
Our human memories are wonderful. Electronic memories store massive amounts of data in chips so tiny they tease the imagination. But the memory of God truly is 'something else' – especially when we take into account the possibility of earlier worlds and many more universes. The divine data-bank defies description. It also means that God keeps every promise he has ever made – because he *is* God. Israel had thought the fulfilment of the messianic promises was a long time in coming, but come it did, though

at a time when much of Israel was unprepared and thinking about other things.

To a child, Christmas seems a long time in coming. The impatience which seems common to much if not all of humanity proves that God's patience is phenomenal. He sent his Son as a child – and most people ignored his coming. This same Son rose from the dead, and most people carried on as if nothing out of the ordinary had happened. This was in a nation whose religion and writings had for centuries been expecting these events. Can we wonder that today much of the world continues to bury its spiritual head in the sand?

Our covenant
The covenant we made, or that was made on our behalf, at baptism is the one that governs our particular mission. We contracted to put God first in our lives, and God for his part accepted us into his family, with all the advantages and responsibilities that go with such acceptance. He will do his part, of that we can be certain. But can God be as certain that we won't let him down? As covenant partners, we need mutual trust and commitment. And Christmas is a good time to review how we are keeping our covenant promises.

Two of a kind
As the old covenants were sealed by the two sides cutting their wrists and binding their arms together till the blood intermingled, so God's covenant with us saw the implanting of his Holy Spirit, so that he shares with his followers the one and the same Spirit: he is in us and we are in him. When we look into the eyes of Christ, we see something of ourselves; and when others look into our eyes, they see (or should see) Jesus. To be two of a kind when the other half is Jesus should so energize us that we go full steam ahead for our Lord; for he is looking to us, his covenant-partners, to share and spread his gospel. Non-believers will not do the work. And the longer the Church takes in getting the gospel published in all nations, the longer will the End of the world be delayed (Matt. 24.14; Mark 13.10). God has promised, and he will not alter the terms of his agreement.

Zechariah's revelation
Zechariah had been dumb for nine months, during which he almost certainly had much time to reflect on what God was doing

in his life. His cogitation had borne fruit – and all who heard his
Benedictus would also have the opportunity to see how God's
promise was coming to fruition. It doesn't always take tragedy or
affliction to bring us to our knees: God knows how to gain our
attention in many other ways. Just now he is doing it through a
little Child. What will this Christmas mean for us – beyond the
cards, presents and parties, beyond even the carol services and
worship? Will it take us into homes where the season is a mere
vacation? Or to homes where trouble seems to be mocked by other
folks' celebrations? Or to homes where the modern 'obligation' of
festivity is too heavy a burden and actually blights the real meaning of the season?

May God help us to spread the *Jesus*-joy of Christmas – with
our covenant partner as our guide!

Suggested hymns
It came upon a midnight clear; O little town of Bethlehem; Unto
us a Boy is born; While shepherds watched.

Christmas Day 25 December 2004
Midnight or early Eucharist **And It Is True!**
Isa. 62.6–12; Ps. 97; Titus 3.4–7; Luke 2. [1–7] 8–20
*'The shepherds returned, glorifying and praising God for all that they
had heard and seen, as it had been told them.' Luke 2.20*

Who would believe?
But who would believe these men of the flocks and fields? Who
would they convince that the impossible had happened, that a
virgin had conceived, a Saviour had been born in a cattle-shed?
There could even have been some among these shepherds who
would see their children massacred by Herod's men, in mistake
for the Child in the manger.

There is no accounting for the ways of God. If a mere human
mind had devised the salvation of the world, wouldn't the saviour
have been born in wedlock, in a palace, with multi-media coverage? But then, belief in that saviour would not have been so great
a step of faith.

Had the first visitors to Jesus been the Sanhedrin dignitaries en

20

bloc, what then? Could Herod's soliders have targetted the wrong baby? No – God planned the nativity with divine foresight, which makes a mockery of human hindsight.

Who will believe?
But we – at this first Eucharist of Christmas – we are the shepherds of this great event. We can join together in celebration, and then return home, praising God for all we have seen and heard . . . and let the partying commence. Or, we can decide that this nativity is too great an event to keep to ourselves, and we can go further afield with the news.

But who will believe? And does it matter, provided we have played our part?

Is the answer to this not a very definite 'Yes'? True, there are more Christians in the world today than ever before (so the Good News has been broadcast by many believers). But there are also more non-Christians than ever before, so the Christians' work of sharing the Good News is surely more important than ever before.

A Child's demands
We come to meet a Child today, with all the love and wonder a baby excites. But children also place demands on us, and the Christ-Child says to us today: 'I cannot go out and witness; I need you to witness for me. I cannot seek out the hurting and heal them; I need you to heal for me. I cannot go to the sorrowful; I need you to comfort them for me. I've given you my Spirit, and I need you to take it to others. I have given you my love, joy, peace; my patience, kindness and generosity; my faithfulness, gentleness and self-control. You are my hands, my feet, my voice!'

Yes, the Christ-Child of Christmas says all this, for he is no ordinary child. And he has given us no ordinary command. Sheer love has called us to his service; sheer love, which grows the more we share it.

The shepherds had been on duty, watching over their flocks; but it was a duty which took second place to the news brought by the angel. Not until they had located Jesus, had spent time with the holy family, and had heard all that Mary and Joseph could tell them, did they return to their flocks. Each of us can draw our own lessons from this.

21

Talking about good news
Bad news gets instant and enthusiastic media coverage. Good news, for one reason or another, is often more difficult to broadcast. Yet at Christmas part of the wonder is that folk in general are more receptive to good news. Can we pray that this wonder will extend into the New Year, and beyond? The world is not so full of joy that it can't cope with a lot more.

On this night, long ago, a little coterie of shepherds on the bleak Bethlehem hillside were bubbling over with joy at what they had seen and heard. And God, as he set the heavens ringing with 'Gloria in excelsis!', must have been joying too. Can we not recall that joyful verse in Job, recalling the first white days of the world:

> when the morning stars sang together,
> and all the heavenly beings shouted for joy. Job 38.7

Surely we, too, can 'bring our praises, to offer to our King'?

Suggested hymns
A Child this day is born; Christians, awake, salute the happy morn; Hark, the herald-angels sing; O come, all ye faithful.

Christmas Day   *In the day: Principal Service*
Born Again   Isa. 52.7–10; Ps. 98; Heb. 1.1–4 [5–12]; John 1.1–14
'To all who received him, who believe in his name, he gave power to become children of God, who were born, not of blood, or of the will of the flesh or of the will of man, but of God.' John 1.12–13

Christmas morning
Are we 'born again' on this special morning? Yes, in a way, we are. Drawn together, in God's sight, to celebrate the birth of his Son, we are renewed and revitalized by his Spirit. We may call it all part of the 'wonder of Christmas' – that indefinable 'something' that brings families together, fills the airwaves with joyful rather than dismal news, and lights up the darkest days (in physical terms) of the year. Christmas – despite, rather than because of, its

commercial attachments – makes new people out of us. Born again to new life, as we celebrate new life, we take up the reins again after Christmas re-energized and reinvigorated. But, for what? To resume life as before? Will Christmas have only recharged our batteries, or will its awe and wonder have infused new life into our spirits and bodies? Shall we leave the manger to return to our pre-Christmas schedules? Or are we looking to God to give us new fields, new work, new opportunities?

Christmas growth

The Baby in the manger did not remain a child for long. He grew, and in growing fulfilled the purpose of his mission. It may be that our own mission is to continue for a further period in the place where God is currently using us – or he may gently (or even quite forcibly) be pointing us towards somewhere or something else. May we, born again in the joy of Christmas, be open to his will; may we, entrusted with his gospel, be ready to hear when he speaks and to move when he directs.

'In these last days [God] has spoken to us by a Son', we shared, in this morning's epistle (Heb. 1.2). Christmas is God's voice in the modern world, no less than two millennia ago. It is God saying, 'I love the world *so much*, look at what I have given.' It is mind-blowing (almost) to conceive of such love – for a world that continued largely unconscious and uncaring of it. But still today – to us who profess to be Christians, as well as to others – God's concern for the world impacts at Christmas. Many will not admit to the impact, but that doesn't negate it. God's heart of love is large enough to embrace the world, and precious enough to be contained in a Child.

Responding to God

How we respond to God's Christmas love will mould our spiritual life for the coming year. We cannot leave a tiny Child alone. We must take him out with us when we leave our Christmas worship, yet not to minister to his needs, but to the needs of ourselves and others. He is not asking to be fed; instead, he offers to feed us with his word. He is not asking to be clothed, but he stands in the hearts of those who are destitute, cold and homeless. This morning, Jesus looks out on the world through the eyes of a child – and a child sees what older and wiser folk sometimes miss.

The famine continues,
His parents are missing,
Abandoned and starving,
No lodging or board;
He's no reason for living,
No reason for living,
Yet pleading with me
Are the eyes of my Lord.

Underneath the old bridge
In a bundle of papers,
For company, garbage,
For pillows, a board,
The homeless exist,
By society forgotten,
But calling to me
Is the voice of my Lord.

I've a life to be living,
And souls to be saving,
A road to be travelling,
A death to afford;
But whoever I meet,
Where I go in his service,
Still drawing me on
Is the heart of my Lord.

If I promise to Jesus
I'll do what he tells me,
I'll go where he leads me,
I'll follow his word,
He will give all the help
I shall need to help others,
So vital to me
Is the love of my Lord.

Suggested hymns

A Child is born in Bethlehem; In the bleak mid-winter; The first
Nowell the angel did say; What Child is this.

Christmas Day *Second Service* **Supreme Encouragement** Ps. 8; Isa. 65.17–25; Phil. 2.5–11 or Luke 2.1–20

'Before they call I will answer, while they are yet speaking I will hear.'
Isaiah 65.24
'Let the same mind be in you that was in Christ Jesus.' Philippians 2.5

Uplift for the soul

To Israel in turmoil, God gave hope. To a nation under Roman occupation, Jesus brought encouragement. God knows exactly how to lift us out of the slough of despond: whether we sink back again, rests with us.

At Christmas, his coming brings a great uplift. And Paul tells the Philippian Christians (and by extension every Christian since) to think like Christ: to replace pessimism with optimism, criticism with encouragement, sadness with joy, doubt with faith. We are here, using God's free oxygen, not to please ourselves but to affirm others in their faith and mission. Enthusiasm and encouragement is infectious. Let us help to spread the godly epidemic! Jesus is our prime example: he could encourage the unlearned and inept to become the frontline Christian missionaries and preachers of the early Church. He could overcome a man's self-doubt or denial, and encourage one to take the gospel to India and the other to Rome.

Holistic approach

We celebrate the Child's birth today. Yet we know what the shepherds did not, that the Child grew into the Man who applied a holistic approach to his ministry unparalleled before. He fed souls with the gospel, after first attending to their physical needs, whether food for the stomach, or healing for the body. It was an all-out attack on the equally holistic approach of the devil, who tries to destroy the soul and bring hunger, sickness and disease to the body.

By the same token, unless our own Christian ministry is holistic, addressing the needs of both body and soul, we may justifiably question how Christian it is – how much of the mind of Christ we have.

Christmas continuum

Our ministry is a continuum of Christmas, even as Christ's was: from nativity to ascension, he had come to do the will of his Father. Conscious of who he was, yet constantly battling against people's unbelief and incomprehension, it was no easy task. Neither is our Christian ministry, but Christmas and its joy makes it easier.

Yet we know that many appear able to celebrate Christmas without Christ. They may hear the bells on Christmas Day and think 'How nice!', but never consider coming to church. They may even send religious cards to each other, without thinking of the illustrations or reading the religious verses inside. How can they do it? With a dichotomy not far removed from that of the priests and people who howled for the crucifixion of the Messiah whom they'd been expecting all their lives. It is perfectly possible. Satan is the arch-manipulator of venom and apathy alike. And unless Christians extend their celebrations to bring the *true* Spirit of Christmas to these non-believers, non-committed, Satan will go on recruiting.

Christmas love

'Love came down at Christmas' – and it's love that will knock down the bastions of unbelief and apathy. Love is the key that God gives us in his Christmas Child, to open hearts still cold and indifferent to the Lord.

There will never be another nativity, another Child in the manger – next time Jesus will come in glory (though again with angels). So let's make the most of the love that has come this Christmas, while the Child is still giving us time to make him known.

Suggested hymns

A great and mighty wonder; Love came down at Christmas; Silent night; What Child is this.

First Sunday of Christmas (or St Stephen; see p. 250) 26 December 2004

Principal Service **This Was to Fulfil** Isa. 63.7–9; Ps. 148; Heb. 2.10–18; Matt. 2.13–23

'Then Joseph got up, took the child and his mother by night, and went to Egypt, and remained there until the death of Herod. This was to fulfil what had been spoken by the Lord through the prophet: "Out of Egypt I have called my son."' *Matthew 2.14–15*

Why, Lord?

Mary and Joseph must have asked 'Why, Lord?' Later, the disciples and members of the early Church; and obviously Matthew also. 'Why, Lord, did the massacre of the children have to be?' And folk would search the Scriptures, where answers were to be found. The flight into Egypt, the massacre itself, the return and settlement in Nazareth – it had all been foretold, though not understood until now. Matthew carefully links each stage of the story with the old prophecies. He is saying, in essence, 'We still don't understand why – but at least these things don't happen in a vacuum; they can be seen to have been forecast.' Whether Mary and Joseph had caught up with the prophecies, or whether they simply obeyed the instructions from the angels, we do not know. But certainly they – particularly Joseph – show a faith and trust which surely leaves us speechless with awe. As we celebrate Christmas, perhaps our worries and troubles fall into a better perspective, in the light of the holy family's trauma, when Jesus was still so young.

Life experience

God alone, in his wisdom, knew why he planned for Jesus to experience life on earth in such a dramatic way, touching the lows as well as the highs that we face, coming through situations that we still think are 'unfair' or 'unjustified'. 'This is life,' God is saying, 'and my Son experienced it, too.' So we should not complain that our path is not as smooth as it might be; we have not been specially targetted for the world's angst any more than was Jesus; if the truth be told, far *less* than was Jesus. If he came through with faith undamaged, so can we overcome our lesser Calvaries.

A great upheaval

Quite possibly Joseph's life had been quiet until the birth of Jesus. So it was asking a lot of a village carpenter to trek around 250 miles into a foreign land (and one with no very happy associations for any Jew), with a wife and young child, and the threat of persecution behind them. Mary might have been able to ride, with her precious Child, on a donkey; almost certainly Joseph would walk most if not all of the way. Probably they took little in the way of tools, clothes or food. How did God safeguard them against robbers on the journey? Once in Egypt, where did they live? Where did Joseph find work? Did they manage to keep the donkey for the return journey? These questions probably don't impact too much on our Christmas celebrations, but perhaps we can take some time to consider them as we look at the cards on the mantelpiece depicting the journey.

Search the Scriptures

We, too, can search the Scriptures and find prophecies, advice and even specific commands for whatever life is bringing us just now. Simply put, that is why we have the Bible. It is our compass, our rule book, our *modus operandi* and manual of instruction. We should not complain that life is hard if we leave our Bibles unopened on the shelves and look instead for answers to the world's problems in the world itself, a world not equipped to give the answers. Or, if our present situation is so fraught that we literally have no Bible to hand, we can follow Joseph's example and simply trust God to show us how he is going to deal with the situation.

Family service input

Encourage the young people (1) to look up other instances of Old Testament prophecies being fulfilled in the New Testament; and/ or (2) to gather data on the Church in Egypt, and work out a prayer programme or mission contact.

Suggested hymns

I cannot tell why he whom angels; Jesus, hope of every nation; Once in royal David's city; Thou didst leave thy throne.

First Sunday of Christmas *Second Service*
Christ the Encourager Ps. 132; Isa. 49.7–13;
Phil. 2.1–11 [or Luke 2.41–52]

'If then there is any encouragement in Christ, any consolation from love, any sharing in the Spirit, any compassion and sympathy, make my joy complete: be of the same mind, having the same love, being in full acord and of one mind.' Philippians 2.1–2

Because of this
Encouragement was Christ's reason for coming. Somehow, God had to show the uncaring, unheeding world that was blithely careening towards oblivion how much he loved us. Would his coming make a difference? Perhaps he wondered later when he returned to glory, leaving eleven apostles with the whole world to evangelize. But the encouragement he gave them, right up to the end, worked; and the ongoing encouragement of the Holy Spirit continues to work. Divine encouragement is the bulwark between our survival and demise: that is the measure of its importance.

Encouraging the minister
Paul himself is looking for encouragement – he has it in abundance from Christ, but he wants a top-up! He asks for his congregation to encourage him by Christian unity. This is not formal unity, such as we today look for between the various denominations – briefly in the Week of Prayer for Christian Unity, and spasmodically for the rest of the year – but committed unity and single-mindedness within the whole of the Philippian congregation. 'Give me this – let me see it in action,' Paul is saying, 'and my joy will be complete.' He has obviously experienced the sadness and frustration of working hard to preach and to live out the gospel, only to see his listeners drifting apart in disunity and disagreement.

Yet Jesus had trodden the same path. His inner circle, his frontline troops, could fall to arguing about position and prestige (Mark 10.37); and in the early Church there had been strong disagreements on the admitting of Gentiles and the question of circumcision (Acts 11.1ff.). Paul himself had fallen out with Barnabas over the seeming defection of Mark from his mission team (Acts 15.39)! Without godly encouragement, none of us would get very far. And Paul knows that he and his Philippian friends need reciprocal encouragement.

The Church's lifeblood

Divine encouragement is the lifeblood of the Church, the impetus of the Holy Spirit, without which our spiritual stamina is non-existent. How energetic and diligent are we, in affirming others, or do we look first for their affirmation?

> *Oh, Master, grant that I may never seek*
> *So much to be consoled, as to console;*
> *To be understood, as to understand.*
>
> *Prayer of St Francis*

If we encourage others, we shall in turn receive encouragement. That is how it works. But if we continually criticize others, then criticism is what we shall receive.

A house divided

Paul knew the danger of a house divided against itself, and he strove to see that internal division did not weaken the Church in Philippi. He had had first-hand experience, on the question of Gentiles and circumcision in the emerging Church. If that had not been thrashed out promptly, Christian history may have looked very different. Disunity in the Church is something the devil is banking on, to delay forward growth, to set back the spreading of the gospel, and thereby to purchase Satan more time to cause more trouble. On this premiss, doesn't disunity seem too high a price to pay – especially when the alternative is something as attractive as encouragement?

Spiritual output

God supplies all the spiritual input we need, but we also need his guidance in the best use of this energy. Our output can never exceed his input; but we can waste spiritual energy, and healing disunity takes a lot of energy. Perhaps, were we to dare to run a sort of 'time-and-motion' study on our spiritual flow (and ebb), we may find impedimenta that could profitably be jettisoned – or even encouraged out of character.

Suggested hymns

Courage, brother, do not stumble; Help us to help each other, Lord; Once in royal David's city; Peace, perfect peace, in this dark world of sin.

Second Sunday of Christmas   2 January
Principal Service   **The Unseen God?**   Jer. 31.7–14;
Ps. 147.12–20; Eph. 1.3–14; John 1.[1–9]10–18

'No one has ever seen God. It is God the only Son, who is close to the Father's heart, who has made him known.' John 1.18

God's human face

Jesus, coming to earth as a man, put a human face on God. 'Who-ever has seen me has seen the Father,' he said on one occasion (John 14.9). And so we can believe that his compassion, kindness, patience – in fact, all the fruits of the Spirit itemized by Paul (Gal. 5.22–23) – blend together to give a picture of God. At no point in Scripture is Father, Son and Spirit portrayed as being more indivisible, identical and understandable.

Yet there is mystery. God made human beings in his likeness, but no two people are exactly alike, in families or nations. And while Jewish Christians will understandably anticipate meeting a Jewish Jesus in glory, Chinese and African Christians will have different expectations. We are not divine alchemists; surely we can believe that a God of love will make himself wholly recognizable to each and all of us.

Why did he come?

More precisely, why did he come as he did? It was almost as though Jesus did not want to be recognized. Certainly on occasion he told people not to make him or his miracles known (though such injunctions were usually disregarded). Was he guarding his identity against the possibility of too early an arrest? Yet surely God, as the Master of time, would not have allowed events to overtake him? These are questions for which we shall probably have to wait until glory for an answer; yet the Lord who made enquiring minds is surely not fazed by our debating them.

Jesus came to show us how much God cared about his creation. Out of sheer love he could not allow humankind to continue its slide away from him. Satan was gaining confidence, and only the coming of Jesus to break the devil's stranglehold on death could save humanity from eternal oblivion.

Such was the importance of the incarnation. We may trivialize it with tinsel trees and holly, but we are tangling here with history's greatest event. The coming of God into the world started in motion the reversal of a trend which, had it been allowed to continue, may have seen the devil presiding over chaos. That could not be, for God had made an immutable covenant with Noah (Gen. 8.22) and with Abraham (Gen. 17.4). Further, innumerable prophecies regarding the Messiah had been made, and needed fulfilment. God could not be untrue to his word. The world had to be saved – and the price of salvation was as high as only Love could conceive. True, no one has ever seen God, but we have seen what he has done, and the Son he has given. Is that not the most munificent down-payment on record, this side of glory?

God in Jesus
The 'divine' in Jesus attracted people to him, not only because he healed and worked miracles, but because he had – he was – something which no one else had or was. In a country riven by insurrections, grumbling and frustrated under a Roman army of occupation, riddled with sickness, disease, corruption and poverty, and with a man-made divide between the religious grandees and the common people, God-in-Jesus impacted. People took note of certain men (and women) that they had been with Jesus. Death threats were issued against Lazarus of Bethany because of his resurrection link with Jesus. Pilate and Herod, sworn enemies before, healed their differences in an unholy alliance against Jesus. Priests in high office lowered their code of conduct sufficiently to bribe the guards at the tomb to commit perjury, in an effort to quash the resurrection truth. And all for a carpenter's son from Nazareth?

God is here now
And after the ascension, God came back, into every believer, in his Holy Spirit. He loves the world so much, he will be with us until there is a new heaven and a new earth. That is, simply, Love.

Family service input
Encourage the young people to illustrate, in whatever medium they choose, the Jesus (= God) of the gospels, and/or how they can 'see' God in today's world.

Suggested hymns
Had he not loved us; Here, O my Lord, I see thee face to face; Praise be to Christ in whom we see; To us a Child of royal birth.

32

Second Sunday of Christmas   *Second Service*
Divine Provision   Ps. 135; Isa. 41.21—42.4;
Col. 1.1–14 [or Matt. 2.13–23]

'May you be made strong with all the strength that comes from his glorious power, and may you be prepared to endure everything with patience, while joyfully giving thanks to the Father.' Colossians 1.11–12a

Mighty strength
How often do we consider the sheer amount of divine help and strength on offer? Blinded by the least of *little* problems, *little* pains, *little* tragedies, God tells us to turn from these to what *he* can give: 'Set forth your case . . . bring your proofs!' he says in our Old Testament reading (Isa. 41.21). A little earlier, in the same chapter, he lovingly tells us, 'Do not fear, for I am with you; do not be afraid, for I am your God; I will strengthen you, I will help you, I will uphold you with my victorious right hand' (v. 10). What more can he say? What more can he give? This is the almighty Lord of heaven and earth talking, and his word is sure.

Not a quick fix
He is not holding out a quick fix, to anaesthetize the part until the next pain comes along. The Royal Way is to build us up until we are strong enough to endure everything, to ride it out with powerful patience – and, in the process, to thank God with joy for the wherewithal to do it. God is not looking for stoical martyrs who, however brave, grind through difficulties persuading themselves and anyone else who will listen that life is a burden worth enduring. The Lord says be a martyr if you like – but do it with JOY, and then others will be encouraged too!

Paul's joyful concern
It was divine joy welling up in Paul that sharpened his concern for the Colossian Christians. Stayed by the Holy Spirit from preaching in Asia, on his second missionary journey (Acts 16.6), he had nevertheless received news of the struggling little church there – battling in a polyglot, sophisticated city against a battery of philosophical and religious arguments. During the two years of his Ephesian ministry, Paul's joyful concern for Colossae reached the Christians there through the faithful Epaphras (Acts 19.10, 26), though Paul himself had not been to the city (Col. 2.1).

33

There is a valuable lesson here for ministers of the gospel (lay and ordained) today: we should not restrict evangelism to 'face-to-face' encounters. So we cannot go to China? But we can pray for the Chinese church, write to Chinese Christians, and extend the hand of Christ to those of China who visit Britain. And the same goes for any country and community in the world. Paul didn't let a little problem like distance prevent him from encouraging a congregation he had never seen. Today, surely he would have used our multi-media technology to the full!

Well, we are using it, aren't we?

Spiritual back-up

The spiritual back-up is here for us, ready and waiting to be used, tailored to our needs and the needs of those to whom we minister. 'Do not fear,' God is still saying; just put the divine help to use.

At a diocesan gathering, the delegates split up into little groups to discuss the subject of 'fear'. Two questions were posed:

(1) What do you fear most?
(2) What overcomes fear best?

And at the end of the day when the data were collated, two recurring answers came up:

(1) The loss of someone.
(2) Encouragement.

Not quite what the organizers had expected, these answers gave much food for thought and material for many sermons. It is always tempting to condense data given in such circumstances – but surely Paul's teaching and the Isaianic reading for today go to the centre of the subject: the thing to fear most (and solely) is the loss of God; the solution is to avail ourselves of his divine encouragement. Easier said than done? Well, let's make a start, 'setting forth our case . . . and bringing our proofs', as the Lord himself invites.

Suggested hymns

A great and mighty wonder; Christ is the world's true light; Jesus, hope of every nation; The great God of heaven.

Baptism of Christ (First Sunday of Epiphany)

9 January *Principal Service* Until Isa. 42.1–9;
Ps. 29; Acts 10.34–43; Matt. 3.13–17

'He will not grow faint or be crushed until he has established justice in the earth.' Isaiah 42.4

'And when Jesus had been baptized, just as he came up from the water, suddenly the heavens were opened to him and he saw the Spirit of God descending like a dove and alighting on him.' Matthew 3.16

A glorious affirmation

His birth had been almost private, except for some shepherds drawn from their night's work by wonders in the heavens. Now the heavens are parted again – but this time in front of quite a crowd gathered at the Jordan, ostensibly to hear the preaching of John.

There have been attempts to rationalize this event; but did the clouds part *only* to let the sun through? No. Doves do not normally alight on a person's head, particularly when it is dripping immediately after baptism. And what of the voice, the *bath qol*, as the Hebrews called it? Thunder does not speak in a language as we know it.

Jesus' baptism was a divine declaration of intent; God telling the world that its long-awaited Messiah had not only been born, but was on the point of beginning his ministry. As the dove had brought the olive-leaf message to Noah, that the floodwaters were receding and life could begin anew (Gen. 8.11), so God with the baptism dove of his Spirit is telling us that new life, new hope is on offer.

> *New life, new hope awakes,*
> *Where'er men own his sway;*
> *Freedom her bondage breaks,*
> *And night is turned to day.*
>
> G. W. Briggs

The new mission

The mission of Christ, in the words of Isaiah 42.4, was to 'establish justice in the world'. He would not leave until this had been accomplished. It's an ongoing mission; for, though he has ascended back to glory, his Spirit is continuing the work – not as a dove descending from parted heavens, but as the greatest dynamo ever conceived in every believer.

Yes, it really needs such power to establish justice in a world that still has a fair mileage to go. Yet in every place where there is a Christian, the heart of justice beats a little stronger. Whatever pressures come against Christ's mission, it will continue until its purpose has been accomplished. This is divine encouragement at its best.

Essential baptism

We don't know how many of the people who came to John for baptism later fell by the wayside. Nor do we know for sure that John actually refused baptism to anyone – though he was caustic in his preaching to the Pharisees and Sadducees (Matt. 3.7ff.). In fact, the nearest John came to denying baptism was to Jesus himself, though this demur was on the grounds of humility and unworthiness (Matt. 3.14).

God could have confirmed Jesus in his ministry at any time; that it took place in the context of baptism is an endorsement of the validity, value and obligation of the rite. By water and the word, changes are made in and to the person baptized, which are unseen but no less real; their very invisibility renders them incalculable, and therefore we should never underestimate the importance of baptism.

How we nurture and affirm the baptized is also important. We know, for example, that John maintained contact with his disciples, even from his prison cell in the fortress of Machaerus (Matt. 11.2ff.): Spirit with Spirit meeting in the baptized gives strength to both the newly baptized and those more mature in the faith. For, until justice has come worldwide, the mission of the baptized goes on. We who are lit up by the Spirit have enough light for all the world. It would be a grave injustice to keep it to ourselves.

Family service input

The young people could be encouraged to design illustrations and choose texts or compose verses for parish baptism cards (including baptism anniversary cards).

A man there lived in Galilee; Christ, when for us you were baptized; Name of all majesty; When Jesus came to Jordan.

Baptism of Christ *Second Service*
Word of Power Pss. 46, 47; Josh. 3.1–8, 14–17; Heb. 1.1–12 [or Luke 3.15–22]

'[Jesus] is the reflection of God's glory and the exact imprint of God's very being, and he sustains all things by his powerful word.' Hebrews 1.3

Jesus is great!
J. B. Phillips once wrote a book entitled *Your God Is Too Small*. It is one thing to place Jesus in the manger at Christmas, but he will not be kept there. We are dealing with the Good Shepherd and the Friend of little children, certainly, but he is so much more. He is a mirror image of God, in all his glory: what God does, Jesus does; what God says, Jesus says – and the words that he says give life to everything. Who can take all that in? Only God – so let's settle for simple, trusting faith that *it is so*. From the very beginning (and, in a way we cannot imagine, even before that), it has been so.

In Isaiah 55, we find:

As the rain and the snow come down from heaven, and do not return there until they have watered the earth, making it bring forth and sprout, giving seed to the sower and bread to the eater, *so shall my word be* that goes out from my mouth; it shall not return to me empty, but it shall accomplish that which I purpose, and succeed in the thing for which I sent it. (Isa. 55.10–11)

God is looking for a return on this investment of his words. We, too, as we sow his gospel seed and share our faith with others, can expect a return. But God's ways are so far removed from the restricted ways of the earth that we may not see the fruits of our labours, but reap the harvest that someone else has sown. Does it matter? No, we can have faith in the Almighty to keep the record straight. He has been in the business far longer than we have.

Every unproductive word

We need to watch our words, for we're dealing with prime seed – seed that can make the difference between life and death, just as natural wheat or barley seed can save whole nations from starvation.

Our Lord knew the value of the seed he was sowing. He once said, very seriously, 'On the day of judgement you will have to give an account for every careless word you utter; for by your words you will be justified, and by your words you will be condemned' (Matt. 12.36–37). And James emphasized the power of the tongue, and what a force for evil, as well as for good, it could be (James 3.2ff.).

Are those whom we meet cheered by our words? Are they brought closer to Jesus? Are they helped through whatever problems they are facing?

By the same token, do we thank God for our friends – those to whom we can turn for support and Christian counsel? Those who love us, and believe we haven't made a permanent job when we mess things up? Those with whom we can share our joys as well as our sorrows?

An investment of trust

When Jesus entrusted us with his gospel it was not as a last resort. On Christians hangs the worldwide commission. If we sit down to think about that for long enough, we shall be overcome by the responsibility. The antidote, therefore, is to be up and doing.

> *Oh, ye heralds of the cross be up and doing,*
> *Remember the Great Command: Away!*
> *Go ye forth and preach the word to every creature,*
> *Proclaim it in every land.*

> *Fanny J. Crosby*

We shall run out of steam before we exhaust all the opportunities; but another will take up the baton ... until all the participants in this gospel ministry eventually meet up on another shore. And who knows what new opportunities and challenges will await us there?

We may rather derogatorily consign Job's three friends to 'non-comforters', but at the beginning of the exercise Eliphaz the

Temanite gives the suffering Job some praise: 'Your words have supported those who were stumbling . . .' (Job 4.4). Whether or not we feel as sorely traumatized as Job was, wouldn't we hope that such an encouragement could be ours?

Suggested hymns
Songs of thankfulness and praise; Spirit of God, as strong as the wind; To the Name of our salvation; With joy we meditate the grace.

Second Sunday of Epiphany   16 January
Principal Service   **God's at Work**   Isa. 49.1–7;
Ps. 40.1–11; Cor. 1.1–9; John 1.29–42
'The next day, John again was standing with two of his disciples, and as he watched Jesus walk by, he exclaimed: "Look, here is the Lamb of God!"' John 1.35–36

Speaking out
And look what John's words led to! Are we as bravely outspoken? When a terminally ill patient recovers, do we exclaim, 'This is God's work!' When a tornado or earthquake changes its line of attack and a community is saved, do we give God the credit? When a war is averted, do we find any number of politicians or diplomats to praise – and relegate God to the next time we have a problem? Is it any wonder that God doesn't work more miracles? If there was one thing that the Baptist was not, it was shy. 'Everyone who acknowledges me before others,' said Jesus, 'the Son of Man also will acknowledge before the angels of God' (Luke 12.8). Acknowledging Jesus in our hearts may keep our spiritual equilibrium in working order, but it probably doesn't cut much ice with anyone else. The Christian faith is a multifaceted animal – social, as well as individual. We need to speak up and speak out for God.

No bad thing
John the Baptist lost his head for acknowledging God and fearlessly speaking out for him. We are unlikely to stand in similar danger, but it would surely be no bad thing if some feathers were ruffled by our Christian witnessing. The alternative – no one taking

any notice through an enervating apathy – would be much more serious.

Satan has been very clever in conditioning people to an increasing acceptance and tolerance of immorality, indecency and sheer shock-horror. When the brain can take no more violence, depravity or scandal, it literally 'switches off', and normal feelings are dampened down into compassion fatigue, chronic spiritual inertia, stoical indifference, or half a dozen other names for the same condition.

Come alive!

Wouldn't we rather live dangerously but honestly, like John the Baptist, than slowly die spiritually, an inch a day, despairing of the world and the people in it?

Let's rather come alive and speak out fairly and frankly. And if we are to be called 'Nutters for God', let's be first-class nutters, remembering always that 'big oaks from little acorns grow'.

John may have had a short life – but it made best-selling, worldwide news.

The Baptists of today

We are, in a way, the Baptists of today. As John acted as a catalyst between Jesus and people who did not know the Lord, so we are divinely commissioned to bring folk to a knowledge of Jesus, to point them in his direction, to show them where he is. A woman was driven to distraction on hearing that her nephew had been killed in a motor accident, in a car being driven by his girlfriend. 'Where was God that day?' she asked.

Wasn't he there, in the deliverance of the girl from serious harm, in the fact that no other car was involved? Wasn't he there, in the immediate call-out of expert, compassionate paramedics? Wasn't he there, in the earlier depositing of the couple's baby with its grandparents?

We may dream up wonderful futures for our young people, but if we believe God doesn't make mistakes, don't we have to give him the best as far as any person's life-assessment is calculated? In recent years we have seen that more than a century was allowed for the Queen Mother; a generation or so less for Mother Teresa; and what may still seem to be an abnormally short span for Princess Diana. Each of these would have done more had they been spared longer. Perhaps each is even more busy in glory.

When Satan pestered God to let him torment Job, God consented. But when the devil went further and demanded Job's life, God very firmly drew the parameters.

He will allow us time enough to make him known – but he will surely expect us to make the most of that time.

Family service input
Co-ordinate the compilation of a parish 'spiritual profile', comprising how the young people see God at work in the parish. Discuss the profile's subsequent circulation/distribution.

Suggested hymns
God of gods, we sound his praises; Great is thy faithfulness; Jesus calls us, o'er the tumult; There is a Redeemer.

Second Sunday of Epiphany *Second Service*
Our Gospel Ps. 96; Ezek. 2.1—3.4; Gal. 1.11–24 [or John 1.43–51]

'He said to me: "Mortal, go to the house of Israel and speak my very words to them."' Ezekiel 3.4
'I want you to know, brothers and sisters, that the gospel that was proclaimed by me is not of human origin; for I did not receive it from a human source, nor was I taught it, but I received it through a revelation of Jesus Christ.' Galatians 1.11–12

The wider gospel
Doesn't this broaden your concept of the gospel? Ezekiel received his message from God – and God told him faithfully to repeat it truthfully word for word. Peter, John and the other disciples received their gospel from the lips of Jesus while he was on earth, and in case they forgot any of the three-year ministry's sermons and teaching God sent his Holy Spirit to remind them of every word ('The Advocate, the Holy Spirit, whom the Father will send in my name, will teach you everything, and remind you of all that I have said to you,' John 14.26). And Paul, in today's reading, rejoices that although he had missed out on the closeness of the Twelve with Jesus, the Lord nevertheless had dealt with him, on a one-to-one basis by revelation. That is why, when he was writing

to the Christians in Rome, twice in a relatively short letter he was able to call this precious teaching '*my* gospel' (Rom. 2.16; 16.25). It was not Paul's authorship, but his Lord's gospel revealed personally to Paul. And he was quietly, Christianly proud of it.

What is our gospel?

What is the gospel that we preach and teach and share? Almost certainly an amalgam of Scripture and revelation – revelation being in this case the guiding hand of God in our lives. God is not teaching and revealing to us new things every day, for us to forget or jettison them because we do not find them word for word in the Bible. They are there – if we search, for all our experiences are to be found there. Paul valued his revelation, but he didn't divorce it from the Scriptures, because he found that even though the New Testament had not yet been written (and, in any case, he was writing most of it himself), the revelations given to him by Jesus could be seen as illustrations or fulfilments of the Scriptures he already knew or had to hand.

Acts 29

Someone has well said that we are now writing the twenty-ninth chapter of the book of Acts. We are, in that our lives may be used by God to help others, in much the same way that the lives of Peter, Paul, Barnabas, Mark and the rest have helped countless millions since the New Testament was compiled. For non-Christians, we are probably the first Bible that they see. It is a sobering thought, because so often with the naivety (or criticism) of unbelief they expect us to be perfect. That is why it is imperative that we should point them to Christ and his perfection, before they demand of us an ideal we cannot give, or, disillusioned by our frailty, they turn away from Christ and his Church.

Praying for revelation

Implicit in Paul's message is an encouragement to pray always for more revelation. The enthusiasm of his followers must be a great encouragement to the Lord – and he will respond. When we have stopped asking God for things, we have lost a vital interest. He will continue to love us, but he will be grieved at our lack of lustre. But with our praying, may we also not be blind to what God is doing and showing to us already: the surprises, the up-lifts, the way problems are being worked out; plans we may make that get changed; new meetings, people and places. Are not all these God's revelations?

> *Lord, give us the eyes of faith to see*
> *beyond the obvious.*

Shared experiences
Shared experinces – between God and humanity, as well as between human beings – are the stuff of which faith is made. God intervenes in our lives in millions of different ways, but the onus is then on us to broadcast his interventions.

Suggested hymns
Go, tell it on the mountain; I sing the almighty power of God; Tell me the old, old story; Tell out, my soul, the greatness of the Lord.

Third Sunday of Epiphany   23 January
Principal Service   **From Darkness to Light**
Isa. 9.1–4; Ps. 27.1, 4–9; 1 Cor. 1.10–18; Matt. 4.12–23

'The people who sat in darkness have seen a great light, and for those who sat in the region and shadow of death, light has dawned. From that time, Jesus began to proclaim: "Repent, for the kingdom of heaven has come near."' Matthew 4.16–17

Darkness of spirit
It was not a physical darkness, but darkness of spirit that first Isaiah and then Jesus inveighed against. Far more dangerous than physical darkness, this is an eternal affliction, a state of 'principalities and powers', all the more deadly because it can approach so insidiously that its presence may pass undetected until its advance has gone beyond the point of no return. At the coming of Jesus, few if any of the Jews would have admitted to being in spiritual darkness. But then, they could look Jesus in the eye and declare they'd never been in bondage, when their history had been punctuated with exile and slavery and they were currently writhing under a Roman army of occupation. And today there are those who will try to defend living an irreligious life by claiming that they are truly free.

God gave us free will – to choose between light and darkness. But since the way of Christ, the light of the world, is *not* darkness it doesn't leave too many alternatives.

Light had dawned
Light had dawned on the Jews, whether the Jews recognized it or not. And today Christ's light has dawned on a world where many still don't recognize it. Now, as then, God does not compel recognition. At any time in history he could have intervened to withdraw freedom of choice from the human race. But what sort of a god would require automatic service from automatons programmed to do no other? Our loving Lord wants us to come to him out of love – love related to the greatest Love of all which suffered at Calvary. We are of far more value to him than the most self-sacrificing Stoics. And he meets love with Love.

Heaven at the door
With Jesus, heaven came to earth. He was a window into glory as he taught and preached and healed, giving himself and all that he had to all who come to him. In the prayer he gave us, he made no distinction of aeons of time between the clauses that so often we separate: 'Your kingdom come, your will be done' (Matt. 6.10). The kingdom *had* come, with him. It could be experienced, however partially (and, since we have not yet moved through the veil to glory, we use 'partially' while realizing its semantic limitations), here and now, wherever folk met up with Jesus and did his will. Today, it's in the hearts of Christians; when we get to glory, it will be in a sense like stepping into another room, and we shall still be 'at home'.

Key of admittance
Yet the key of admittance to heaven – here and herafter – remains the same. Repentance. The most dedicated Christian cannot obtain admittance while carrying any unconfessed, unforgiven sin. One would imagine that such unwelcome impediments could be jettisoned quickly and without regret. Some sin can, while other sin some folk tend to cling to as though it were a passport to heaven instead of a barrier. Sometimes, we confess a sin, yet take it back and worry over it, for all the world as if we doubt God's ability or willingness to forgive – or even because life may (in the short term, at any rate) seem a bit easier if we break or bend a rule here

44

and there. Sin is sin. There is no such thing as a large or small sin, a black or a white sin. It's all sin, and it's all bad news. 'Repent, and get rid of it!' Jesus is still saying – or heaven will not come close.

Light of our lives
The more we accept Jesus and his light into our lives, the less sin will be able to get established; and the quicker we deal with sin's advances, the more time we shall have for the work of God. The world of 2005 stands in even greater need of Christ's light than it did in the time of Isaiah or in the first century AD, beause there are more people today who don't yet have Christ's light.

That's the bad news. The good news is that there are more people today than ever before who do have his light. It's how we shine it out that will make a difference.

Family service input
Encourage the young people, in these cold, short January days, to plan a parochial 'Week of Light', highlighting ways in which the light of Christ can percolate from the church through the parish.

Suggested hymns
Brightest and best; Light's abode, celestial Salem; O, worship the Lord in the beauty of holiness; The people that in darkness sat.

Third Sunday of Epiphany *Second Service*
For What We Receive ... Ps. 33; Eccles. 3.1–11; 1 Pet. 1.3–12 [or Luke 4.14–21]
'Although you have not seen [Jesus Christ], you love him; and even though you do not see him now, you believe in him and rejoice with an indescribable and glorious joy, for you are receiving the outcome of your faith, the salvation of your souls.' 1 Peter 1.8–9

By faith
We are receiving salvation now, by faith. That is why Jesus could say that he had brought heaven near. We don't have to wait until glory to be saved. Salvation is ours, by belief in Jesus now. It lends a new, richer meaning to Jesus' beautiful promise:

In my Father's house there are many dwelling-places. If it were not so, would I have told you that I go to prepare a place for you? And if I go and prepare a place for you, I will come again and will take you to myself, so that where I am, there you may be also. (John 14:2–4)

One prepares a room for a known arrival, a scheduled appointee. Heaven doesn't deal in scratch accommodation or double bookings.

Our joy
Is our faith so wonderful that the joy is indescribable? If we are dedicated to sharing it with others, we usually try to find the right words so that they may be drawn to Christ. Yet there will almost certainly be deep feelings, revelations, joys and longings, that are secrets between Jesus and ourselves – for who can sound the depths of God's love? Our English is a rich and beautiful language, but there are parts of our faith too deep and beautiful for words: times of precious, wordless prayer, when salvation is real and heaven is close. God gives us these times as his gifts. Treasure them, for they come when he knows we need them most. Some are for sharing – again, when the time is right.

In season
'For everything there is a season, and a time for every matter under heaven,' said Koheleth the Preacher (Eccles. 3.1). We in our time can consider ourselves especially blessed, because we believe in Jesus without actually seeing him (John 20.29). We may not have been given that beautiful verse if Thomas had not insisted on seeing as a prerequisite to believing in the resurrected Christ. Thank God, then, for Thomas and his doubting!

Yet many would not give thanks, because there are many like Thomas around today who seek for proof rather than faith. They will not commit themselves to Christ, yet run after the gambles of the world, which can take wings and depart before their eyes.

It was Tertullian, the fiery preacher of the early Church, who sighed after patience but never caught up with it, who said: 'Can anyone who looks at a single rose doubt the existence of God?' Too often the answer to this is 'Yes'.

If a resurrection could not convince some folk, what chance has a rose? Each time such unbelief occurs there must flow a tear from the Father-heart of God.

Belief into love

Because God is love he calls forth a reciprocal love from us. Belief grows into love, and strengthens all the while. And love grows into trust. If you look back along your Christian life you will see this clearly. It's a certainty. But it all follows from that initial, all-important *fiat* – Yes, Lord, I believe; be it done to me according to your will. And if we are as bold as Mary in our faith, we keep on praying it: do what you will with me, Lord.

An abundant response

The response of Jesus is munificent: we receive 'the outcome of our faith, the salvation of our souls'. The contract is magnificently unfair, the wonder is that anyone should refuse it.

While we are still given time we might be able to make a Christian difference in someone's life. In fact, with the Lord on our side (Ps. 118.6), we should not be content with only one life changed for the better.

Suggested Hymns

As with gladness men of old; Father God, I wonder how I managed to exist; For my sake and the gospel's, go; I cannot tell why he whom angels worship.

Fourth Sunday of Epiphany (or Presentation of Christ in the Temple, if transferred from 2 February; see p. 263) 30 January
Principal Service **Glory Revealed** 1 Kings 17.8–16; Ps. 36.5–10; 1 Cor. 1.18–31; John. 2.1–11

'Jesus did this, the first of his signs, in Cana of Galilee, and revealed his glory; and his disciples believed in him.' John 2.11

God's provision

God had provided for Elijah by multiplying the oil and meal of the widow of Zarephath (1 Kings 17.8ff.), and he showed a similar over-riding of physical constituents in changing the water to prime wine at Cana. This same power is understood by Paul in his letter to the Corinthians as 'the source of our life in Christ Jesus' (1 Cor. 1.20).

God himself. He may do us the honour of involving us in his miracles, as he involved the widow and the catering staff at Cana, but the sheer authority behind what he does leaves us marvelling. His workings are not to be explained step by step, because they are – humanly speaking – inexplicable. We who are inordinately proud of our intellect must accept this, and rest on trust.

> *In some way or other, the Lord will provide,*
> *It may not be my way,*
> *It may not be thy way;*
> *And yet, in his own way,*
> *The Lord will provide.*

> Mrs I. J. Cook

And it is glory
The evangelist John called it, simply, 'glory'. Jesus at Cana 'revealed his glory' – that is, showed a power that was super-human, supernatural, inexplicable. It was God at work, as in the widow's pantry at Zarephath centuries before.

So, 'glory' is 'otherness', an indefinable extra that takes no account of the laws of physics, chemistry, biology and medicine that by contrast bind us within fairly rigid parameters. 'Glory' knows no bounds and observes no parameters. 'Glory' can translo-cate and is no servant of time. 'Glory' is not subject to the laws of gravity or material as we know it; Jesus could pass through walls and doors, and could be so empowered by 'glory' as to glow on the Mount of the Transfiguration.

A tantalizing thought
The fact that Mary could so confidently appeal to Jesus, and then calmly order the servants to do as he directed, raises the tantalizing thought that Jesus had already at some time and place given his mother an indication of his glory. We are so familiar with the Cana wedding that we can take Mary's part for granted. But there seems to have been such a special bond between her and her son, that it would be understandable for her to have somehow had a foretaste of his power.

The generosity of Jesus
It is an indication of Christ's generous love that he could use his divine power in such a homely, social setting as the wedding breakfast. No eloquent sermon was preached, no overt healing to save a soul, just a guest coming to the rescue to save the blushes of the catering manager and keep the jollity going a little longer. What a kind heart of love our Lord has! May we, too, resolve not to be overly primly pious or long-faced in his service!

Strengthening the bond
The miracle, however, had a more serious side, if not a calculated effect. It strengthened the bond between Jesus and his disiples, and probably set the seal on their commitment. After all, the converted water was not ordinary wine, but streets ahead of what had already been drunk. 'God gives with no niggardly hand' as Professor F. F. Bruce used to remark at this point to his students.

May we, too, be generous in our service for God. May we also resolve to pray especially for those undertaking marriage vows, remembering how Jesus blessed a wedding celebration so lovingly and generously.

Family service input
Encourage the young people to start an in-depth project on the 'glory' of God, using the pointers in this sermon and following them up with concordances, commentaries, etc. The project could be widened to include older members.

Suggested hymns
Be thou my vision; God of grace and God of glory; Thine be the glory; To God be the glory.

Fourth Sunday of Epiphany   *Second Service*
Refreshed by Love   Ps. 34; Gen. 28.10–22;
Philemon 1–16 [or Mark 1.21–28]

'I pray that the sharing of your faith may become effective when you perceive all the good that we may do for Christ. I have indeed received much joy and encouragement from your love, because the hearts of the saints have been refreshed by you, my brother.' Philemon 6–7

There is hope
There is hope, Paul believes, that someone who could give him such encouragement and refreshment would also have it in his heart to show magnanimity towards the young Onesimus and take the lad back into his service. Paul presses home the appeal even further: take him back, Philemon, not as a slave but as a friend, for I, Paul, believe he has proved his worth. We may reverently deduce that Paul's plea would not fall on deaf ears.

Godly pleas
Praying for others, and physically interceding between two parties as Paul was doing, is as vital today as then. Whether the dispute or misunderstanding has been of long or short duration, often all that is needed is an intermediary to effect a rapprochement. It takes courage, for often one or both parties at the outset is opposed to any healing of the division. Paul entered into the business fired up and 'refreshed and encouraged' by Philemon's love and concern for his ministry. It was the best of beginnings.

Looking for the good
The closer we look for good in others, the more we shall find, and the stronger will be the foundation for our dealings with them. It is still so true that upright, godly people (such as Philemon obviously was) can spend their lives in helping many others yet fail to see close at hand someone with whom they have a grievance, or who has a grievance against them.

What it costs
If we happen to be the intermediary, we don't need telling what the exercise costs in sheer spiritual courage and compassion. But if we are one or other of the parties at variance, we may not appreciate all it has taken for the modern-day Paul to enter the fray. It's far easier not to get involved ('They'll think I'm an interfering busybody!'), and to ignore the chance of healing other people's differences. If one goes in with good intentions but as clumsily as an elephant treading on eggshells, the situation may indeed go from bad to worse. Any exercise of rapprochement needs prayer, and we can only guess at how long Paul had prayed and sought godly advice before he wrote his letter to Philemon. Perhaps, indeed, it was the outcome of several earlier attempts

that had been aborted. As it now stands, it's a model of prayerful concern and diplomacy, encouragement and love.

Spreading good news
We can infer, from Paul's generous praise of Philemon's ministry, that the folk to whom he ministered, as well as Paul's companions, had talked about his goodness. There's not such a surfeit of good news in today's world that more spreading of praise and appreciation wouldn't come amiss. Bad news travels fast enough. May we, as Christians, play our part in godly gossiping; when we find good, let's broadcast it. The ministry of Philemon had given not only Paul but also young Onesimus hope, that the lad could return home. And let's not forget Onesimus' worth: for his part, his loyalty and service to Paul had made him worthy of the plea to Philemon. It was a case of mutual encouragement and refreshment all round.

The Christian life
Yes, the Christian life is the best of all lives – but it's even better for the uplift that such refreshment gives. Let's not wait until we write our sympathy cards and letters before we tell our family and friends, our fellow-workers and worshippers how precious they are to us. We won't look for it, of course, but we just might get a bit of refreshment in return!

Suggested hymns
Christ is our cornerstone; Help us to help each other, Lord; Lift high the cross; Songs of thankfulness and praise.

Sunday next before Lent   6 February
Principal Service   **Bowled Over**   Ex. 24.12–18; Ps. 2 or Ps. 99; 2 Peter 1.16–21; Matt. 17.1–9
'When the disciples heard this, they fell to the ground and were overcome by fear. But Jesus came and touched them, saying, "Get up and do not be afraid." And when they looked up, they saw no one except Jesus himself alone.' Matthew 17.6–8

A natural reaction

It was only natural for the disciples to be bowled over by the glory on the mountain. They'd gone up there with Jesus, probably expecting a sermon or two, and even a picnic. Then Jesus was lit up by glory. That in itself seems not to have fazed them. Nor does the appearance of the long-dead Moses and Elijah (also glorified, Luke tells us, Luke 9.11) prove too much for the mere mortals. We're not told how the disciples recognized the prophets – perhaps in the conversation Jesus called them by name to make identification certain. But Peter, James and John prostrated themselves in terror, hiding their faces from the sight and sound of the strange 'bright' cloud and the voice from heaven that followed.

What was the cloud other than surely the shimmering. *Shekinah-*glory of God. We don't know how long Jesus let them tremble, but they did not obey his command to 'Get up' immediately; they 'looked up' and saw that the cloud had gone, Moses and Elijah had vanished, and Jesus was there alone with them.

Do not fear

'Do not be afraid.' Did Jesus expect them to witness such happenings without fear? Yes, apparently. Does he expect us to go through whatever life sends without fear? Yes, it would seem so. Can we take comfort from the fact that sturdy Galilean fishermen got terrified every now and then? Yes, but that was before God implanted his Spirit in them at Pentecost. Never afterwards do we hear of them being afraid. Therefore we, with the same Holy Spirit, *have the spiritual means not to fear.*

The number one command

Jesus tells us not to fear, more often than anything else he commands – certainly more frequently than he tells us to 'love our neighbour'. It's a measure of God's love and concern for us. He knows the deleterious effects of fear not only on our physical bodies, but on our spirits. So he tells us not to do it. Fear, in its many and varied forms, is of the devil. It is bad news. And yet we still treat our Lord's command more like a mild suggestion, or break it with impunity. Satan must feel satisfied with his progress so far in getting his mankind so conditioned to fear.

How can we break the habit and take on Jesus's prime command with the respect due to it? Only by constantly and consistently praying for guidance, off-loading our burdens on to God and refusing to take them back.

Standing firm

Who knows what more the disciples may have seen, up there on the mountain, had they not let down their spiritual guard and succumbed to fear?

'Well, they were still young in the faith!' So they were, and we who still let down our guard at times should not throw the first stone. But the implication is there: when we do take fear on board, what may we be missing that God is waiting, willing and wanting to reveal to us? When our stomach is churned into knots with terror and foreboding, and our mind paralysed with fear, how can God get through? Note that Jesus made contact again with the disciples *after* the glory had faded and gone. What had they missed in the meantime?

If we could only see how that invisible link with God is *blocked* when we accept fear into our lives, perhaps we should be quicker to send it back to where it belongs – in Satan's lap.

Family service input

Arrange a workshop on 'Fear and its overcoming', and encourage the young people to bring fear into the open, turn the spotlight on to it and destroy it, . . . applying then the process to their life and experience.

Suggested hymns

Christ upon the mountain peak; Christ whose glory fills the skies; Fight the good fight; 'Tis good, Lord, to be here.

Sunday next before Lent *Second Service*
Assumptions of Old Ps. 84; Ecclus. 48.1–10 or 2 Kings 2.1–12; Matt. 17.9–23 (or 1–23)

'How glorious you were, Elijah, in your wondrous deeds! . . . You were taken up by a whirlwind of fire, in a chariot with horses of fire.' Ecclesiasticus 48.4a, 9

Moses and Elijah

The deaths of both Moses and Elijah had been unusual, to say the least. Moses, we are told, 'was buried in a valley in the land of Moab, opposite Beth-peor, but no one knows his burial place to this day' (Deut. 34.6). Elijah's departure was much more dramatic, as the horsedrawn chariot of fire whirled him up and away from the watching Elisha (2 Kings 2.11–12). In the non-canonical apocrypha and pseudepigrapha, there is a book written in Aramaic on 'The Assumption of Moses'.

Whether the assumptions of Moses and Elijah had any bearing on their presence with Jesus in the transfiguration experience, is not certain. They could simply have been representing the old 'Law and the Prophets'. The main reason seems to have been to show that death (however it is perceived to come) is not the end; those who have 'passed on' have not passed out of God's cognizance, God's purpose or God's love. In ways in which as yet we cannot understand, they are enjoying a freedom which is streets ahead of physical life as we know it.

Foretastes of glory

It's as though God is so thrilled with the success of Jesus' sacrifice opening up glory to those who believe in him, that he simply must give us glimpses and foretastes of the best that is yet to come. And as we prepare to enter the sombre, penitential season of Great Lent, it's good to reflect on this. God could have inspired a Bible with no visions of glory, but God in his love chose otherwise. When we are buffeted by pain, tragedy or fears, or when we hold the hand of someone mourning the loss of a friend, we have hope to give and to hold on to, that this life is leading to a fuller, richer, more free experience.

'But nobody has yet come back to prove it!' This is often alleged, and yet in the transfiguration Moses and Elijah did return; after his resurrection, Jesus also returned; and the incidences of sightings, hearings, feelings of the so-called 'departed' continue to increase. In a multitude of ways, God is saying: 'Believe me, I am parting the veil between this life and the next all the time. Feed your faith and starve your doubts!'

Once again, he doesn't need to do it, but he is doing it out of love.

The value of the past
In the transfiguration, God was also showing the value of the past.
We need it, as a foundation for the greater foundation stone of
Christ and our Christian faith. We need the faith of the people of
the past to encourage us. In the Gospels Jesus teaches us how he
valued the past, primarily because it foreshadowed and
undergirded his message and his mission.

But, now . . .
Throughout his preaching and teaching, Jesus emphasized the
change from the past to the present. This . . . and that . . . has
happened in the past, BUT NOW, I tell you . . . Time and again,
the message is that we are to move forward, with the experience
of the past, to new growth and new outreach. The past will not
be jettisoned or left behind – the transfiguration shows us that –
but it will be there in a new way, a new form, because it cannot
die. What God has breathed life into can never die. The past points
up the present and the future; in so many ways we shall probably
read only a small proportion of the signs. Twice the compiler of
Proverbs tells us not to remove the old landmarks (Prov. 22.28;
23.10). They are there for a purpose – just as are the landmarks
along our personal road of life. Where have they led us? Did we
follow them when we should? What is the landmark we have our
eyes on at the moment? We need to pray constantly for grace to
read aright all the signs God is giving us.

Suggested hymns
Christ upon the mountain peak; Eternal light! Eternal light!; Jesus,
these eyes have never seen; Lord Jesus, once you spoke to men.

Ash Wednesday   9 February
Principal Service   **For Our Sake**   Joel 2.1–2, 12–17
or Isa. 58.1–12; Ps. 51.1–17; 2 Cor. 5.20b—6.10;
Matt. 6.1–6, 16–21 or John 8.1–11

*'For our sake he made him to be sin who knew no sin, so that in him
we might become the righteousness of God.' 2 Corinthians 5.21*

55

Exposed to awfulness

Have you ever thought how demeaning and distasteful it must have been for the spotless Lamb of God to be exposed to the awfulness of sin? How terrible it must have been for the Jesus of glory to go to a place so filthy horrible as hell! But he went through with it – because he loved us so much, and wanted so much to win our salvation. Jesus voluntarily tarnished himself with our sin, that he could burnish us with his righteousness. And he will never be the same again, for he now bears Calvary's scars as a grim and blessed reminder. Nor shall we ever be the same as we were before we met Jesus, for the scars of our sin have been so subsumed into his wounds that we are now able to stand before him in the purity of righteousness.

This blessed thought was the joy of Paul's life: 'There is therefore now no condemnation for those who are in Christ Jesus,' he encourages the Roman Christians (Rom. 8.1). What's he talking about? those with good memories would ask, recalling the arch-persecutor of the early Church and the man who had consented to Stephen's death. But Paul knew what Jesus had revealed to him (see, for example, Eph. 3.3), and he was not speaking out of turn.

Great Lent

On this first day of Great Lent we come to the altar rail for the imposition of ashes and wear the smudgy cross at least for the rest of the day. What does it say to those who meet us, and perhaps ask us about it? Only that we've been to church on Ash Wednesday? We need to have our answers ready (cf. 1 Peter 3.15), for, please God, we shall be asked. If the ashes of last year's palm crosses are to mean anything to others, we need first to be certain about their meaning and message for ourselves.

The cross is an identification with the sufferings of our Lord, albeit on a smaller scale – and predominantly today with his temptations. Therefore we are committing ourselves to following his example, of using the word of God *every time* to defeat the temptations of Satan. 'It is written . . . it is written . . . it is written . . .' (Matt. 4.4, 7, 10). Back in the 1950s, Billy Graham was famous for his phrase 'My Bible says . . .', which prefaced many of his illustrations. The more we make God's Bible our Bible, the more we shall be able to quote it.

Satan hates hearing the word of God – so that's reason enough to give it to him. But we need to be wary: the devil is not averse to quoting it back to us with his own slants and inuendos (cf. Matt. 4.6). Let us pray for a right discernment and use of God's word. In Jesus, we are the righteousness of God; that is a big plus. Also, since the devil tangled with Jesus in the wilderness, he has received the body-blow of Christ's triumph at Calvary. That's another point in our favour. For Satan, constant irritant as he is, is only a shadow of his pre-Calvary self. Remember that when next he comes knocking.

The difference of Lent
Is this Lent going to make a difference to our lives? Or are we going to let the purple altar furnishing, the extra mid-week (often ecumenical) services, even the ashy cross of today, come and go as an interesting but inevitable part of the year's cycle? Outward signs are important, but they are not *the* most important; and we could really observe Lent without any of them. If we want to draw closer to Jesus this Lent, in the solitude of our hearts, we need to look for him in the wilderness. He was virtually lost to the world for those forty days, as he fought in the *secret* and *uninteresting* desert for victory against the devil.

   Lent at its closest to Jesus needs to be in spiritual communion with him.

Suggested hymns
Christian, dost thou see them?; Father of heaven, whose love profound; Forty days and forty nights; Lord, in this thy mercy's day.

Ash Wednesday   *Second Service*
Practical Christianity   Ps. 102; Isa. 1.10–18;
Luke 15.11–32

'Learn to do good; seek justice, rescue the oppressed, defend the orphan, plead for the widow.' Isaiah 1.17

Lent with Jesus
Lent with Jesus, at its simplest, is, as we saw in today's main service, drawing aside spiritually with him, as he temporarily left the busyness of the world to meet and overcome Satan in the desert. But not many of us can do this on a full-time basis. We

must draw aside at least for some part of each day, if only because Jesus obviously felt it was essential for his mission – if he needed forty days' preparation, we need some too. Many of the monks of former days did precisely that, withdrawing from society and fasting (with varying degrees of rigour, according to inclination, location and climatic conditions) from Ash Wednesday until Easter.

The social gospel

Yet we are not monks in the Syrian or Egyptian deserts. We're in the social world, committed to preaching the social gospel that, as our text from Isaiah shows, did not begin with the New Testament. Drawing aside with Jesus benefits our souls; drawing aside with him in order to share his gospel better with others will benefit other' souls as well. That is surely observing Great Lent in the best and most positive way. Our virtuous glow may deepen if we give up chocolate and sugar, but will that exercise help anyone else's soul (or even ours, to any noticeable degree)? Lent is a two-way process, of reaching in (to the innermost depths of our souls) and reaching out (to others). We should not worry over-much about getting the balance right: take it to God and reason it out with him. As Isaiah 1.18 says: '"Let us argue it out," says the Lord.' In his good time he will make his Lenten purposes clear to us. And Lent does come round each year for a purpose.

Waking Israel to realization

In our text God was trying to waken up Israel to a realization of her responsibilities – social, as well as spiritual. Individuals and nations come apart when the balance of these two responsibilities is out of kilter. They were always together in the life of our Lord, as he preached and healed, taught and fed the hungry, expounded the Scriptures and raised the dead. Today there are many parishes looking at the question of the spiritual and social balance: has the Church got it right, or if not how can it regain that balance? Are we, as a Church, ministering to all the needs of all the people, or to some of the needs of a few? Perhaps the Lord is asking our own community to 'argue it out'.

The community centre

Sometimes, rather cynically, a churchyard is referred to as 'the dead centre of the community', and with a vestige of truth maybe.

But who would want such a negative title to be the sole designation? The Church should be the centre of the community, for all the reasons given in our text from Isaiah. Lent is an appropriate time to evaluate whether this is in fact the case, or whether some of these functions have been gradually hived off elsewhere.

Just occasionally, the media broadcast news of folk seeking sanctuary (usually for political asylum) in a church, and some people show surprise that this tradition is still operative. If it was claimed in our own church, how would we react, having our text in mind? Do people come to the church in our place for justice, or do they go somewhere else?

The degree to which the Church is involved with the community can be an indication of the scope of its ministry – holistic or partial. Perhaps it need not change. Perhaps it cannot change. Perhaps it should not change. Dare we pray:

> God grant us the serenity
> to accept the things we cannot change;
> Courage to change the things we can –
> And wisdom to know the difference.

Suggested hymns
Abide with me; Judge eternal, throned in splendour; Lord, her watch thy Church is keeping; Through all the changing scenes of life.

First Sunday of Lent   13 February
Principal Service   **A Difference of One**
Gen. 2.15–17; 3.1–7; Ps. 32; Rom. 5.12–19; Matt. 4.1–11

'Therefore just as one man's trespass led to condemnation for all, so one man's act of righteousness leads to justification and life for all. For just as by one man's disobedience the many were made sinners, so by the one man's obedience the many will be made righteous.' Romans 5.18–19

One makes a difference
From the very beginning it has been so. Created by God as individuals, each of us matters and one makes a difference. It had taken one to compromise with sin and thus to condemn many to

the consequences. It took one to go to Calvary and redress the balance. If anyone thinks their life does not impact on others and make a difference, let them read and reread Paul's fifth chapter to the Romans. At home, at church, at work or play, we are accumulating the difference our life is having on others – maybe thousands, millions of others. But the meeting we fail to attend, the service we miss, the letter we neglect to write, or the phone call we say we're too busy to make, all mean that the differences here that might have been possible have been forfeited.

Because one man ran the gauntlet of temptation by Satan in the wilderness, and emerged from the contest as Victor, we have Great Lent. We can build on the example of Jesus and make a difference this Lent – in church, home or business. God may bring us to a place of change, or a plateau of respite; an opportunity to share Christ, or a time of quiet, interior reflection; a time for action, or a time for withdrawal from the world's helter-skelter. Whatever, however, whenever, let us pray for grace to discern his purpose in bringing us to another Great Lent when he could just as easily have ushered us into glory. His purposes for us have yet to run some mileage. Depending on how we use Lent, by the time it makes way for Easter he may have shown us considerably more of ourselves and of himself.

Classic preparation

The wilderness experience was Jesus' preparation for ministry: classic preparation, seeking God's will away from social and economic distractions. Abraham had done the same, centuries before; so had Moses, Elijah, Ezekiel. With slight variations the practice had proved its value, time and again.

But spiritual distractions could not be left behind, even in the wilderness. And they still have a habit of accompanying us wherever we go.

But where Satan goes, God goes too. The psalmist sang:

> *Where can I go from your Spirit?*
> *Or where can I flee from your presence? . . .*
> *If I take the wings of the morning*
> *and settle at the farthest limits of the sea,*
> *even there your hand shall lead me.*

Ps. 139.7, 9–10

We may withdraw from all normal life in Lent, yet God – and Satan – will still be with us in the desert, as they were with Jesus. Does it seem a fair exchange? No, it's magnificently unfair, for the odds are stacked heavily against the devil. God has legions of angels on whom to call if necessary to come to our aid. That is their raison d'être, and they are proficient in their calling. There are legions of them, yet every one can make a difference. It needed only one angel to call forth Mary's world-changing 'fiat' (Luke 1.26); one angel to send the holy family to safety in Egypt (Matt. 2.13); and one angel to open the tomb on Easter morning (Matt. 28.2)

Perhaps it will take only one Lent to make the biggest difference yet in our lives. We can never fathom how one God can work so intricately and so intimately in the lives of millions of people, day after day after day. But isn't it wonderful to know we are not one of a crowd?

'I have called you by name, you are mine,' says God (Isa. 43.1). It would be hard to get more personal than that, wouldn't it? As we reflect tonight on what we have done for God today, let us remember that no one else has done precisely the same. Every time we promise something for him, remember no one else has made the very same promise. Ours can make such a difference, with his blessing.

Family service input
Encourage the young people to make a file on as many facets of the parish and church life as they can, and of the gifts, skills, talents, etc. that comprise the whole.

Suggested hymns
Father, hear the prayer we offer; Father, I place into your hands; Lead us, heavenly Father, lead us; O Jesus, I have promised.

First Sunday of Lent   *Second Service*
Calling on God   Ps. 50.1–15; Deut. 6.4–9, 16–25; Luke 15.1–10
'Offer to God a sacrifice of thanksgiving, and pay your vows to the Most High. Call on me in the day of trouble; I will deliver you, and you shall glorify me.' Psalm 50.14–15

Gratitude and promises
It's an exceptional bargain: in return for our gratitude and dili-
gence in keeping promises, God has contracted to bring us out of
trouble. There is one final condition: that we give him the credit
and not ourselves or anyone else. It means remembering to say
'Thank you' (which, too often, we don't); and keeping a record,
written or mental, of the promises we make to him and to others
in his name. 'Oh, I'm sorry, I completely forgot!' is no way to
evade a promise made; promises should be sacrosanct. Does God
break his?

Provided we have done our best to keep these conditions, then
we can justifiably call on God's help when we need it. Yet the
Father-heart of God's love is so great, he helps us *before* we have
perfected our Christian ethic, often a long time before. And we
need to show our gratitude by giving him the glory – as Jesus
did. We are wonderful people, who do wonderful things, but it's
Christian policy to keep all this wonder a secret and instead to
point others to our wonderful God.

God's timing
Notice that God doesn't tell us to anticipate trouble. If we worry
about it before it actually comes, we are loading ourselves with
an unnecessary burden (and anticipated trouble often doesn't even
come). To get a car moving you turn on the ignition at the time
you want to move, not a day or a week before. God offers us help
'in the day of trouble', not a day or a week before. When we really
need it, he will give us the help.

But we are seemingly programmed now to forward planning,
complicated and far-distant pensions and insurance schemes. It's
small wonder that so often God's timing throws us out of kilter.

'In quietness and in trust shall be your strength' (Isa. 30.15). It's
a good text to illuminate for Lent.

A lesson in trust
As the plane kicked the air behind it over the Atlantic, the pilot
radioed through to the cabin for all seatbelts to be fastened, as
they were running into turbulence ahead. Soon the aircraft was
plunging and rolling, and many of the passengers became nervous.
A woman sitting next to a small boy watched in surprise as, uncon-
cerned, he continued filling in a crossword in his comic.

'Aren't you frightened?' she asked, at length. The boy looked up at her and grinned. 'Why should I be scared? It's my Dad in the cockpit!'

Should we, as Christians, give way to panic when, even on the wildest, worst days, it's *our* Dad – our Abba – in the cockpit, firmly in control, not only of us and our machinery, but of the very elements themselves. We'd do well, also, to reflect that whatever may happen this Lent, come Easter we shall be celebrating this same wonderful Dad's power to raise the dead. He has brought us this far. He's not likely to desert us now.

Call on God
But when trouble comes slamming into our lives, it's sometimes tempting to seek a quick fix – perhaps a friend or neighbour, perhaps a fellow-worshipper, perhaps we ourselves, if we put the grey cells to work, can come up with a solution. But God tells us to come to him for help. He doesn't deal in quick fixes, or *any* solutions, but *the* solution, the right one, for each and every problem. Because, by the time we appeal to him for help, he's already got his foresight on what is in our future; he knows exactly how to solve our present problem the better to equip us for the next situation or experience.

No other help on earth comes within miles of competing with that!

Suggested hymns
O help us, Lord, each hour of need; Seek ye first the kingdom of God; What a Friend we have in Jesus; With joy we meditate the grace.

Second Sunday of Lent   20 February
Principal Service   **No Condemnation**   Gen. 12.1–4a; Ps. 121; Rom. 4.1–5, 13–17; John 3.1–17

'[Jesus said] "Indeed, God did not send the Son into the world to condemn the world, but in order that the world might be saved through him." ' John 3.17

Blame in the right place

Why didn't Jesus condemn the world? Wasn't it in such an awful state that condemnation would have been thoroughly justified? But God is a God of justice, and apportions blame only where blame is due. There was one culprit guilty of causing the confusion and sin in the world: Satan. He had used people as his instruments, as pawns in the deadly game he was playing; but God saw through the devilish machinations to the power behind them. Out of pity, love and justice, Jesus was sent to save misguided and manipulated humankind.

Is it any wonder that Satan is so venomous against anyone who reminds him of the man who won at Calvary?

Satan's wiles

The devil is still manipulating wherever he can – and he's become so proficient at hiding behind his victims, it's all too easy for us to blame the instrument rather than the operator. The sinner's fault lies in compromise with Satan: that is bad, but one day the devil will have to answer for the greater crime of perpetuating the evil in the first place. He has his followers: those who see him as their master, and whom he has so befuddled and deluded that their 'gospel' has everything topsy-turvy, with Satan the good god and the Almighty as evil; sin as the force that can rule the world, and good as weak and ineffectual. Christians may be asked to tangle with these Satan-adherents face to face, in which case Satan in them will come up against God's Spirit in us. But we need not wait for a confrontation: we can pray against Satan and his forces at any time and in any place, particularly in Lent when we are focusing on Jesus' victory over the devil in the wilderness. Satan quails before a prayer offensive. We may never know what evil we avert or destroy with our prayers – but God will know.

Honouring salvation

It's just one way of honouring the sacrifice of Christ that brought our salvation. Since Calvary, no one *needs* to be lost to the good; and we, in the prayerful strength of Christ, have the means to recall those now heading for destruction. We can also affirm and encourage others to say 'No' to Satan.

> *You're starting, my boy, on life's journey*
> *Along the grand highway of life.*
> *You'll meet with a thousand temptations,*
> *Each city with evil is rife.*
> *The world is a stage of excitement,*
> *There's danger wherever you go;*
> *But if you'd be true to your manhood,*
> *Have courage, my boy, to say 'No!'*
>
> H. R. Palmer and Ira D. Sankey

Christlikeness

If we want to be like Christ, therefore, we must quash any feelings of condemnation, censureship or judgement. God is the Judge: he may safely be left to take all the judicial steps that are necessary. Our mission is to continue the showing of love to the world that Christ began. Hating the sin but loving the sinner is far from easy; folk are quick to accuse Christians of double standards, spinelessness, and much more that should cause us no lost sleep if we are sensible. Surely, if God loved the world so much that he gave his most precious gift, we can afford also to love even when it's not reciprocated, or when it's misunderstood. It may be many years afterwards, but if we have played our part, someone somewhere will remember that Jesus smiled on them.

Is your heart breaking? You can still smile. Are you misrepresented, pilloried, ostracized? You can still smile.

> *There are many sorrows that will pass like shadows,*
> *There are many burdens that will disappear*
> *When we learn to greet them with a smile to meet them,*
> *For a smile is better than a frown or tear.*
>
> *You can smile, when you can't say a word;*
> *You can smile, when you cannot be heard,*
> *You can smile, when it's cloudy or fair,*
> *You can smile anytime, anywhere.*
>
> Alfred B. Ackley

Family service input

The very young can be encouraged to make 'smile' cards, with texts such as 'Jesus loves you!' inside. Older ones can either paraphrase the gospel reading or compose a hymn on it.

Suggested hymns
Blessed assurance; Fill thou my life, O Lord my God; I cannot tell
why he whom angels worship; Thy hand, O God, has guided.

Second Sunday of Lent   *Second Service*
The Penalty for Ingratitude   Ps. 135; Num. 21.4–9;
Luke 14.27–33

*'The people spoke against God and against Moses: "Why have you
brought us up out of Egypt to die in the wilderness? For there is no
food and no water, and we detest this miserable food!"' Numbers 21.5*

Spoilt children?
Who has not been told, when a child, 'If you don't say, "Thank
you", I'll take your present away!' (or words to this effect)? And
the Israelites in our lesson are acting like spoilt, ungrateful children. Why haven't they grown up, we may wonder, but, given a
similar situation, would we be any more mature? We'd like to
think so.
  'The grass may look greener . . .' until one gets to the other side.
Certainly the sun-baked wilderness was less inviting environmen-
tally than the equally sunny but fertile Nile delta of Egypt. True,
they had been hard-worked and badly treated slaves in Egypt,
whereas in the wilderness they had their freedom; but ingratitude
is ungracious and selectively forgetful at any time. God had given
them freedom, safety, food and water sufficient for their needs.
Yet with the capriciousness of the selfishly spoilt, they wanted to
exchange this for a few melons, cucumbers and garlic cloves of
an oppressive, alien land.

Gratitude to God
'Count your blessings', says the old hymn, but how often do we
follow its advice? It's a good exercise on retiring for the night:
sleep overtakes one before the tally is complete, but it helps to
inculcate a grateful heart. As an indication of our spiritual gratitude quota, we can reflect on how grateful we are for what others
do for us. If we are forgetful of friendships and kindnesses, then
almost certainly God is missing our thankfulness as well. Jesus
highlighted the value of gratitude in the episode of the healing of

ten lepers; only one of whom returned to give thanks for his healing. The point was made clear, though Jesus phrased it in a beautiful way saying that only one had given glory to God.

Making the point
It's reminiscent of the diplomacy of John Wesley. Travelling one day in a carriage with a boorish companion whose language was filthy with swearing, Wesley after a little time quietly interposed: 'I beg of you, sir, to grant me one request; kindly stop me, as soon as you hear me using any profanity.' The other subsided immediately in shame.

Throughout the wilderness wanderings, God was alternately cajoling, encouraging and reprimanding his chosen people. That they eventually reached the Promised Land was more a tribute to the Lord's love and patience than to Moses' leadership or even Joshua's courage – though these must have mitigated to some extent the ingratitude and moodiness of the multitude in general.

Gratitude today
We can look at the Church today and thank God that he continues to work out his purpose in a world that still knows how to be ungrateful and capricious. The work that Jesus began is spreading further and further, and we have never had the Bible in so many languages. Christian texts and teaching are reaching millions more people through the Internet, as modern technology makes distances shrink every day. It's an exciting age in which to live, and we need to thank God for giving us mission and ministry at such a time. But many things do not change, and we must thank him that this also is true: the word of the Lord, as strong and true as ever; the love of Christ in the eyes of a believer; the power and prayerfulness of corporate worship; and, perhaps best and most exciting of all, the challenge of living in the certainty of God's love, yet the glorious *un*certainty of what he may do next!

Thank you, Lord, for all of this – and for so much more.

Suggested hymns
Give me oil in my lamp; Now thank we all our God; Songs of thankfulness and praise; We thank you, Lord, for this fair earth.

Third Sunday of Lent   27 February

Principal Service   **Christian Character**   Ex. 17.1–7;
Ps. 95; Rom. 5.1–11; John 4.5–42

*'We boast in our hope of sharing the glory of God. And not only that,
but we also boast in our sufferings, knowing that suffering produces
endurance, and endurance produces character, and character produces
hope; and hope does not disappoint us, because God's love has been
poured into our hearts through the Holy Spirit that has been given to
us.' Romans 5.2b–5*

The character history

Paul traces the growth of what we call 'Christian character', from
the initial trauma of suffering through patient endurance, to the
hope that laughs at difficulties and dangers – for it knows they
are but transitory, and that even the sting of death has been drawn,
once for all time, at Calvary. He is well qualified to run this delin-
eation, for Paul has suffered more than most, endured more than
most, and yet lives by the hope that, in Jesus and for Jesus, it has
all been worth the struggle. It has been said that only the soil that
has been deeply ploughed can yield the best harvest, and the blade
of life's plough has surely cut deep furrows in Paul's life.

A part of life

Suffering is a part of life. We don't like it, and when we can we
try to avoid it, or mitigate it, or anaesthetize it. There seems at
times to be no pattern to it, and certainly no justice in it. Some
people suffer a lot, yet are modern-day saints in their faith and
good works; while some who break (or at least bend) society's
rules appear relatively free from trauma. While some cope well
with grief, pain or burdens of other kinds, others have a low
resistance and are quickly brought to despair. Some believe that
suffering is sent by God to test them, others that Satan is the author
of all that is bad and that sufferers have thus done something to
deserve their trouble.

Surely God *allows* suffering, but he should not be seen as sending
it. What was Jesus doing healing people with all kinds of sickness
and disease if God had inflicted them with it in the first place? It
is true that there are good and bad ways of enduring suffering,
and godly endurance builds character. But if Satan is slow to see
that, it's not our problem.

Hope for eternity

In the strength of endurance, hope grows; and being Christian hope, it grows beyond the grave. We make our long-range schemes and take out our long-term insurances. These are hopes of a kind, but the greatest hopes of eternity are far, far superior. What *are* these hopes? Hopes of an ongoing, never-ending ministry? Hopes of reunion with friends of days past? Surely all these and more, much more, for our God is the Lord of infinity.

With Paul, we can strengthen our hopes by laughing – yes, laughing – at difficulties, slapping Satan down time after time with the imperishable word of God; looking defeat, disaster and depression eyeball to eyeball and kicking them back where they belong – at the yawning black hole where Satan's front-door stood before Jesus powered down to hell and ripped the old devil's furniture off its hinges. That's how to deal with trouble. Paul called it triumphing over principalities and powers; we can call it following in our Master's footsteps.

The more we build Christian character, the more like Jesus we shall look to Satan. And as often as the devil is stupid enough to tangle with us, so he will find that we *are* like Jesus. If we are to cultivate holy boldness, let's make sure we are good at our gardening.

We can reflect, too, that Paul had overcome a large handicap. He had been the arch-persecutor of the Church. With conversion and confession behind him, God would have had no problem in forgiving and forgetting – but human memories and prejudices rarely have anything approaching the generosity of God. We are unlikely to have to live down such a reputation.

Family service input

Encourage the young people to collect data on Christians in the news (today or in history), who show great Christian character.

Suggested hymns

A safe stronghold our God is still; Holy Spirit, Truth Divine; I heard the voice of Jesus say; Jesu, our Hope, our heart's Desire.

Third Sunday of Lent *Second Service*
Be Bold! Ps. 40; Josh. 1.1–9; Eph. 6.10–20 [or John 2.13–22]

'I hereby command you; Be strong and courageous; do not be frightened or dismayed, for the Lord your God is with you whereever you go.' Joshua 1.9

'Pray also for me, so that when I speak, a message may be given to me to make known with boldness the mystery of the gospel, for which I am an ambassador in chains. Pray that I may declare it boldly, as I must speak.' Ephesians 6.19–20

A divine imperative
God could not speak more plainly: 'I command you: Be strong . . . do not be frightened' (Josh. 1.1). But throughout both the Old and New Testaments, the imperative is the same: 'Don't fear; be bold.' Is it because the Lord knows that this, of all other commands, is the one we are the most likely to break? Do we regard fear as 'legal', just because its prohibition is not included in the Decalogue? Would that really have made a difference?

One difference is very, very obvious: as soon as we take on board the Lord's command, and make the great effort that is needed (it is a great effort, let's be honest) to let him take the strain, his peace composes our minds, relaxes our tensions and allows us to get on with living. The reality that this process usually needs to be repeated many times a day is because we have become so proficient at fearing, it comes naturally. The devil must be delighted at the success of his machinations, for fear takes nations into war, fills the hospitals, mortuaries and crematoria, and causes untold heartache. Yet still our patient, loving God is saying, 'I command you *not* to fear!'

Bold ministry
Paul had learnt the hard way about overcoming fear: through grievous bodily harm, shipwreck and sheer antipathy. He outlines the problems he had come through with deep feeling. He had suffered 'far more imprisonments, with countless floggings' than the other ministers of Christ:

> Five times I have received from the Jews the forty lashes minus one. Three times I was beaten with rods. Once I received a

stoning. Three times I was shipwrecked; for a night and a day I was adrift at sea; on frequent journeys, in danger from rivers, danger from bandits, danger from my own people, danger from Gentiles . . .

The list of his vicissitudes goes on; read all about it in 2 Corinthians 11.23ff. Yet the strength of Christ kept him going. Had he tried to soldier on alone – still worse, succumbed to fear – many people would have been denied his ministry, and our New Testament would have been much shorter.

Mutual aid
But Paul also knew the value of mutual aid. In asking the Ephesians to pray up extra boldness for him, he was involving them in an important way in the gospel ministry. We tacitly accept that ministers will pray for their congregations – and even for each other; but Paul had early discovered the value of reciprocal prayer from his various congregations and communities. Whether lay or ordained, the privilege and power of prayer is such that we can pray boldness into another's life, in the full assurance that such prayer will find a welcome response in the Father-heart of God.

Encouraging freedom from fear
We are back with that buzz-word: ENCOURAGEMENT! Every one of us needs all the encouragement we can get, to be free from fear. It will take all the prayers we can pray, and all the prayers that others pray; it will take a conscious and repeated effort on our part, and all the attention that we can possibly give to God, to get rid of fear. Yes, it is that serious. But if we are clinging to fear ourselves, we are not likely to be much help in encouraging others to become free of theirs.

Switching the current back on
When fear is there, faith is not (Mark 4.40), and so the live current between God and ourselves is disconnected. Abort fear, and regain faith – and, *voila*! the current is reconnected, and we are able to function again as the Christians we want to be.

Suggested hymns
Fight the good fight; Let us sing to the God of our salvation; Onward, Christian soldiers; Stand up and bless the Lord.

Fourth Sunday of Lent (Mothering Sunday)

6 March *Principal Service* **Inner Peace**

Readings for Mothering Sunday: Ex. 2.1–10 or
1 Sam. 1.20–28; Ps. 34.11–20 or Ps. 127.1–4;
2 Cor. 1.3–7 or Col. 3.12–17; Luke 2.33–35 or
John 19.25–27

*'And let the peace of Christ rule in your hearts, to which indeed you
were called in the one body. And be thankful. Let the word of Christ
dwell in you richly; teach and admonish one another in all wisdom, and
with gratitude in your hearts sing psalms, hymns, and spiritual songs
to God.' Colossians 3.15–16*

Deep in the heart

The more of God's word we have in our hearts, the more we shall
sing and praise and share with gratitude the joy of our faith. Our
Lord's mother is a wonderful example of this. On the day when
she and Joseph presented the young Jesus in the Temple, and
Simeon warned her of the sword that would pierce her soul (Luke
2.35), she was able to continue the care of her son, because she
had stored up in her heart the promises and prophecies God had
made. 'Mary treasured all these words and pondered them in her
heart' (Luke 2.19). The peace of Christ ruled in her heart and
sustained her through his childhood years, through ministry and
right to the foot of his cross at Calvary (John 19.25f.). Paul tells
the Christians at Colossae to 'be thankful', to show 'gratitude', for
this wonderful peace, which grows with sharing and never leaves
us. We may at times smother it – with fear, or even forgetfulness
– but once implanted, it remains, waiting with the patience of its
Implanter, to be rediscovered.

Showing gratitude

On Mothering Sunday, probably more than on most other days,
we show gratitude: for our own mothers, for Mary and for Mother
Church. In the Father-heart of God there is a special love which
on earth is translated into mothers. Strong and yet tender, authori-
tative and yet patient and forgiving, it's a 'one-off', which most
of us have known and some of us have given. And the value of
motherhood was underlined by God, in giving a mother to Jesus.
Our Lord could have started his life on earth in a million different

ways, but God chose Mary to be the unique *Theotokos* (Mother of God), and her beautiful life has been an example to all mothers. By the grace of God, she gave to Jesus something that no other could give, and his love and care for her in his hour of deepest agony on the cross reflected this.

Mother Church
Mary was still there, in the earliest days of the Church. We don't know the extent of her influence in those dramatic, often fraught days in Jerusalem; but it's surely significant that relatively quickly the Church became known as 'Mother Church'. Particularly in the stormy and exciting medieval period, the Church was seen as caring for her children almost literally as a mother: it was the place of spiritual comfort, joy, worship and praise; the place of community and family bonding; the place of art and culture, husbandry and crops; the place of healing and caring for the sick, with its great monastery gardens, infirmaries, tithe barns and thousands of rolling acres around its many granges.

Some of this, of course, has changed with time. But still today the Church is 'Mother Church', caring for the spiritual needs of her children, and at least involved in if not operating the provision for their physical needs. We have only to visit countries or communities where there is no church to realize what we should lack if we didn't have Mother Church to welcome and embrace us.

Reciprocal love
But a mother, to give of her best, needs the reciprocal love of her children. Jesus gave to Mary the devotion and support of a loving son. We show our mothers today how we love them, with our flowers, cards and presents. How do we show our love for Mother Church? The ways are as many as the opportunities God gives. May we pray for grace to use them to the full, with the peace of Christ in our hearts and thankful praise sending the Lord the message that it is a pleasure to live in his love.

Family service input
Provide or arrange earlier that the children bring flowers to make up into posies for mothers, those who have lost mothers, and those who are mothers in all but name.

For Mary, Mother of the Lord; For the beauty of the earth; Jesus, good above all other; Lord of all hopefulness.

Fourth Sunday of Lent   *Second Service*
Walking in the Light   Principal Service readings:
1 Sam. 16.1–13; Ps. 23; Eph. 5.8–14; John 9.1–41

'Live as children of light – for the fruit of the light is found in all that is good and right and true.' Ephesians 5.8b–9

An airway of light
Before we came to the Lord, there was a blockage – spiritually speaking – between us and his light. We were, effectually, in darkness. But when the light of Christ's love penetrated our hearts, it was as though a channel, or airway, of light was unblocked, and we could see everything (to use a common expression uncommonly) 'in a different light': Christ's light, which is as different from ordinary light as the light of a candle is from the sun. We can live now according to his light, but he doesn't compel us: we can choose to carry on as before, keeping our faith secret and pulling up no trees for God. Such hypocrisy would be idiotic, but the choice is ours.

The light walk
Walking in the light means living with the spotlight of Christ on all that we do and say. That's what the world sees. It also means that Christ is illuminating all that we think; the world only notices the outcome of some of our thoughts; the Lord sees every one of them from birth. So, we have nothing to hide? Being human, this is usually qualified to some extent. 'But, Lord, we're trying – and with your help, we'll make it!' A prayer such as this, from the heart, will elicit a loving response from a God who also has faith that we'll make it.

In some ways, the world's scrutiny is worth more than a few thousand candle-power, for it knows, with the keen eye of criticism, what it expects of Christians. And if we fall short of these expectations (and who but Christ is yet perfect?), the world is quick to turn up its spotlight to a higher power still. But it's not a gloomy picture: walking in the light of Christ gives us, literally, a lightness to the world's distractions that otherwise could prove serious. It means we don't need to rack our brains with double-dealings or subterfuges – which really tax that grey matter and do nothing for our medical bills. The world is full enough of sharp practice and secrets. 'Nothing is covered up that will not be uncovered,' said Jesus on one occasion, 'and nothing secret that will not become known. Therefore whatever you have said in the dark will be heard in the light, and what you have whispered behind closed doors will be proclaimed from the house-tops' (Luke 12.2–3). That is multi-media coverage on a divine scale. Whose life but Jesus' will bear such scrutiny? If God, in the generosity and kindness of his heart, did not operate a shredding policy for confessed sins, we should have no hope.

Constant light
Natural light is always changing with time, weather and the seasons; but Christ's light is constant. We can hide it, if we choose; but it's still there. We can shield it with sin; but it's still there. Yet by divine alchemy, we can walk tall in it and share it, and – constant though it is – it burns brighter. Don't try to understand my light, says Jesus. Just make the most of it – there's plenty in reserve.

Just as we need light to go about our daily lives, we need Jesus' light to be Christians worthy of the name. Christians worth their salt. If we believe we're not shining enough with his light, we can ask him to show us how. If, after an honest assessment, we think we're beaming out pretty brightly, we can still ask him for more light – so long as we're prepared for such a big prayer to be answered.

Children of light
'Live as *children* of light,' Paul counsels. Children don't agonize for long about *how* they'll put a gift to good use: they just get on with using it and getting the most out of it. They don't worry about its wearing out, or getting broken, or going missing. They simply enjoy using it. I want you to be like that with the light of Christ, Paul is saying.

It's very good advice.

Give me oil in my lamp; I heard the voice of Jesus say; Light's
abode, celestial Salem; The light of Christ has come into the world.

Fifth Sunday of Lent (Passion Sunday)

13 March   *Principal Service*   **For Your Sake**

Ezek. 37.1–14; Ps. 130; Rom. 8.6–11; John 11.1–45

*'Then Jesus told them plainly, "Lazarus is dead. For your sake I am glad
I was not there, so that you may believe. But let us go to him."' John
11.14–15*

For his friends

Jesus was constantly thinking of his disciples, that small but varied
band of men who would shortly be entrusted with his Church's
worldwide mission. He knew their preparation time was short,
yet because it was long enough for God's purpose it had to be
long enough for Peter and the others. In the same way today, God
is concerned about our ministry, giving us encouragement and
opportunities *for our sake*, as well as for him and for his Church.
The sheer personal love and care for his friends is as strong as
when Jesus spoke these words to the Twelve. When we seem to
be under pressure from all sides, we should look up: God deals
in encouragement, and the pressure will not come from his direction. He is wanting us to make good, and the way he has chosen
is by our overcoming (in Christ's strength) the pressures of Satan,
not by lifting us out of the way of them.

Not lacking in courage

The *cri de coeur* from Martha and Mary also brought out a hitherto
undetected courage in Thomas. He thought it was foolhardy for
Jesus and his team to court danger near Jerusalem. But if such
was on Jesus' agenda, so be it, they'd all face it together. At this
stage in his training, Thomas' courage was stronger than his faith
in his Master's judgement; the last thing that he could understand
was that Jesus had his disciples' spiritual welfare at the forefront
of his decisions.

But God was going to reveal more of himself, his purpose and
his power in the raising of Lazarus. It was part of a building up

of encouragement and spiritual stamina in the future missionaries: stamina that was to convince them that the impossible had happened at Easter, and to send them out to convince others.

'We saw it'
They would be able to say, 'We saw Lazarus raised, after four days. Jesus did it. We don't know how, but he did it.' And what do we say today? That people in Africa, Asia, Latin America are being raised by the same power, but, closer to home, it 'doesn't happen like that'? Let us reason it out with God in prayer and believe that *for our sakes* God will work his miracles in his timing. Revivals come in waves. We need to be primed and ready for the next!

Testing beyond the limit?
It would probably seem to Martha and Mary that their faith had been tested beyond the limit: the anxiety of Lazarus' illness (for how long we don't know); the uplift when their message had been despatched to Jesus ('Surely he will come soon!'); and the (justifiable) depression when no word or sign of him came; and then Lazarus died. As if the funeral (which would be on the day of death) had not been traumatic enough, their Best Friend had let them anguish for four more days. And wouldn't someone in that time rub salt into the wound: 'Where's your healer-friend Jesus? Doesn't he care?'

But the sisters stood remarkably firm, both believing that even at the time he eventually came he could do *something*.

Sometimes we're told today that Jesus tests his greatest friends the most. Perhaps he does – after all, it's not our business how he tests anyone but ourselves. But he will never test anyone beyond their endurance. Martha and Mary stood the test, and came out of it well. Jesus had faith that they would. He had delayed for their sake, too.

For our good
'We know that all things work together for good for those who love God, who are called according to his purpose,' Paul later told the Roman Christians (Rom. 8.28). *All* things. But we often operate on a more selective level: 'Lord, this time, surely, you don't mean me to go through all this?' Yet when the trauma is past, and – somehow! – we have come through, how often do we thank God and give him the credit for knowing what was best for us?

Encourage the young people to share any testing time they've had, or that someone close to them has had, and discuss where God was in it, and how it came – to pass.

Suggested hymns
In Christ shall all be made alive; Jesus, the Name high over all; O Breath of Life, come sweeping; Revive your Church.

Fifth Sunday of Lent *Second Service* Great Is the Lord's Faithfulness Ps. 30; Lam. 3.19–33; Matt. 20.17–34

'But this I call to mind, and therefore I have hope. The steadfast love of the Lord never ceases, his mercies never come to an end; they are new every morning: great is your faithfulness.' Lamentations 3.21–23

In the depths
We can be in the deepest depths of sorrow, tragedy, weakness. Yet, so long as we 'call to mind' the faithfulness of God, that invisible bungee-cord of prayer will get us up to the surface again. It really will. You don't think any trouble Satan can trundle into your life is stronger than God's faithfulness, do you? The knowledge of this powerful faithfulness took Jesus safely from lower depths than we'll ever now have to experience, to the *right* side of the tomb on Easter morning. That is some strength. It was strong enough to convince men and women of the veracity of the resurrection, and to send them out to start conquering the world for Christ. That was some mission.

And what can that same strength persuade us to do today? It's ready, waiting and able to power us into completing the conquering of the world for Christ. Or are we trusting God for a smaller blessing?

The daily miracle
When God woke us this morning, he had our daily miracle on his mind – or we should not be here. Every day is new, with new life, new hope and new work, but all bending towards the mission for which Jesus lived and died and rose: the saving of the world.

Does it occupy our thoughts? Probably not too frequently, for we have church buildings and quotas to deal with, and a thousand and one other things. God knows about these, too, but he is still faithful to his mightiest mission of all.

Refreshing sleep

New every morning the world awakes, and its people with it. Some of us try to turn night into an extra day, snatching more hours of work until we drop exhausted (or dead) from lack of sleep. 'It is in vain that you rise up early and go late to rest,' sang the well-adjusted psalmist, 'eating the bread of anxious toil; for he gives sleep to his beloved' (Ps. 127.2). God knows we need our sleep, to rise with each new day. If we allow him to 'pace' us, we shall have more energy to do more for him. Sleep also allows God to give us dreams: visions, revelations, counsel and encouragement. Some of our dreams are meant as teaching, and we recall them in detail on waking; others are for the enjoyment and refreshment of the moment. We may not recall any part of them, yet we know on waking that 'we have had a good night'. May we thank our faithful Lord for it before we give the credit to a soft mattress or duvet, the open window, central heating or whatever springs to mind in our search for a reason. God's mercies indeed 'never come to an end', but we channel many of them unwittingly to other sources.

Start of the Passion

It's good on this Passion Sunday to reflect how the faithfulness of God saw Jesus (and the Eleven) through the trauma of the Passion. Our Lord knew that the world's salvation hung on his success in breaking the power of death. Did he know what hell was like? We do not know. He certainly did by the end of the week. And because he went all the way to hell, we shall never need to. Our souls, lightened of their load of sin, will not sink to the underworld, but soar as on angels' wings to the place God has prepared for us.

His faithfulness has convinced him that we shall reach our eternal destination. How's that for divine encouragement?

Suggested hymns

Come, let us with our Lord arise; Great is thy faithfulness; My soul, there is a country; We give immortal praise.

Palm Sunday 20 March *Principal Service*
For a Price Isa. 50.4–9a; Ps. 31.9–16; Phil. 2.5–11;
Matt. 26.14—27.66 or Matt. 27.11–54

'Then one of the twelve, who was called Judas Iscariot, went to the chief priests and said, "What will you give me if I betray him to you?" They paid him thirty pieces of silver.' Matthew 26.14–15

Evil in a dark corner
When Jesus rode into Jerusalem he did it openly, in broad daylight, for all to see; he cleansed the Temple of the money-changers and dove-sellers, in full view of the Temple hierarchs and worshippers; he went on to teach daily in the Temple, hiding nothing, doing nothing in secret. We are not given many details of Judas Iscariot's evil transaction with the chief priests, but the inference is that it was conducted in secret, probably in an inner chamber at or near the Temple. Since our Lord's entry into the city, people were flocking to hear him; the priests would scarcely have dared to discuss his betrayal openly with Judas, for fear someone would overhear and leak the plan to Jesus or the other disciples.

Fore-ordained
The betrayal had been prophesied (e.g. Ps. 109.8; cf. Acts 1.12), yet no one but Jesus knew who would be the betrayer. Right up until the act, Judas could have pulled out of the arrangement. But someone else would have stepped into his shoes: there was a dreadful inevitability about it. We know he had been helping himself to the mission funds (John 12.6), yet Jesus, fully aware of the embezzlement, did nothing about it. Perhaps he knew that the leopard in the Twelve would stick to his spots.

The Judases of today
Judas lives on today in those who make compromise with Satan and play Jesus false. It was a sixteenth-century Judas who 'shopped' William Tyndale as he worked on the Continent to complete the Bible translation and get it back to England. As a result of the betrayal, Tyndale was executed.

But not all modern-day Judases are so overt. Some sit tight when the altar call comes at a convention, rather than publicly admit to being on the Lord's side. Others, with a shrug or a turning away, decline to give a reason for the faith that is in them.

Do not be ashamed to own him,
Or obey your Lord's command;
In your every word and action
Show the world just where you stand.
When temptations throng around you,
Closer hold his nail-pierced hand;
You have joined his blessed service;
Show the world just where you stand.

Lizzie de Armond

Jesus made an entry

As the little donkey stepped out on the greenery, and the bruised sap scented the air, the procession slowly wound down the Olivet road, across the Kidron and up to the towering walls of Jerusalem. Jesus was making an entry in a telling way; and the crowds were equally overt, shouting and hailing him, while in the Temple the well-established *bureau de change* conducted its business with equal preoccupation and enterprise.

Contrasts

It's perhaps not surprising that Holy Week should begin like this, for it is a time of contrasts until the grand finale next Sunday. Those best equipped and educated to expect the Messiah go about their business and plan in secret his arrest and arraignment – while the object of their venom wins the attention and hearts of the unlettered and untasselled. Come Friday, a weak-willed Roman governor and an Idumaean puppet-ruler will settle their differences, and the Son of God will die between two thieves.

But life will go on, after Friday.

Family service input

Encourage the young people to compose or illustrate hymns or prayers to present at the Good Friday service(s).

Suggested hymns

All glory, laud and honour; At the Name of Jesus; O sacred head; Ride on! ride on, in majesty.

Palm Sunday *Second Service* What More Was There To Do? Ps. 80; Isa. 5.1–7; Matt. 21.33–46

'And now, inhabitants of Jerusalem, and people of Judah, judge between me and my vineyard. What more was there to do for my vineyard, that I have not done in it? When I expected it to yield grapes, why did it yield wild grapes?' Isaiah 5.3–4

God in tears

Jesus wept over Jerusalem (Luke 19.41), as the proud vindictive, turbulent city crouched like a honey-coloured lion in the sun. He knew it was only days away from howling for his crucifixion. Centuries before, God had given his tenderest care to that same vineyard, and had been repaid by indifference, petulance, rebellion and immorality. What more could God have done?

The miracle is that today, when many in the world still reject God, he still has not given up on us; he still honours his desire to save his humankind. He will not be untrue to himself – but he can do no more than he has done. Jesus will not come to die again. When next he comes, it will be as Judge, and the sheep will be sorted out from the goats. Two men will be working in a field; one will be taken, and the other left. Two women will be working at a mill; one will be taken, and the other left (Matt. 24.40f.). The writing is on the wall.

On deaf ears

Don't we sometimes feel that our gospel message is falling on deaf ears? The media saturate the airwaves and bookstalls with news of Satan's machinations (though they attribute blame elsewhere). We can reflect on higher morals of yesteryear, and even wish the shadow could go backwards in the dial of Ahaz (cf. 2 Kings 20.11; Isa. 38.8). People who used to avoid Christians on a Sunday morning, in a tacit acceptance of shame at not attending worship, now go about their business or pleasure with the attitude, 'You're doing your thing, and I'm doing mine.' What more can we do that has not already been done?

Kindness – coercion – conflict?

For the Church to accept with equanimity that 'our way' and 'their way' can co-exist with mutual agreement is surely no kindness to those outside the fold. Jesus commissioned us to make disciples, to take the gospel to as many as possible. Therefore, we must not give up or give in. During the monastic centuries, there was not a little coercion, and penalties were often imposed for non-attendance at worship. But history has shown that this was not the complete answer to the problem. God wants loving sons and daughters, rather than a compulsorily adopted family, or a household of slaves kept against their will.

So, is persecution the answer? If it was a crime to be a Christian, many would escape scot-free for lack of evidence. It's nevertheless true that in parts of Asia, Africa and South America, where religious persecution is still strong, the Church is also strong, and growing. One would imagine the Christian life is challenge enough, without persecution and conflict thrown in. There is even a touch of irony for folk to be drawn to a loving God by the threat of persecution. Yet history has shown that the Church in whatever part of the world has been suffering most, has grown the strongest. It seems that with the conflict, the 'cords of love' also strengthen:

> I've found a Friend, oh, such a Friend!
> He loved me ere I knew him;
> He drew me with the cords of love,
> And thus he bound me to him.
> And round my heart still closely twine
> Those ties which nought can sever;
> For I am his, and he is mine,
> For ever and for ever!
>
> The Revd J. G. Small

Is love indeed what the world needs, but doesn't know it?

Suggested hymns
A charge to keep I have; I feel the winds of God today; Love divine, all loves excelling; Thou, true Vine, that heals the nations.

Monday of Holy Week   21 March   Through the
Eternal Spirit   Isa. 42.1–9; Ps. 36.5–11; Heb. 9.11–15; John 12.1–11

'For if the blood of goats and bulls, with the sprinkling of the ashes of a heifer, sanctifies those who have been defiled so that their flesh is purified, how much more will the blood of Christ, who through the eternal Spirit offered himself without blemish to God, purify our conscience from dead works to worship the living God?' Hebrews 9.13–14

Within God himself
It was God working through every divine operation, on our behalf: the Son through the Spirit offering himself entire (unblemished, complete) to the Father. In almost shocking terms, God was tearing himself apart, to come together for us against the world's sin. The Almighty was going to great lengths, for you and me. He was taking trouble to give us freedom, light and life – a hope for eternity, an infinity with him. The sheer effort made the earlier animal sacrifices pale into insignificance. Yet there were those who blindly continued to trust in those sacrifices, to live by sight and not by faith.

Living by faith
It was not the 'soft option' to accept the Christian life and to live by faith. It's still hard – so hard, that many choose not to take up the challenge. They will not trust God with their short life on earth and have the prospect of trusting him for the hereafter. To those who have taken up the cross, it's incredible that such an offer as that of Jesus should be spurned. Paul, in presenting the case for believing in the resurrection, argues that if we put our trust solely in what the world has to offer, where are we left but in despair? And, 'if for this life only we have hoped in Christ, we are of all people most to be pitied', he goes on (1 Cor. 15.19). Even belief in Christ should not – does not – end with the grave, or what *are* we believing in? If we believe in Christ now, we are implicitly believing in his birth, life, teaching and death. Do we, with any vestige of consistency, stop right there? We cannot deny his resurrection, if we have gone so far along the road of belief. To red-pencil, or blue-pencil, the Bible to suit ourselves is a dangerous operation. Throughout the three short years of his ministry, Jesus went to great lengths to ground what he was saying and doing –

who he was, and what was to come as a result of his mission – in the prophecies of earlier centuries. He came not to fulfil an odd two or three prophecies, but every one that had been made. God is nothing if not thorough.

Consistency counts
In a world where progress depends on trust – yes, even in secular matters – we need trust and consistency to shine out of the gospel we share. We don't need to excavate the Scriptures for it: it's right there in every word. But it must form the bedrock, the thrust of our ministry. Outsiders looking in at the Church need to be aware of the consistency of our gospel. It can be a sobering thought, that we are the first Bible many people see; by our lives and our witness, Christ is evaluated. We love him, because we trust him, and because we have proved his consistency. Others need to love him through the gospel we share – the gospel of trust.

Holy Week
At the start of another Holy Week, as we prepare for the extra services, and hear (probably many times) the Passion story unfold yet again, may we be led by God further into the constancy of Christ. He knew what lay ahead, yet he went forward, calmly, deliberately, with complete trust in the constancy of God to see him through.

Suggested hymns
Lord, through this Holy Week of our salvation; Oh, for a faith that will not shrink; Once, only once, and once for all; Through all the changing scenes of life.

Tuesday of Holy Week 22 March We Wish to See Jesus Isa. 49.1–7; Ps. 71.1–14; 1 Cor. 1.18–31; John 12.20–36

'Now among those who went up to worship at the festival were some Greeks. They came to Philip, who was from Bethsaida in Galilee, and said to him, "Sir, we wish to see Jesus."' John 12.20–21

Those whom we meet
These Greeks were very open about it, and Philip responded positively – as one would have expected of a disciple. He went straight to Andrew, who was well known as a bringer of people to Jesus (John 1.41; 6.8–9), and things moved on from there. Some of the people we meet are as open as the Greeks, and ask us about Jesus and how they can come close to him (in other words, 'see' him in faith); but others are more hesitant, and either talk about other things and are too shy to broach what is uppermost in their minds, or watch from a distance, hoping to learn from the things we do and say. We may never know how many people our lives have touched for Jesus (or how many we have turned away from him), which points up our responsibility as Christians to present as close a picture of Jesus as we possibly can, in all of our lives.

The first move?
Almost certainly, by the time someone actually comes out with a question about Jesus, they have had much heart-searching, and the question is not their first move towards him. It could have been a birth, a marriage or a death that made them question whether this life is the answer to their ponderings; it could be the loss of a job, an illness or accident; it could even have been a wonderful holiday, a friend's gift, a visit to a cathedral or country church. God has an infinite number of ways in which he can plant the first seed of Christian awareness in a person's heart. And, of course, it may be something that you or I have said, perhaps quite a time ago, that has met up with the Lord somewhere in a person's heart and eventually comes to the surface as the question, 'How can I see Jesus?'

He is everywhere
Jesus is everywhere to be found, as one of our modern hymns says:

> *The famine continues, his parents are missing,*
> *Abandoned and starving, no lodging or board;*
> *He's no reason for loving, no reason for living,*
> *Yet pleading with me are the eyes of my Lord.*

Chorus
Jesus is everywhere, in everyone I meet,
Whether at home or abroad, in friend or in stranger I greet;
Jesus is everywhere, he's everything to me,
He claimed me for his own, on Calvary.

Underneath the old bridge, in a bundle of papers,
For company, garbage; for pillows, a board,
The homeless exist, by society forgotten,
But calling to me is the voice of my Lord.
Chorus

I've a life to be living, and souls to be saving,
A road to be travelling, a death to afford;
But whoever I meet, where I go in his service,
Still drawing me on, is the heart of my Lord.
Chorus

If I promise to Jesus I'll do what he tells me,
I'll go where he leads me, I'll follow his word,
He will give all the help I shall need to help others,
So vital to me is the love of my Lord.

Suggested hymns
I heard the voice of Jesus say; Jesu, our Hope, our heart's Desire;
Lord, through this Holy Week of our salvation; We sing the praise
of him who died.

Wednesday of Holy Week   23 March
With Perseverance   Isa. 50.4–9a; Ps. 70; Heb. 12.1–3;
John 13.21–32

'Therefore, since we are surrounded by so great a cloud of witnesses, let
us also lay aside every weight and the sin that clings so closely, and let
us run with perseverance the race that is set before us, looking to Jesus
the pioneer and perfecter of our faith.' Hebrews 12.1–2a

Physical and spiritual

The race of life needs both physical and spiritual stamina. When Paul used the sporting metaphors in his letters of encouragement to the churches, he would not be thinking only of the Greeks' preoccupation with fitness and sport, but also of the considerable time in his earthly ministry that Jesus had spent in restoring the sick, infirm and dead to life and health. God did not design our muscular bodies as a mere exercise in art and design, but to be put to good use in his service. And, as every athlete worth their salt competes to *win*, so does the Christian need perseverance, sometimes against all the odds, to keep on to the winning-post.

Perseverance fatigue

There are times when the sheer effort of keeping on keeping on seems too much. Those are the times when, if we pray him to, God shows us more of himself. Once we get our eyes off the problem along the track and focus on the finishing-post and God himself, he is able to move in on our trouble and attend to it – perhaps not in the way for which we are looking, but he will act. He will work on it for us, as he worked for Martha and Mary when Lazarus died. Their faith didn't falter, even though for some time they didn't understand why Jesus was acting in such a way. Whatever our trouble is – and we all experience trouble of some kind – we are not to slacken in perseverance, to take our eyes off God, to let go of faith. God is in control, if we have given over the problem to him. He will not let us down. He took his Son through the Holy Week of our salvation, and brought him out very convincingly the other end, via the tomb. Do we believe his power to be any less great today? Do we even for a moment entertain the thought that he doesn't love us enough to bring us through our troubles? There is a way out of every problem, and God knows it (1 Cor. 10.13).

The twin relay

We don't run the race of life alone: it's run in tandem with Christ, the pioneer who sets off with us, and the perfecter who sees to it that he also finishes with us. It is a twin relay, in which he is always just ahead, experiencing everything before we do, standing between us and the competition, the opposition. He paces us, so that if we keep our eyes on him we shall neither be overtaxed nor lose the race through inertia. God expends a lot of energy in helping us, if we'll only focus on him and give the credit for progress where the credit is due.

The cheering crowd
Paul appreciates the uplift and encouragement a cheering 'home crowd' can give to competitors. We've got such a crowd, he tells his readers, in the saints of former days, and the angelic legions. They are all gunning for us, says Paul. Can we let them down? Can we see our loved ones there, praying us on? Who, with such a loyal and dedicated home crowd, could fail to win the race?

Of course, Satan hopes we'll ignore all this spiritual back-up. It interferes with his plans to persuade us to realize our inadequacies and abandon the struggle. We can surely deny the devil this satisfaction – and in so doing, experience some of the joy that kept Jesus steady through the trauma of the Pasch.

Suggested hymns
All for Jesus, all for Jesus; Children of the heavenly King; Let saints on earth in concert sing; Lord, through this Holy Week of our salvation.

Maundy Thursday   24 March   Special Revelation
Ex. 12.1–4[5–10]11–14; Ps. 116.1–2, 12–19;
1 Cor. 11.23–26; John 13.1–17, 31b–35

'For I received from the Lord what I also handed on to you, that the Lord Jesus on the night when he was betrayed took a loaf of bread, and when he had given thanks, he broke it, and said, "This is my body, that is for you. Do this in remembrance of me."' 1 Corinthians 11.23–24

Personal input
All the four evangelists – Matthew, Mark, Luke and John – either experienced the Last Supper at first-hand, or presumably heard of it from others who had been there. Though Paul of course had no written gospel to hand, one would have expected him to have been told about such an important event from Peter and the rest. But apparently not: he tells us that his eucharistic knowledge comes from Jesus himself: part of the personal, one-to-one input that the Lord gave him to set him up in the ministry. The others,

he admits, had had the honour of being with Jesus – but he had the special honour of personal revelation.

It's an indication of the value of the Last Supper that Jesus gave Paul such a revelation; arguably, too, his is the first written record. And for two millennia the Christian Church has faithfully followed the Lord's command to 'Do this in remembrance of me'. Through periods when the Mass was celebrated in a language alien to many of the worshippers, the observance continued. Today, in around 2,500 tongues, the Eucharist is the main service in most churches, with substantial lay as well as ordained participation at the altar.

The Last Supper
But there was no thought of worldwide celebration in the disciples' minds as they watched Jesus break the loaf and call it his body, and lift the cup and call it the new covenant in his blood. Paul had not been there, but he must have questioned the disciples after his revelation; he must also have meditated many times on the significance of the event.

Jesus wanted his sacrifice to be a focal part of worship in the Church; of that, we can be sure. This was not merely an offshoot, still less a continuum, of the worship of his day – but a new covenant, new-made, drawing a line under what had been before, and directed towards the End of the world and eternity. It was at one and the same time a remembrance and a looking forward. When we take the bread and wine, we are remembering the greatest event in history, and anticipating the greater event of eternity – infinity concealed in a tiny wafer and a sip of wine.

Our great Saviour
How great is our Saviour? As big as every Eucharist that has been and that is to come. We call him Friend, Brother and Shepherd, and so he is; but he is so much more. His sacrifice came at the highest-ever price. Yet he asks us to commemorate it in the simplest of ways, in the sharing of two simple staples of life – bread and wine. We dress it up at times with elaborate liturgy and beautiful music, yet the simple act of eating and drinking at the centre of the observance has remained essentially unchanged.

Understood in probably as many ways as there are communicants – from a simple memorial to transubstantiation – it continues to remind us of the night 'when he was betrayed', the night when a great trust was placed in eleven men, and another great trust was broken by the twelfth.

May we solemnly renew our trust in Jesus, as we share his body and blood today.

Suggested hymns
And now, O Father, mindful of the love; Author of life divine; O thou, who at thy Eucharist did pray; We hail thy presence glorious.

Good Friday   25 March   *Principal Service*
Giving up the Spirit   Isa. 52.13—53.12; Ps. 22; Heb. 10.16–25 or Heb. 4.14–16; 5.7–9; John 18.1—19.42

'After this, when Jesus knew that all was now finished, he said (in order to fulfil the scripture), "I am thirsty." A jar full of sour wine was standing there. So they put a sponge full of the wine on a branch of hyssop and held it to his mouth. When Jesus had received the wine, he said, "It is finished." Then he bowed his head and gave up the spirit.' John 19.28–30

The end?
Had it been a mere man who hung on the cross, the words of the Preacher could have been applied: 'The dust returns to the earth as it was, and the breath returns to God who gave it' (Eccles. 12.7). But this was the incorruptible Son of God, not dust of the earth; the living, dynamic Holy Spirit, not mere breath. While human beings came to earth to live, Jesus came to die: his death was the purpose not the accident of his life. He had to die to live, while mere humans were living to die.

And because Jesus died, we, like him, die to live – for his death altered the purose of humankind. Now the focus was on eternity, and everything that was to happen on earth would have new meaning because of Calvary.

Day of wrath, and day of mourning
Whether we sing the *Dies irae* or not, Good Friday is different. Although the world increasingly demands its business, for many this is a day of quiet, sombre services; of remembering what it cost the sinless man to suffer – and a recognition of the debt we

owe. The travesty of his trial, the cruelty of Calvary, the numbness of sorrow and inevitability as the afternoon wore on. We travel the Via Dolorosa, in our 'Stations', Vigils and Complines, singing hymns that we may not sing again for a whole year. There is a solemnity about Good Friday, as muffled bells ring out, altars are either stripped or draped in purple, and congregations leave the churches more quietly than on a normal Sunday.

What is it? An indefinable, poignant remembrance of a tortured day two millennia ago, a day when a high official asked a bound prisoner standing before him bruised and bleeding: 'What is truth?'

A question of today

It is still being asked today. What is truth? Is it true that a man could suffer for the whole world, and still love and pray for his torturers? Yes – because love is stronger than hate.

Is it true that he is alive today, in more ways than we can imagine? Yes – because Life is stronger than death.

It's true, because it was Truth incarnate to whom Pilate's question was addressed; and the procurator read 'Not guilty' in the eyes that looked into his.

He tried to save one man, and failed. But that man went on to save a world of believers. We can reflect on the truth of Good Friday today because we know what followed. But there are those for whom Calvary is still a mystery. Some of them will ask us about it – if not today, then sooner or later. Shall we have an answer ready? Will the Jesus of Calvary have so penetrated our hearts that his truth will spring to our lips? May no one ever come to us in hope and leave in doubt.

Meditation

Where are you, Lord? Where have you gone? The outward form hangs limply on the bloodstained cross. You are no longer here. Your once-beautiful face has the dreadful pallor that tells me you yourself have gone. You lived. You died. For me. And now, is it all over?

No, for you – for me – *some thing* is only just begining. It's called 'the future', and I cannot see, feel or understand it. No one has yet lived it, to come and tell me what it is. The tomb stands waiting, Lord – but will it be you whom Joseph and Nicodemus carry there – or only the form of God who walked the earth?

You cannot die, Lord. You will go on for ever living in my heart – for there is no cross there, only you. The cross – you left it behind, Lord, at Calvary.

Suggested hymns
Forgive them, O my Father; His are the thousand sparkling rills; It is finished! Blessed Jesus; See, the destined day arise!

Good Friday   *Second Service*   Reconciliation
Pss. 130, 143; Gen. 22.1–18; John. 19.38–42 or
Col. 1.18–23

'And you who were once estranged and hostile in mind, doing evil deeds, he has now reconciled in his fleshly body, through death, so as to present you holy and blameless and irreproachable before him.' Colossians 1.22–23

The awesome, awful cost
Good Friday brings home the awfulness of it all. Something so dreadful as death could not be defeated at any lower cost; but the sheer horror of our Lord's Passion comes home today. Heaven's eternity came at a high price: the price we pay is service. Paul tells his readers that for the promise of hope, he has become a servant of the gospel. He's given up everything: a bright, ecclesiastical, legalistic career (for he had trained under the leading lawyer/priest of the time, Rabban Gamaliel, Acts 22.3), the respect of his peers, and an assured income. He chose instead a life of service, with constant ministry, often to unresponsive and hostile audiences; hard travelling, with many vicissitudes; recurrent persecution and injury – but at the same time, the joy of bringing people to a knowledge of his Saviour, and the prospect of a blessed eternity.

Quiet reflection
As another Good Friday draws to its close, and the tension of Calvary evaporates into the sombre quietness of the sepulchre, where is Jesus in our lives? If we are in the midst of struggle, suffering or pain, is he reminding us that he has so recently and convincingly been there also? Does his victory give us courage to

stand firm and see out our trouble in his strength? Or, are we so burdened that all we can do is to throw ourselves at the foot of his cross and find rest in his peace? He will not leave us there for long, because he himself did not linger at Calvary. But the respite will give as strength, to get up and get on.

Or is life so good at the moment that we find it hard today to enter into the grief and anguish? We should thank God for our present blessings, yet they are possible because of Calvary. With the trauma past and the tomb sealed, can we not return to gaze at the now-empty cross and quietly rejoice that the greatest love of all time made it possible?

Our personal visit

Whether we come to the cross or keep vigil at the tomb, at the close of Good Friday we make the pilgrimage as personal beneficiaries of Christ's sacrifice. Caiaphas, Annas and the priests; Pilate and Herod; and the crowds who shouted, 'Crucify!', could never say that their 'visit to Calvary' had changed their lives, because they all thought that Jesus had died *for someone else*. Only when we appreciate that he suffered for us does our pilgrimage mean anything. Belief takes us across the divide from pain to peace, from death to life. There is a part of every Christian that is spiritually in glory now, by virtue of being spiritually alive. That is the blessing by which we may end Good Friday, but for which the disciples had to wait until Easter Day to experience.

> God loved the world so much, he gave us Jesus,
> To show us how to walk his Royal Way;
> He came to teach us how to love each other,
> To preach his word, baptize and heal and pray.
> He came to save the world from dark destruction,
> From compromise with Satan, prince of sin;
> Through torture, passion, death and resurrection,
> He paid the price of Calvary, our souls to win.
>
> God loves the world today, and still is pleading
> For us to spread the news to every land;
> To follow Love, wherever Love is leading,
> To show his peace, where war's on every hand.
> To share his joy, where sorrow strength is taking,
> To speak his truth, where rules corruption's sway;

O Holy Spirit, kindle an awakening
Of fervent zeal in all your Church on earth today!

(Tune: The Londonderry Air)

Suggested hymns
Beneath the cross of Jesus; Glory be to Jesus; It is a thing most
wonderful; When I survey the wondrous cross.

Easter Eve (not the Easter Vigil) 26 March
The Peace of the Garden Job 14.1–14 or
Lam. 3.1–9, 19–24; Ps. 31.1–4, 15–16; 1 Peter 4.1–8;
Matt. 27.57–66 or John 19.38–42

*'Now there was a garden in the place where he was crucified, and in the
garden there was a new tomb in which no one had ever been laid.' John
19.41*
*'So Joseph took the body and wrapped it in a clean linen cloth and laid
it in his own new tomb, which he had hewn in the rock.' Matthew 27.59*

Kindness in sorrow
Not for Jesus the common grave where the bodies of crucifixion
victims were thrown, but a quiet garden, a new tomb and the
kindness of friends whom compassion had brought into the open.
The women were there, to watch. Jesus in death was not alone.
They didn't know what was going to happen: probably they
thought that nothing would happen. They would later watch the
soldiers and the priests arrive to seal the tomb (Matt. 27.65–66) –
but even this didn't impact enough to stop them preparing anointing oils for the Sunday morning. Grief had numbed them into
quiet, subdued acquiescence; the anguish of Good Friday had
passed, leaving them drained of everything but sorrow.

Bereavement ministry
The Jesus of the tomb on Easter Eve calls us to reflect on how we
minister to the bereaved, and the care we give to our dead. The
outward formalities of death today have become so well established that in the very observance of them is a sort of comfort –
a scheduling of the days of anguish when we are usually too numb

95

with grief to do anything else: the funeral director, doctor and coroner; the priest, the family members; discussing the funeral arrangements – even assessing numbers for the meal afterwards. It all helps, in some unreal way, to get us through the first few days. It's only when the service and the meal are over and the visitors have left that the grief surfaces so painfully, and life with all its demands is claiming an attention that we feel unable and unwilling to give.

We know what Mary Magdalene, Joseph, Nicodemus and the others did not yet know on Easter Eve – that the parting is not for ever. But that doesn't take away all the grief of the moment. We shrink in horror and dread from any parting. Our grief is therefore in some way as painful as theirs, for, while we may have hope, we still (like them) do not know the actual time or place of future reunion. God has stepped into our lives very convincingly, and has placed us in a situation which is beyond our control and not of our choosing. We feel helpless and very vulnerable.

Natural uncertainty
Feelings of uncertainty at a time of death may be natural, but if they stand in the way of our helping the bereaved they need to be addressed. We need to seek God's help and guidance in coming alongside those who are hurting, not necessarily to talk, but to love and to listen. The worst thing we can do is to keep our distance, as though in some way the bereaved have become infectious in their loss. Nicodemus and Joseph bonded together in their grief (John 19.38–39); Mary Magdalene was joined in hers by 'the other Mary' (Matt. 27.61; 28.1; Mark 16.1ff.); Peter and John were together as they ran to the tomb on Easter morning (John 20.3). Grief borne alone can literally be unbearable. May God give us grace to help share the burden, even as today we join together at the tomb of Jesus.

> Let us love as you have loved us;
> Jesus, show us how to care;
> Melt our anger and frustration,
> Give us willingness to share.
> Give us hearts to sing your praises,
> Love to help a friend in need;
> Joy to sing in celebration,
> Faithfulness in word and deed.

96

My God, I love thee; not because; O come and mourn with me
awhile; Resting from his work today; Rock of ages.

Easter Vigil 26–27 March **Heaven and Earth**
Are Moved Ex. 14.10–31; 15.20–21; Ps. 114;
Rom. 6.3–11; Matt. 28.1–10

'After the sabbath, as the first day of the week was dawning, Mary
Magdalene and the other Mary went to see the tomb. And suddenly
there was a great earthquake; for an angel of the Lord descending from
heaven, came and rolled back the stone and sat on it.' Matthew 28.1–2

Cosmic rejoicing
Heaven and earth were moved to rejoice at Jesus' victory over
death – but at a human level realization was slow to dawn. It was
so unbelievably wonderful! Somehow, when Jesus had foretold
his resurrection, no one seems to have seriously taken it on board,
so that when it came to pass the surprise took some time to take
effect. The reversing of time on the dial of Ahaz had been dramatic
enough (2 Kings 20.9ff.), but that had happened a long time
ago. The raising of the widow's son at Nain (Luke 7.11ff.) and
the raising of Lazarus (John 11.43 ff.), however, had been so
recent that surely some would have had faith to believe that Jesus
could not stay dead. Hindsight is a wonderful thing: perhaps we
should have been taken as much by surprise as Mary and the
others. Millions of people today still don't believe in the greatest
event.

The city of shocks
Jerusalem had suffered an earthquake on the Friday afternoon,
at the climax of the Passion (Matt. 27.52f.), when graves had
shuddered open and there had been resurrections of the dead. Yet
these seem to have left the city strangely unmoved. The quake on
Easter morning was different: its effects may have been slow
initially, but the city was going to experience the phenomenon of
hitherto frightened men and women proclaiming with fervour the
truth of the resurrection. The chief priests were going to have to
cope with the fact of the empty tomb, the broken seals, the sleeping

guards – and the increasing number of witnesses of the risen Lord.
An awesome amount to explain away, if it didn't really happen.

New life

Dawn breaks on Easter morning to new Life with a capital 'L':
Life that in a wonderful, poignant way had not been before. Jesus,
since before time, had lived in glory; but now his glorified body
is different: it carries the scars of Calvary, as an everlasting sign
of what he has done out of love for the world.

Is the world worthy of such love? No. We accept it, but we have
not earned it. Our sin was the cause of it, our salvation its reason.
There is no fairness in any of it – but only God's magnificent,
totally lovely unfairness. The Sun of Righteousness shines in
believers' hearts on Easter morning, whatever the weather is
doing. And somehow, by God's grace, we have to get that Sun's
light to every nation on earth. And then Christ will come, the
second time around. He will come, as he has promised (Acts 1.11)
– and this time, everyone will know.

Winter has passed

Winter has passed, and the whole world looks new at Easter. But
it's the Easter joy in our hearts, not the daffodils nor even the
fragrant Easter lilies, that can make the real difference in lives of
those still in the winter of unbelief. If we bring the risen Christ to
even one person today, the angels will sing and the heavens rejoice
(Luke 15.7): such is the power of the Easter Jesus. Of course, he
is alive every day, and every day we are under orders to evangelize; but today is his very own – and how we celebrate it is a
measure of our resurrection joy.

Suggested hymns

Comes Mary to the grave; Good Joseph had a garden; Jesus Christ
is risen today; Light's glittering morn.

Easter Day 27 March *Principal Service*
The First News Acts 10.34–43 or Jer. 31.1–6;
Ps. 118.1–2, 14–24; Col. 3.1–4 or Acts 10.34–43;
John 20.1–18 or Matt. 28.1–10

'Jesus said to [Mary], "Woman, why are you weeping? For whom are you looking?" . . . "Do not hold on to me, because I have not yet ascended to the Father."' John 20.15, 17

From the depths

From the depths of sin and despair, Mary had found such a faith in Jesus that her loyalty and trust drew her to the tomb, and thus to the honour of being the first to hear the wonderful news. And it's as though Jesus, to draw out even more faith in her, asked the 'stranger's' question with a smile. Don't you recognize me, Mary? It was surely not that he looked like someone else, but that grief and fears had blinded her perception. Grief and fears have a habit of doing that, paralysing not only our minds but also our senses: Mary didn't even recognize Jesus' voice.

Well, why should she? The last cry he had given at Calvary, in anguish and yet triumph would still be ringing in her ears (Matt. 27.50; Mark 15.37; Luke 23.46).

But now he stands before her, and as she dashes the tears from her eyes, she prepares to embrace him. But for some reason he holds back. 'I am not yet ascended; don't hold on to me.' We can reverently believe that somehow, resurrection changes and power were still taking place in his risen body. Or, perhaps he didn't want Mary to press into his wounds; perhaps the sight of them would have been too much for her. Indeed, she may have seen them – or recognition of her Lord may have dawned without such poignant supporting evidence. Then again, in his new, resurrected state, he was not bound by natural physical laws as before; perhaps, in fact, she would not have been able to hold on to him.

In the event, it didn't matter. Nothing mattered, beyond the blessed fact that he had risen. He had promised, and he had kept his promise – as, being God, she should have known he would.

Our promises

At baptism, when we enlisted in Christ's army, we (or our elders on our behalf) made equally solemn promises, which we affirmed

99

at our confirmation. We accepted the Great Commission, which we carry now for all time. Only when the gospel has been published in every nation shall the Commission be completed, and the New Life begin, with a new heaven and a new earth. God will keep all his promises, and he is looking to us to keep ours. The Easter joy that thrills us today is in our lives to thrill others – many others. Today, as in first-century Palestine, Jesus is saying (even more strongly, with resurrection power): 'Look around you, and see how the fields are ripe for harvesting' (John 4.35). The poor are still with us, the sick still need healing, the dead raising from sleep, and God's joy still needs to lift hearts that as yet have no hope. It needs Easter people to do the work, for Christ has no hands but ours.

Easter encouragement
The resurrection was the best encouragement that any world could ever receive; but, as with all encouragement, some folk were so preoccupied they didn't notice. Some of our well-intentioned work for Jesus will be ignored, some will be resented, and some will make the difference between death and life in someone's life.

After Mary left Jesus, alight with joy and Easter sparkle, the Lord would know that his Passion had not been in vain.

But – then, as now – no work for God is ever in vain.

Family service input
Encourage the young people – and, if possible, the wider congregation – to compile an Easter hymn collection, either of their favourite Easter hymns, prayers and stories, or of new material they compose, for use in the period during the Easter season and, maybe, beyond. Perhaps other churches in the parish could join in the project.

Suggested hymns
All in an Easter garden; He is Lord, he is Lord; Now the green blade rises; The day of resurrection.

Easter Day *Second Service* **Easter Glory**
Pss. 114, 117; S. of Sol. 3.2–5; 8.6–7; John 20.11–18 or
Rev. 1.12–18

*'In the midst of the lampstands I saw one like the Son of Man clothed
with a long robe and with a golden sash across his chest. His head and
his hair were white as white wool, white as snow; his eyes were like a
flame of fire … He placed his right hand on me, saying, "Do not be
afraid; I am the first and the last, and the living one. I was dead, and
see, I am alive for ever and ever; and I have the keys of Death and of
Hades."' Revelation 1.13–14, 17–18*

Jerusalem – and glory
Jerusalem gives us precious sightings of the risen Jesus, but John's
vision gives us extra Easter joy, of Jesus perfected and glorified.
He has risen, and we should look up today as in spirit we rise
with him; in our daily life we meet him as Mary did, recognizing
him not as the gardener, but as the Lord, nevertheless able to cope
with the meeting at the tomb, rather than with the splendour of
glory. One day, our glory will come – but now he is 'Rabboni',
Master, our Jesus. Troubles may surround us on all sides, trying
with insidious weight to drag us down, but today is Easter Day,
and Christians even under stress don't go around in doom and
gloom. Sing, shout for joy, and joy will conquer, with resurrection
power.

The Easter signpost
Easter is a signpost to glory. The history of the world – past,
present and future – met at the Calvary crossroads. Jesus pointed
his Church one way, while much of the world careened along
another road. The Easter road starts out from the empty tomb and
ends with the vision of glory revealed to John. In short, it gets
better and better, and the best is yet to come.

If we had been asked to pinpoint on the globe the numbers of
Christians on Easter morning, the task would soon have been
done (in fact, the disciples of Jesus were not yet then known as
'Christians'; that came later, in Antioch, Acts 11.26). But let us
tackle the job today – and who could count the number? The
Easter road *is* getting better and better, wider and wider, longer
and longer; and nearer and nearer to its conclusion.

But the best is yet to be, which is why it is good to share John's vision on Easter Day. The glory points up also what it must have cost Jesus to leave such splendour, to work out the world's salvation.

> I will sing the wondrous story
> Of the Christ who died for me,
> How he left the realms of glory
> For the cross on Calvary . . .
> Days of darkness still may meet me,
> Sorrow's path I oft may tread;
> But his presence still is with me,
> By his guiding hand I'm led.

> Francis Harold Rawley, 1854–1952

Mary's transformation
The first Easter was a time of transformation, not only for Jesus (for, although he still had the wounds of Calvary, his body was different from what it had been), but for Mary and the disciples also. Sorrow was transformed into joy, and fear into faith. Mary had proved that her conversion was for real, and had been rewarded munificently. Peter and the others, paralysed with grief at their denial and desertion, were likewise rewarded, not with even a gentle rebuke but with Christ's sheer joy at 'mission accomplished'. No examination of his friends' failures, but instead a message to be up and doing, and to broadcast the good news.

Whatever troubles we have had before this festival day, can we, too, leave them with the Easter Jesus and go out with new hope, new faith, new courage and new joy, to carry on the good work.

Suggested hymns
Alleluia, alleluia, hearts to heaven and voices raise; Good Christian men, rejoice and sing; The Lord is risen indeed; The strife is o'er.

Second Sunday of Easter   3 April
Principal Service   **Jesus Is the Messiah**   Acts 2.14a, 22–32; Ps. 16; 1 Peter 1.3–9; John 20.19–31
'*Now Jesus did many other signs in the presence of his disciples, which are not written in this book. But these are written so that you may come*

to believe that Jesus is the Messiah, the Son of God, and that through believing you may have life in his name.' John 20.30–31

Beyond belief?

We're all familiar with the saying, 'It beggars belief.' But that's not true of the resurrection. We have God's word for it, here in John's Gospel. He has given us in his word something wholly believable: God would not demand of us what we could not give. He has given us ample evidence for belief, and if we decide not to use it, then it's not his fault. Jesus appeared after his resurrection to a large number of witnesses from varying walks of life. St Paul describes these appearances in detail:

> He appeared to Cephas, then to the twelve. Then he appeared to more than five hundred brothers and sisters at one time, most of whom are still alive, though some have died. Then he appeared to James, then to all the apostles. Last of all . . . he appeared also to me. (1 Cor. 15.5–8)

That's an impressive list of witnesses by any standards. And we know, says John, only a minute fraction of what he did while on earth. But the fraction is sufficient for us to believe.

God's dealings

And God, in his dealings with us today, reveals to us all we need to know to work out his purposes in the world. Jesus is the Messiah, and his work of Messiah goes on until every person has been given the chance to believe. Until the gospel has been shared with someone, how can they believe? Paul asks:

> How are they to call on one in whom they have not believed? And how are they to believe in one of whom they have never heard? And how are they to hear without someone to proclaim him? And how are they to proclaim him unless they are sent? (Rom. 10.14–15)

He could speak with conviction, for he, if anyone, was seeing conversion at first hand, across a wide spectrum of creeds and cultures.

Parochial mission
How are we sending the gospel out? By word of mouth or the written word? By doorstep or tele-evangelism? The ways of gospel ministry are wider and further-reaching today than they have ever been before. While we praise God for these advances, our praise needs to be backed up (as was Paul's) by practicality at the grass roots. Paul was not bound by parochial limits, and our boundaries were surely not drawn to restrict the spreading of our gospel ministry.

What is the Messiah we are proclaiming? A king? Yes, and more. A priest? Yes, and more. A prophet? Yes, and so much more.

> *Jesus, my Shepherd, Brother, Friend,*
> *My Prophet, Priest and King;*
> *My Lord, my Life, my Way, my End,*
> *Accept the praise I bring.*

John Newton, 1725–1807

He is all things to all people. In him, a believer finds total assurance, satisfaction and a meeting of every need. And he will go to great lengths to get his gospel message through.

Eric Liddell, the athlete of the 1930s who trained for the 100 metres, made headlines when he pulled out of the race because it was scheduled for a Sunday. He ran instead in the 400 metres, for which he had not trained; it was held on a weekday, and he won. Later, as a missionary, he was taken prisoner in Shanghai. The younger men in the camp, bored with the restrictions of prison life, organized a hockey match on a Sunday and asked Liddell to be the referee. He refused, and the match ended in a free fight. The following Sunday, after much prayer, he did referee a match, to keep the peace. Like Jesus who could break the sabbath rules to further his message, he could have said with Paul: 'I have become all things to all people' (1 Cor. 9.22).

The gospel with which the Messiah has entrusted us is, truly, the word for everyone.

Family service input
Encourage the young people to plan a Gospel Marathon of continuous readings, publicized throughout the parish, *or* a system of daily readings in which the whole parish is invited to participate.

Come, ye faithful, raise the strain; How sweet the Name of Jesus
sounds; Now is eternal life; This joyful Eastertide.

Second Sunday of Easter   *Second Service*
Prayer Comes First   Ps. 30.1–5; Dan. 6.1–23 or 6.6–23;
Mark 15.46—16.8

*'Although Daniel knew that the document had been signed, he continued
to go to his house, which had windows in its upper room open towards
Jerusalem, and to get down on his knees three times a day to pray to his
God and praise him, just as he had done previously.' Daniel 6.10*

Right priority (1)
Prayer was going to come first with Daniel, no matter what the
laws of the Medes and Persians said. Would we stand out for God
in an alien crowd? Well, we might one day have our answer to
that put to the test. Centuries before Paul put it into words, Daniel
was living out the truth that 'My God will fully satisfy every need
of yours according to his riches in glory by Christ Jesus' (Phil.
4.19) – yes, even to taming a den of ravenous lions. Nothing is
too hard for God.

Right priority (2)
Jesus, on Easter morning, had one aim in mind: the preparation
of the disciples for mission. 'Tell [the] disciples and Peter that he
is going ahead of you to Galilee', the angel had been told to
inform the women at the tomb (Mark 16.7). They could discuss the
resurrection to their hearts' content *after* delivering that message –
but it was a question of priority!

Right priority (3)
As a follow-up to these two lessons, can we reflect on our priorities? Daniel's number one was prayer; Jesus' was mission. Both
have played a major part in the growth and vitality of the Church
ever since. Paul didn't lie awake at night worrying about the
church roof or the parish share. For one thing, mission kept him
so busy he would be ready for sleep at night. By the same token,
we can weary ourselves with parochial minutiae, until we too

sleep soundly – but what percentage of the day has been given to items that neither Daniel nor Jesus would have made a priority? We are given as many hours in the day as they were given. Has our church got its windows open to God, spiritually speaking? Are we so intent on mission that we put it before local matters?

Uncommon Christians

God is still looking for uncommon Christians, men and women who stand up and stand out for God. They may be considered square pegs in round holes by some, but in all probability folk said something of the sort about Jesus. Peter had so stood out on the night of the arrest (both his Galilean accent and his slicing of a man's ear attracting such attention) that he resorted in desperation to lying when challenged in the high priest's courtyard. He stood out, but not up, for Jesus on that awful night. It's not much good doing only half the job: the part we fall down on cancels the part we get right. We can play safe and choose to go with the crowd. Our head well down, we'll avoid the awkward situations and the brickbats. We'll also risk being called mediocre – and surely the occasional brickbat is preferable to that (cf. Rev. 3.16).

> *Dare to be a Daniel!*
> *Dare to stand alone!*
> *Dare to have a purpose firm!*
> *Dare to make it known!*
>
> P. P. Bliss

In the monasteries and convents, individualism was discouraged; but today's Church needs it if we are to get this world evangelized and the End of time ushered in. We need the Billy Grahams, Reinhard Bonnkes and Paul Yonggi Chos – and, oh so many more, to dare to be a Daniel and to stand out for God.

> *Oh, send us, Lord, we'll go where you direct us;*
> *Give us the means; we trust you for our all;*
> *We are prepared and primed for any service;*
> *Let us not stay, once we have heard your call!*

Suggested hymns

Give me the faith that can remove; Soldiers of Christ, arise; Stand up and bless the Lord; Stand up, stand up for Jesus.

Third Sunday of Easter   10 April
Principal Service   **Spiritual Heartwarming**
Acts 2.14a, 36–41; Ps. 116.1–4, 12–19; 1 Peter 1.17–23;
Luke 24.13–35

'They said to each other, "Were not our hearts burning within us while he was talking to us on the road, while he was opening the scriptures to us?"' Luke 24.32

Heartburn that is welcome
This is heartburn at its best, its spiritual high. John Wesley recorded in his *Journal*, on the occasion of his so-called 'second conversion' at Aldersgate, that his heart was 'strangely warmed'. It's the sensation that a preacher sometimes gets when he or she feels taken over by the Lord in the pulpit. Prepared notes go for a burton, as – literally – one warms to the work and God provides the message. It's the same sensation (for want of a better word), also, that comes when surprised by beauty – a sunset, an opening flower, a vast mountain range, snow-capped and glistening in the sun. The analogy is not exact, for the heartwarming or burning is different each time; but it's not a physical phenomenon. God is at work.

On the Emmaus road
Just as he was at work on the Emmaus road. It had been a long day, beginning before sunrise with Mary at the tomb – and even now it had not ended. The hot afternoon slid into evening, and the journey of some seven and a half miles, with Jesus expounding the Scriptures all the time, would take quite a while: one doesn't walk fast when one is talking. Jesus was preparing the ground for his appearance to a group of his disciples in Jerusalem later that evening. On his implanting the truth of the resurrection in the minds of these two travellers, rested their return to Jerusalem fully convinced and capable of convincing the others. And then, after Jesus had clinched the matter, appearing through a locked door, the first Easter Day would at last be over.

It didn't really matter how long it had lasted: Jesus didn't need sleep any more. He was the same in some ways, but very different in others; and for the next forty days or so, his disciples would have to come to terms with this.

Jesus the heartwarmer
Does Jesus warm our hearts today? Of course he does, for he's the same, yesterday, today and for ever. We can't kindle a spark of life in a kindred spirit unless Jesus has first warmed our hearts. Centuries before Christ, God had told the prophet Ezekiel: 'I will remove the heart of stone from [the people of Israel's] flesh, and give them a heart of flesh' – a heart that could respond to the Lord's warming – 'so that they may follow my statutes and keep my ordinances and obey them' (Ezek. 11.19–20).

On Easter Day Jesus needed to warm the disciples' hearts, which had turned stoney with grief. At times, we are called to do the same. Doesn't it remind you of John the Baptist's words at the Jordan, just before the start of Jesus' ministry? John told the assembled crowd: 'I baptize you with water ... but [Jesus] will baptize you with the Holy Spirit *and with fire*' (Matt. 3.11). John was not talking about baptism as we know it. Jesus very probably didn't baptize anyone (John 4.2): he called men and women to his way, his work, his witness and mission. It wasn't for the faint-hearted, but for those who could stand the heat.

White-hot for mission
If we pray him, Jesus can heat us to white-hot fervour for ministry and mission. Is he having his way with you, or are you 'off the boil'? Easter with its high excitement and awe-inspiring power, its beautiful services and triumphant music, is a good time to get spiritual heartburn. Pray also that yours will set someone else on fire for Jesus.

But, watch out! The devil doesn't like red-hot, still less white-hot, Christians; and he's pretty smart at trying to smother the fire with a wet blanket – if we'll let him.

Family service input
Encourage the young people to come up with ideas of how Christians can get spiritual heartburn. If possible, put the ideas into practice.

Suggested hymns
Colours of day; Give me oil in my lamp; Jesu, our Hope, our heart's Desire; We have a gospel to proclaim.

Third Sunday of Easter   *Second Service*
Every Piece Counts   Ps. 48; Hag. 1.13—2.9;
1 Cor. 3.10–17 or John 2.13–22

'Now if anyone builds on the foundation with gold, silver, precious stones, wood, hay, straw – the work of each builder will become visible, for the Day will disclose it, because it will be revealed with fire, and the fire will test what sort of work each has done.' 1 Corinthians 3.12–13

All we do
Whatever we do for God – even if we do nothing – is superimposed as a record for 'the Day', and will be tried in the divine fire of srutiny. Useless material, such as hay or straw, will be very quickly sorted out. While we can, let us see that our work is of the highest possible quality – up there in the 'gold, silver and precious stones' strata.

We can only wonder at how the growth of our lives and the growth of the Church looks to God's eyes, as each day each person adds another piece here, another piece there. It's not our business to evaluate anyone else's contribution (John 21.22), but to maintain as high a standard as we can in the contribution we are making, whether it's the preparation of a sermon, the stocking of a tombola at the church fête, baking a batch of scones for a neighbour, or giving God quality quiet time in prayer. If we set out to do everything for the glory of God, he will bless the work: in the magnificently unfair banking system of the holy and undivided Trinity, if we give God the credit on earth, he will see that we get it in heaven.

Every minute counts
The reward is great, but so is the responsibility, for every minute counts. God has lent us time, but it all belongs to him, and he's interested (with eternity in view) in how we use it. He knows what he has eternally lined up for us, and, if we are open to his leading, he will guide us into situations and experiences destined to prepare us for what he has in store for us. This thought should make life here all the more exciting – and also help to keep our eyes on what matters most to God. Jesus didn't suffer so that we could watch more TV or accumulate stocks and shares and pensions: our longest-range insurance policies fall far short of those operated by the holy and undivided Trinity.

Timely advice

Paul's was timely advice for the little church, set as it was in the bustling, cosmopolitan commercial city of Corinth. The site of the Isthmian Games, Corinth was noted also as much for its corruption and immorality as for its trade and commerce. Be careful! Paul is warning. Get your priorities right, for everything you do will, on 'the Day', come under the scrutiny of God. When the Auditor of the holy and undivided Trinity goes to work on the Grand Account, he will miss nothing.

In this scrupulous accounting is great encouragement. For he will pick up also all the good that has ever been done to his glory, even the multitude of *little* good deeds and words that we add to our Christian tally every day without noticing: it all figures in the Grand Account. We can safely leave the recording with God. We have enough to think about without keeping our own tally. Nor should we clutter up our minds with remembering the faults of those who cross our paths – though we may remember at least some of the good that they do!

Selective memories

God has given us wonderful memories, though as we get older we persuade ourselves they become more selective. So long as we select God and his word and work as our priority, we should not go too far adrift. Jesus acknowledged our inability to remember everything. That was partly why he sent his Holy Spirit: 'The Advocate, the Holy Spirit, whom the Father will send in my name, will teach you everything, and remind you of all that I have said to you' (John 14.26). This same blessed memory will take care of our life's record – every minute of it.

Suggested hymns

Be thou my guardian and my guide; My times are in thy hand; New every morning is the love; Take my life, and let it be.

Fourth Sunday of Easter 17 April
Principal Service **Discernment** Acts 2.42–47;
Ps. 23; 1 Peter 2.19–25; John 10.1–10

'When he has brought out all his own, he goes ahead of them, and the sheep follow him, because they know his voice. They will not follow a stranger, but they will run from him because they do not know the voice of strangers.' John 10.4–5

Freedom of choice

God doesn't make it impossible for us to deviate, driving us ahead of him, with his eye on us, ready to whip us back into line if we break ranks. Where would be the challenge, or the exercise of faith, in all that? He goes ahead, not smoothing out every stone in our way but experiencing whatever lies ahead, so that he knows we can cope because he has been there first. But while he is 'up front', on the reconnoitre, his sheep can wander if the inclination takes them. They can take heed of another voice, a stranger's; but our Lord has faith in us that – like natural sheep – we are inclined, more often than not, to sheer away from a stranger.

Sometimes, however, sheep go contrary to nature, and break the rules. And so do we, trotting off along byeways not chosen or examined first by God. Then we wonder why things go wrong, and we complain to God that he's let us down. The long and short of it is, we've landed ourselves in a mess.

'They will not follow a stranger,' Jesus says, of his own sheep. Wow! Don't we like to modify that into, 'They should not follow a stranger'? What if we do wander off after someone else? Well, Jesus doesn't stop us: we've been given freedom of choice, and God is not going to file for repossession this side of the grave. But when our new 'guide' has proved false, or when we've come to our senses, the Good Shepherd doesn't leave us wandering. He comes to look for us. And he doesn't stop looking until he finds us.

> *And all through the mountains thunder-riven,*
> *And up from the rocky steep,*
> *There arose a cry to the gates of heaven:*
> *'Rejoice! I have found my sheep!'*
> *And the angels echoed around the throne:*
> *'Rejoice! For the Lord brings back his own!'*
>
> Elizabeth C. Clephane

111

A world of strangers
There are many strange voices in the world today, ready and willing to draw us off into paths of their own – paths which may look so much more interesting and alluring than the one along which our Lord is leading. We may even enjoy the new experiences – for a while. But the realization of our position – precarious, because we have opted for a less than true guide – will come, sooner or later; and the progress we have lost on God's chosen path may be irrecoverable. Deviation is dicing with death, and we should not entertain it.

> God leads us through no darker rooms
> Than he's been through before;
> He that unto God's kingdom comes
> Must enter by this door.
>
> Richard Baxter, 1615–91

God's way at times may seem dark, but if it's his way, it's the one we should be walking, and it will get lighter if we stay on it. By contrast, the way of a stranger may start out promisingly, but the road surface will deteriorate until (spiritually speaking) we are either cutting our feet to ribbons on sharp stones or sinking in the Slough of Despond.

The flock of Christ
As a shepherd doesn't have only one sheep in his flock, so the sheep in Christ's flock give each other mutual aid and encouragement. Each of us comes to Christ on our own; no one can be a Christian by proxy. The Church is, or should be, a fellowship of believers, a flock of sheep; in this community and companionship is the basis for giving and receiving the fruits of the Spirit (Gal. 5.22–23).

So, if we see one of the flock tempted to break ranks, can we do something about it? Yes, Christ has provided for that. We can pray for the tempted sheep, that it stays in the fold, or returns if it has gone wandering; or, if we believe God is encouraging us to do it, we can have a quiet word with our friend and be guided by God as to what to say: there are right, and wrong, ways, and if we pitch in blindly with even well-intentioned advice we can do more harm than good.

'The prayer of the righteous is powerful and effective.' Never has James 5.16 been more apposite than in this context.

Family service input
Encourage the young people to work on a collage of 'The Fold of Christ', for display first in the church and then if possible in schools etc. in the parish.

Suggested hymns
Great Shepherd of thy people, hear; I was a wandering sheep; Loving Shepherd of thy sheep; Thou Shepherd of Israel and mine.

Fourth Sunday of Easter   *Second Service*
One in Christ   Ps. 29.1–10; Ezra 3.1–13; Eph. 2.11–22 [or Luke 19.37–48]
'So he came and proclaimed peace to you who were far off and peace to those who were near; for through him both of us have access in one Spirit to the Father.' Ephesians 2.17–18

No difference
As Paul told the Galatians, 'There is no longer Jew or Greek' (Gal. 3.28), so now he is saying to the Ephesians, 'There's no difference since Calvary between Jew and non-Jew, because Jesus gave his blood, his life, for *all*. And all means all.' Paul and the apostles have matured in the faith sufficiently to take this great truth on board (after, it must be admitted, more than a little heart-searching).

So, what is the matter with the world today, when many of the Jews still attend their synagogues and non-Jews go to their churches? When Palestinians and Jews war against each other, Ireland and Cyprus are still divided, and the Church of the Holy Sepulchre in Jerusalem is almost continually the scene of religious difference if not outright conflict? What is wrong, after two millennia? Why doesn't the world take heed of God's word? While there is discord and dissension, the blood of Christ still flows. How long, Lord, how long?

The best way

Jesus came to show us the best way, but the stark truth is that so often we settle for an alternative route. With the inevitability that anticipated the betrayal of Jesus, so at the End of the world many will have been called but relatively few will be chosen. Satan, stirring trouble wherever he can, has been allowed time by God to stalk the earth like the wounded lion he is. Some of his power was stripped convincingly from him at Calvary, but he still has enough to make the Christian life a challenge. And, if the devil's success rate of 75 per cent, as indicated in Jesus' parable of the sower, still applies, we may expect discord and dissension in the world until Jesus comes.

Our own outreach

But there is still time to work against the advances of Satan. We are Christians, on our 'home ground', on land created and nurtured by God. Satan is the interloper, however he may try to persuade us otherwise. How is our own outreach coming along? Is our altar open to everyone? Is our church best known not for its stained glass or magnificent music, its immaculate graveyard or peal of bells, but for the welcome it gives to Jew as well as non-Jew, poor as well as rich, destitute as well as affluent, irrespective of creed, culture or colour? As the well-known hymn says, 'they'll know we are Christians by our love'.

Will they, *everyone*, really?

Then – and now

It has often been said, without too much thought, that the early apostles preached only to those who were either disaffected or disillusioned with their lot, or those who had been followers of Jesus or John the Baptist anyway. Certainly these latter would form an important element in the emerging Church; but Peter, and particularly Paul, preached to audiences from a wide range of ethnic and credal backgrounds. Even in Jerusalem, with its army of occupation, its three main languages of Hebrew (Aramaic), Latin and Greek, and its polyglot of nationalities, there was great variety. The situation then was not so very different from that of today, when nationals intermingle among the countries, and an even greater polyglot of language can be heard virtually any-where. And, as then, not all non-believers were disillusioned with pagan creeds: Paul had often to overcome deep-seated resentment and prejudice of a gospel that conflicted with, say, the cult of Artemis or the Eleusinian Mysteries, Mithras or the doctrine of the Stoics.

When someone from another persuasion comes knocking at the door, or God brings us together in any of a thousand other ways, do we invite them in for dialogue, to witness to them of Christ – or do we close the door (metaphorically or actually) in their face?

Jesus died so that all may live.

Suggested hymns
Immortal, invisible; He's got the whole world in his hand; In Christ there is no east or west; The God of Abraham praise.

Fifth Sunday of Easter   24 April
Principal Service   **God in Christ**   Acts 7.55–60; Ps. 31.1–5, 15–16; 1 Peter 2.2–10; John 14.1–14

'[Jesus said] "Do you not believe that I am in the Father and the Father is in me? The words that I say to you I do not speak on my own; but the Father who dwells in me does his works. Believe me that I am in the Father and the Father is in me: but if you do not, then believe me because of the works themselves."' John 14.10–11

Getting the message
Wouldn't even Philip get the message? And what about us, who have the words to hear and read over and over again – does the point sink home with us? Yet it was a very daring declaration of Jesus, for does it not mean that in him God died on the cross? No, because Jesus *gave up* his Spirit (John 19.30; cf. Luke 15.46) at the point of death, reclaiming it at some time before his resurrection, perhaps even before he powered through hell: the actual timing is not important.

God was in Christ, reconciling the world to himself, making hearts into what they had been created to be – focused on him, orientated to his purpose. He had set his seal on the mission of Jesus, and he would see that mission through.

Giving the glory to God
Just as John the Baptist had pointed people to Jesus, so Jesus with mind-blowing humility gives the glory and kudos to God. I can do nothing of myself, he tells his friends, before the climax of his mission. But after the resurrection, when he has resumed his glory, he can tell them: 'All authority in heaven and on earth has been given to me' (Matt. 28.18). This is the authority that sends us out with his Great Commission, the authority that will surely see the gospel published in all nations – simply because the Lord has spoken, and his word lives for ever.

Talking deeds
Deeds ('works') often speak louder than words. Repeat these words of Jesus to a nominal believer and they'll probably come as a surprise. But that believer will know at least the salient points of the water turned to wine at Cana, the feeding of the 5,000, or the death of Lazarus. Fair enough, Jesus acknowledges. What I have done seems to have made an impact. If you don't take in what I am saying, think about what I have done, and believe. Look around you: this is God himself, God the Father, at work.

It is as though Jesus realized that, however united and single a view he may have of God, people needed to focus on the three operations that still apply in the thinking of the Church today: Father, Son and Holy Spirit. One day, when we see God in all his splendour, we may understand more how one can be three, and three can be one. One day, though, we may not need to understand. What is more important, in the short term, is how our 'works' are glorifying God. Or are they building up our own image? The world today loves a 'self-made man' (or woman), though it seeks with vindictive perversity to knock him off his pedestal as soon as he mounts it. There is pressure to be 'well thought of', to 'have a good name'. Didn't the author of Proverbs say, 'A good name is to be chosen rather than great riches, and favour is better than silver and gold' (Prov. 22.1)? But the answer lies in the latter clause: provided the name is 'good' in the eyes of God, its assessment by the world (which usually judges by wealth) is irrelevant. If works (of whatever kind) can be done only by compromising the Christian's good name, then they are the wrong sort of works. A Christian's name is not his or her own, but Christ's – and we should guard against sullying his name by anything we do or say. The converse should give us encouragement: by speaking out for Christ, we are showing Satan up for the devil he is, and anything we can do to darken Satan's name further must be good. The Lord in us will give us all the encouragement we need for such work.

The answer to prayer
Jesus was himself the answer to prayer while on earth. Yet the mystery of prayer is such that, although the Father was in him, he needed to be seen to be praying to him. He needed to command his disiples to pray, 'Our Father, who art *in heaven*'. In a very real way, heaven had come to them: the kingdom, in Jesus, was near them.

When we have understood this mystery, we shall be in heaven.

Family service input
Encourage the young people to discuss/illustrate (1) the 'works' of Jesus that have impacted most on them; (2) the 'works' in today's world that impact most on the Church.

Suggested hymns
As the hart pants for the water; God of grace, and God of glory; Tell out, my soul; We have a gospel to proclaim.

Fifth Sunday of Easter   *Second Service*
Come not to Sojourn, but Abide   Ps. 147.1–11;
Zech. 4.1–10; Rev. 21.1–14 [or Luke 2.25–32[33–38]]

'Then one of the seven angels who had the seven bowls full of the seven last plagues came and said to me, "Come, I will show you the bride, the wife of the Lamb." And in the spirit he carried me away to a great, high mountain and showed me the holy city Jerusalem coming down out of heaven from God.' Revelation 21.9–10

Coming together
In this wonderful vision of the New Heaven and the New Earth, everything comes together – and everything is destined to last for ever. God will come, not to sojourn (as did Jesus for a few years), but to abide, to 'dwell' (v. 3) with us. Our hymn will have come, not to pass but to stay:

117

Not a brief glance I beg, a passing word,
But as thou dwell'st with thy disciples, Lord;
Familiar, condescending, patient, free;
Come not to sojourn, but abide with me.

Henry Francis Lyte

And his bride (the Church, New Jerusalem) will come to the Lamb. John, familiar with the mountains of Judaea, the snow-capped peak of Hermon and the mountains of Asia Minor, would not be exaggerating when he called New Jerusalem's a 'great, high mountain'. It would be some height, of that we can be sure. God wouldn't deal in economy provision for eternity.

The richness, the radiance and the sparkle of the New Jerusalem should be a great encouragement to the Church, presently militant in earth. We are working towards that glory, but we shall not reach it unless we have fulfilled our mission here. Are we really militant enough to warrant the title? We fight, each in our own life, against Satan and his evil; but are we fighting as a Church? Certainly as a worldwide Church we hardly present a united front: if we did, Satan would feel the pressure a lot more. The Week of Prayer for Christian Unity goes some way, but nowhere near far enough; we need prayer for unity every week of the year, and, more than that, prayer to be translated into action. We shouldn't need to be reminded of the frailty of a house divided against itself.

Internal divergence = collapse

Some years ago, a tiny village (less than 30 souls) was faced with annihilation when a nearby quarry firm sought permission to extend its already large operation. At the ensuing public inquiry, the village mounted a united opposition – and won. A few miles away, a similar village inquiry heard evidence from another community where opinions for and against a proposed opencast mine were fairly evenly divided. That village lost its battle, and the mine went ahead.

Satan is going to do nothing to heal the divisions within the Church, but everything to widen them. However gentle, meek and mild we may feel called upon to be in certain situations, on this particular point we can and should be as unequivocally militant as God can show us how; and God is a fighter. We have the best possible teacher. He dwells with us: now, as his Holy Spirit, and in eternity in his fullness. We are equipped, moreover, with his armour. He has given us all it takes to get the gospel round the world and the New Covenant signed, sealed and delivered. What are we waiting for?

On the move
In parish after parish, we are on the move – towards unity, towards mission, towards full evangelism. We're getting there, but we've still some way to go. We shall keep on moving forward: the Holy Spirit will see to that. He cannot fail, for he is God.

Suppose, given advances in effort and technology, we were to complete our Bible publishing in all the world's languages tomorrow: what aspects or portions or gifts or activities or missions of your particular church would you consider might be eligible for translocation, transformation, transmutation to a jewel of the New Jerusalem?

Suggested hymns
Abide with me; Jerusalem, my happy home; Jerusalem the golden; Light's abode, celestial Salem.

Sixth Sunday of Easter   1 May
Principal Service   **Loving Revelation**   Acts 17.22–31; Ps. 66.8–20; 1 Peter 3.13–22; John 14.15–21
'They who have my commandments and keep them are those who love me; and those who love me will be loved by my Father, and I will love them and reveal myself to them.' John 14.21

Way of love
The way of love for the Christian began with Jesus' giving of his laws, and our acceptance of them. As we take these commands into our hearts, the Holy Spirit in us goes to work and translates the commands into action. Our working-out of them proves to Jesus that we love him, and the equation comes full circle as God loves all who love Jesus, and as we become what he intended we should become when he created us. Call it the 'Love walk', the 'Love way', and walk in it – this is the gist of Jesus' teaching. Anything else is less than God's best.

Non-discrimination

We are not to discriminate between what we consider greater or lesser, comfortable or uncomfortable, obligatory or mere suggestion: Jesus simply says, keep my commandments. When he says love, we are to love; when he tells us, don't be afraid, we are not to be fearful (and he tells us not to fear, more often than all the other commands put together).

Yes, Lord, I will not fear. Can we make such a brave promise? No, there should be no heroics necessary. We are simply to make it, as a quality decision to keep a quality command. Can I really jettison this thing that is bugging me, and let God take the strain? Yes, for the alternative is to forfeit the love of Jesus, the love of God. If we were only to keep this in our minds, instead of allowing them to become paralysed by fear, we may make more progress in the fight against fear.

Faith v fear

Faith and fear are continually competing for the upper hand in our lives – which is only to be expected, since God is the master of faith, while Satan is the master of fear. We are either serving one master, or the other. At no one time can we serve both, and there's no question about which master we should ditch: the problem lies in putting theory into practice.

The new commandment

It was not a new law that said 'Love your neighbour', but Jesus tacked a new piece on to it: 'A new commandment I give to you, that you love one another, *as I have loved you*' (John 13.34; 15.12). That means laying down our wills, our inclinations, desires, ambitions – our very lives – for Jesus. It's the biggest of asks, but he has calculated that we can do it, and for us to protest otherwise would be wasted effort. Yes, Lord, we give you the best: you know us so well, we can't get away with false modesty, any more than with over-confidence.

Would it help us to have an interim report from God on our progress to date? Then look into the eyes of those whom God causes you to meet – the familiar and the not-so-familiar. What you see there is a good guide. We can hide our feelings with words, but our eyes tell a truer story. Do we see love reflected in another's eyes? Trust? Joy? Or something else? Reflect also on the trust you place in your best friends: God has placed even more trust in us. Is he living dangerously? No, God has no fear of anything or anyone. When we work out what that means, it's a God-size helping of encouragement!

Possession brings obligation
There are many even today with no access to a Bible, and no prospet as yet of getting one. They literally don't have the commandments of Jesus. If they die before receiving them, will they have another chance? Or will Christians who could have shared the word with them, but didn't, be held responsible? We need to teach all whom we can, while we can, and leave the rest to God. But all those who already have the commands of Jesus are under a sacred obligation to keep them – and that does mean us.

Family service input
The young people could divide into four groups, each group taking a Gospel (if numbers permit, each person being given a chapter) from which to extract all the commands of Jesus that they can find. Discussion/illustration can follow. The artistic could perhaps design banners, wall-hangings, etc., featuring these commands.

Suggested hymns
Love divine, all loves excelling; My Jesus, I love thee; Oh, the love of my Lord is the essence; The God of love my Shepherd is.

Sixth Sunday of Easter   *Second Service*
Tree(s) of Life   Pss. 87, 36.5–10; Zech. 8.1–13;
Rev. 21.22—22.5 [or John 21.1–14]
'On either side of the river is the tree of life, with its twelve kinds of fruit, producing its fruit each month; and the leaves of the tree are for the healing of the nations.' Revelation 22.2

An avenue of beauty
This gives us a vision of an avenue of beauty, an arbour of life on either side of the river in the New Jerusalem. It doesn't make any difference if there are twelve trees, each with a different kind of fruit, or twelve fruits in variety on each tree. But why will the

'nations' need healing in the new covenant age? It has been suggested that nations as yet unknown to those on earth will meet up with us there – nations as yet unevangelized, for the ministry of whom our work on earth has prepared us. Yet it's still unclear what healing purposes the foliage of these trees will be used for.

Currently, God has given us earthly 'trees of life', in that all of his natural plant world is increasingly found to be either good for one's day-to-day health maintenance, or a cure for sickness, disease and pain of one sort or another. In fact, the Elder (*Sambucus nigra*), to take one example, has so many medicinal properties in all parts of the plant that it has been called 'God's medicine chest'.

Forward planning
John is shown in his vision the lengths to which God has already gone in his planning for eternity and for our part in it. And the inference from these verses of John's vision is that the skills we have been allowed to hone on earth will be of use also in eternity: medicine, for instance. And why should it not be so? Would God be likely to give us learning that would be obsolete in a few years' time? No. Look back through history and you will see that learning has always been given to meet successive needs and circumstances. We may find it difficult to think globally now – but it's a lot easier than it would have been two thousand years ago. So, what of eternity? Shall we be thinking *universally*, in the widest sense of the word? With these visions, God is inviting us to get excited by the prospet – and almost certainly reality will exceed our present thinking, as God's purposes eternally unfold.

Keeping the ground under our feet
But for the time being we need to keep the ground under our feet, for unless we utilize this time of preparation well, we can hardly hope for more and greater work – here, or hereafter. In a world where technology and the desire for wealth have meant a reduction in simply being a good neighbour, can Christians help to reverse the trend? Do we actually know the folk next door, or next-but-one, or across the street? If we were in trouble, could we go to them for help? Then, if not, they will probably not come to us either, but seek help elsewhere or suffer alone. Perhaps they go to another church? Does it matter? Or, don't they go anywhere near a church? Then it does matter. A priest writing recently in one of our national newspapers admitted with commendable

but anguished honesty that he could not visit all his 'own' parishioners, in their homes, hospitals, schools or even prisons. Yet he felt also that he was letting down those Christians of other churches, as well as of none. 'One person cannot do it all,' he said.

What, then? With eternity in view, do we step out in faith and ordain more priests, or commission more laity to specific parochial ministries? Or, each and every Christian, do we extend the 'good neighbour' policy – yes, giving it, if you like, a specific designation or organizational set-up – but getting the job done? Or (if we haven't already) we shall reach the stage where we have *too few* labourers in the harvest, and people perishing for lack of spiritual food.

God has thought of fruit, and healing for the nations in eternity. And he has provided the means of healing sore and saddened hearts *now*, through his Holy Spirit and his word. But the means of getting this nourishment to starving souls, he has left to us.

At present, we have only one little floating ball, one earth, to concern us.

Suggested hymns
External ruler of the ceaseless round; Help us to help each other, Lord; There is a land of pure delight; When I needed a neighbour.

Ascension Day   5 May   My Witnesses
Acts 1.1–11 or Dan. 7.9–14; Ps. 47 or Ps. 93;
Eph. 1.15–23 or Acts 1.1–11; Luke 24.44–53

'[Jesus] replied, "It is not for you to know the times or periods that the Father has set by his own authority. But you will receive power when the Holy Spirit has come upon you; and you will be my witnesses in Jerusalem, in all Judaea and Samaria, and to the ends of the earth."'
Acts 1.7–8

Antidote to sorrow
The last thing Jesus wanted, as he prepared to leave the earth, was for the disciples – on whom the mission of the Church rested – to be prostrated with grief at his going. Buoyed up by the reality of his resurrection, he then built on their joy by a promise and a command: power would be given them to witness through all

the world. The sheer magnitude of the commission could have overwhelmed them, but for the relief that they would not be dependent on their own power, but God's. It proved the antidote to sorrow, and God is still working along such lines today. We can 'reduce' his method to the simple 'work and encouragement' package, which may not do his love and concern justice; but the method works today as well as it worked two millennia ago. And, as then, God's 'encouragement' invariably precedes his command to 'work'; with the former, he gives the means to do the latter.

Expectation

As they returned to Jerusalem after Jesus' ascension, the disciples would be filled with expectation. And they were not kept waiting for long before the Holy Spirit came at Pentecost very convincingly with all the power they needed.

So, what did the ascension mean to these men, who in the past few weeks had been on a virtual roller-coaster of emotions, from deepest anguish, remorse and terror, to the highest peaks of joy and exhilaration? The resurrection had been a watershed: it had drawn a line very firmly under all that had gone before. Things would never be the same again. The power that had opened the tomb had rubbed off on to them; the glory of the resurrected Lord had shone on them. Fear had been miraculously, divinely banished from their lives; and the worldwide mission, hinted at and spoken of by Jesus before the Passion, which had seemed then an improbable if not impossible vision, now seemed not only likely, but convincingly their life's work. New life, new hope had risen in their hearts, and they felt (and probably looked) new people.

> For you who revere my name, the sun of righteousness shall rise with healing in its wings. You shall go out leaping like calves from the stall. And you shall tread down the wicked, for they will be ashes under the soles of your feet, on the day when I act, says the Lord of hosts. (Mal. 4.2–3)

The Lord had acted, and the sun of righteousness had risen for Peter and the other disciples.

Has our sun risen?

What does the ascension mean for us? Has the sun of righteousness risen in our hearts also? We come on to the scene when the work of gospel mission is so well under way that we may even believe that 'soon, and very soon' the whole world may have heard the good news. We have, by God's grace, the power of his Holy Spirit to get the work done – and we have his authorization to get it done. What more are we waiting for? We can, in a manner of speaking, 'stand looking up towards heaven' (Acts 1.11) – but the disciples were quickly told not to hang about doing something so unprofitable.

Suggested hymns
Crown him with many crowns; Hail the day that sees him rise; Hail to the Lord's anointed; Thou art gone up on high.

Seventh Sunday of Easter (Sunday after Ascension Day) 8 May *Principal Service*
This Is Eternal Life Acts 1.6–14; Ps. 68.1–10, 32–35; 1 Peter 4.12–14; 5.6–11; John 17.1–11
'[Jesus said] "And this is eternal life, that they may know you, the only true God, and Jesus Christ whom you have sent."' John 17.3

Only true
There could only be one God, for only one could keep the world and the universe in perfect balance. Therefore he must also be true, for only truth could be so consistent and constant throughout history. Therefore, the believable and the provable lead us with every confidence to trust what seems at first sight to be unbelievable and unprovable: if God made the visible world, he could also be born of a virgin and rise from the dead. This is not naivety, but firm belief; not wishful thinking, but sheer, strong faith. Yet the power of evil is such that many still don't believe, still have no faith.

God is one: not only in uniqueness, but simply. There is no contradiction in him. Through and through, he is one, he is God, he is true, without hesitation, deviation or repetition. Simply one, whole truth. That is why, as soon as we believe in him, belief grows, faith grows, trust grows. There are no hidden twists and turns with God. We may not be sure of what he will do next, but we can be absolutely sure of *him*. It was this absolute assurance that saw Jesus from the beginning to the end of his mission.

Knowing Jesus

If we know God, we know Jesus, for he and the Father are one. These words of Jesus run counter to the claim by some that God can be known even by those who reject Jesus. 'The glory that you have given me, I have given them,' said Jesus to his Father, of his disciples, 'so that they may be one, *as we are one*' (John 17–22). One whole, true God; very God of very God. So, the more we know Jesus, the more God reveals himself to us. And the more he reveals, the more truth and singleness of heart and purpose takes us over. It can be very hard to stand true in a world that seems largely not to know the meaning of the word. But Jesus tells us it can be done: it must be done; and he has faith in us that it will be done.

Knowing Jesus gives us faith, also, that it can be done. If we hold on to truth, we may be overtaken in the short term by those intent on 'getting on' at any cost. But to trample on truth for fame or fortune is, literally, to dice with death. If we are faithful to Jesus in the little things of life, he will lead us on to greater things.

Sacred v secular

The secular world doesn't understand the Church's way of life – in business, social relations or anything else. It demands security, protection and a hidden agenda as a fail-safe. In contrast, the Church knows its security is vested in the Bank of the Holy and Undivided Trinity, its protection in legions of angels, and its agenda is not hidden but open and above board to all who can read or hear the Scriptures and who believe in Jesus. We look to him, to live – and he's with us.

> There is One so sympathetic,
> Who fills my soul with peace;
> He knows my every little care,
> And does my joys increase.
> And while I trust in his dear love,
> From sorrow I am free,
> And I can never grieve because
> My Lord's with me.

> He knows my little failings,
> How weak I sometimes feel,
> And in his loving kindness
> His strength he does reveal.
> He guides my footsteps on the road,
> And helps me tenderly;
> And I can never fall because
> My Lord's with me.

Mary O'Connor

Family service input
Encourage the young people to (1) illustrate Mary O'Connor's hymn, or (2) compose an extra verse for it.

Suggested hymns
Immortal, invisible; Jesus is God! the solid earth; Lord of our life, and God of our salvation; Walk thou with me.

Seventh Sunday of Easter   *Second Service*
Enlightened Hearts   Ps. 47; 2 Sam. 23.1–5; Eph. 1.15–23 [or Mark 16.14–20]

'I pray that the God of our Lord Jesus Christ, the Father of Glory, may give you a spirit of wisdom and revelation as you come to know him, so that, with the eyes of your heart enlightened, you may know what is the hope to which he has called you.' Ephesians 1.17–18

Inner light
Paul is thinking along two lines: wisdom and enlightenment. We need both for positive Christian living. Wisdom is essential: to discern which voice is speaking – that of God or that of Satan; when we should speak, and when we should be silent; when we should move, and when we should stay. And enlightenment is equally essential; for where there is no vision, the people perish. Enlightenment, as Paul seems to use it, covers present understanding of the Scriptures, as well as vision of the future.

Both wisdom and enlightenment are ongoing, and we can never have too much of either. But it's easy for even a committed

Christian not to have enough; and often when at last we get around to asking God for either or both, he seems to say: 'My child, I've been waiting only for you to ask. Why has it taken you so long?' And yet his rebuke comes surely with a smile, for he knows we shall come crying when we are desperate, but he wants to hear from us before we're taken right to the wire.

In the natural, our hearts work like Trojans in the darkness behind our ribs; but God's light takes no account of flesh and bone, and makes even X-rays seem dim. His light penetrates into the parts nothing else can reach, so that we have inner enlightenment, inner wisdom and power, which, if we stick with God, makes us impervious to fluctuating, external influences. But Satan is constantly playing us another tune, one that harps on our vulnerability, our weakness and inability to cope: 'You no-good, pathetic, delusioned wimp! Fancy imagining you could make any difference! You're way out of your depth! Get back where you belong!' No, he doesn't come at us so blatantly, or even we should cotton on to what he is about. He is far more devious, for he employs the stratagems of busyness, distraction, tiredness and peer pressure – all designed to get our minds off God, and feel good while we're about it.

Satan, get back where you belong!

More of God

Simply, the more of God we can take in, the better equipped we shall be to meet not merely a selection of Satan's ploys, but every one. We should feel it wholly natural to take a reading 'sabbatical' every so often: not necessarily to go away from home or work, but for, say, a week to read only the Bible: no newspapers, TV or radio. Even while pursuing our normal schedules, giving the word of God first place in our reading for a week would do much to clarify our thinking, and therefore our praying. We need godly input more now than ever before – because society has never before been so preoccupied with business and pleasure to cram into every moment.

When, for example, was the last time we read the Book of Revelation, put ourselves into John's shoes, and got excited at the prospect of eternity? When we book a holiday, we usually spend a fair amount of time reading up about what's in store and what a variety of authors have written about the place. Yet many Christians have only the sketchiest of knowledge about what the writers of Scripture have to tell us about the hereafter.

Enlighten us, Lord!

When we are faced with hard questions – of life, death and eternity; of sin, pain and spiritual apathy; of glory, hope and joy – have we the wisdom of God's word in our hearts to answer our questioners?

Enlighten us, Lord!

When people of all ages – but perhaps mostly the young – ask us about the wide and still increasing range of Bible versions, are we sufficiently familiar with their variety to give our questioners a considered reply, instead of just picking every time on our particular favourite?

Enlighten us, Lord!

And he will – until Satan can't find any darkness on which to home in. If we pray for all the light he can give, God will respond – for in him is no darkness at all, and he is giving us himself.

Suggested hymns
A safe stronghold our God is still; Lord of all hopefulness; Meekness and majesty; The people that in darkness sat.

Day of Pentecost (Whit Sunday)   15 May
Principal Service   **Gift of the Spirit**   Acts 2.1–21 or Num. 11.24–30; Ps. 104.24–34, 35b; 1 Cor. 12 3b–13 or Acts 2.1–21; John 20.19–23 or John 7.37–39

'Divided tongues, as of fire, appeared among them, and a tongue rested on each of them. All of them were filled with the Holy Spirit and began to speak in other languages, as the Spirit gave them ability.' Acts 2.3–4

Diversity of gifts
The collection of languages was exactly what the disciples needed for the foreign mission fields. The question of language had probably been exciting their minds for the past ten days or so since Jesus' ascension. But he had commissioned them for world evangelism, and they must have had faith that he would deliver the necessary equipment before they set out. And how dramatic was the delivery!

Have we not all, when struggling to learn a foreign language, prayed that a similar gift would be ours? Yet those tongues were given when needed most. Today there are others going to foreign parts who are still helped with the languages. Do we, in our particular parish, need other tongues? If we do, we shall be given them – in any one of God's diverse ways. But he may decide that another gift of the Spirit is more important for us just now, and that is what he will give us. The Holy Spirit is so powerful, he never runs out of any particular gift.

Joy abounding

When Jesus was born, the event was relatively low-key, though the heavens rang with music over the shepherds' fields. When he rose from the dead, it took him quite a time to convince his friends that it had happened. And when he ascended, it was almost in private.

But when the Holy Spirit came, there was much more drama. God intended to catch the attention of quite a crowd; with so many witnesses, even the Jerusalem ecclesiastical hierarchy couldn't say it hadn't happened. Joy abounded – after the initial shocks of wind and flame – and power flowed, power that could be seen, felt and heard; power to change the world. It's still coursing through any situation or circumstance where Christians are making a difference. Satan is no match for this divine power, so the further the Spirit advances, the further the devil has to retreat. One day there will be no place for him to hide. The End will come, and Jesus in glorious power.

Power for all

It's a mark of the generosity of God's love that at Pentecost a tongue of flame came to rest on each person present. There was work for all to do, and every person needed to respond. In his new Church, God would have a place for everyone. It's the same today: if anyone feels like joining the Church as a comforting diversion, he or she will soon be disillusioned. The Spirit's power is generously given – but to be used, and used as fully as possible, in God's service.

Pentecost was a practical commissioning for the worldwide mission that is not yet complete. And when it is, very likely God will have some further work lined up for us in glory!

Spirit-fire

Why should the Spirit be given in flame? Yes, certainly the 'tongues' of fire brought languages to the receivers; but surely the fire spoke also of warmth and light, the love of God warming the stony hearts of unbelievers, and the light of Christ bringing the gospel into dark, pagan, sin-infected areas of the world, to hearts darkened by aliena- tion from God. The Church had been born – in a very dramatic way – and the gospel message would soon be on the move out of Jerusa- lem in all directions. Did God know on the day of Pentecost that nearly two thousand years later we would still have nations to evan- gelize? Yes, because God knows everything. And if we get disheart- ened when we look at the work still remaining to be done, let's reflect that God also knows the day and exact time when the song has gone right round the world.

Family service input

Download the Lord's Prayer in as many languages as possible from www.christusrex.org/wwwl/pater. Encourage the young people to learn these, for incorporation in intercessions, Bible groups, parish outreach, etc.

Suggested hymns

Come down, O love divine; O Holy Ghost, thy people bless; Spirit of God, unseen as the wind; Veni Creator Spiritus.

Day of Pentecost   *Second Service*
The Invitation Is to All   Pss. 67, 133; Joel 2.21–32;
Acts 2.14–21[22–38] [or Luke 24.44–53]

'In those days I will pour out my Spirit; and they shall prophesy. And I will show portents in the heaven above and signs on the earth below, blood, and fire, and smoky mist. The sun shall be turned to darkness, and the moon to blood, before the coming of the Lord's great and glorious day. Then everyone who calls on the name of the Lord shall be saved.' Acts 2.19–21

A great day

Joel's prophecy looks forward to this 'great and glorious' day, and it would surely have been among those prophecies sought by the

131

disciples in their prayer meetings following Christ's ascension. Questions such as 'How will the Spirit come? What signs will there be? Has such a day been foretold?' would have surfaced, and would have had the literate, or those with friends in the Temple, searching the Scriptures, while the rest trawled through their memories for prophecies heard from childhood. And Peter had homed in on Joel when the Spirit came, as being one such prophecy which was now much nearer fulfilment, if not the actual day.

The Lord, it seems, was so keen to send the Spirit that the day of Pentecost was barely three hours old when he came. And the news was not as slow to take effect as the resurrection had been on Easter morning. The fiery, vocal Holy Spirit made an immediate impact.

Calling on the Lord

'Every one' who calls on the name of the Lord in that day will be saved. This is pretty embracing – yet some will still not turn to God. And the Lord who said, sadly, that even a resurrection will not move them, knows that some will remain obdurate. Like the pagan prophets on Carmel, they will call after their 'Baal', whether Baal is of material or spiritual form. Some will trust in their bank balances, their multi-million estates; others will believe that their sharp practices will find them a loophole to escape; others will bribe their deities of wood and stone with fatalistic nerve; and others will bow before Satan, believing that at last his reign is beginning. God alone knows the percentages – but of the many that have been called, relatively few will 'call on the Lord' in that day.

> Oh, Lord, I want to be among the number,
> When the saints go marching in.
>
> Traditional

But now . . .

But now is the time when we can, if we will, still help to bring others to the Lord. Do we care enough to keep on doing this for as long as we can? This is no time for compassion fatigue. There are still people estranged from God, or even ignorant of him, for whom our ministry can make a difference. Our encouragement

132

may in fact be the means of giving them an eternity with God, instead of – somewhere else. That is the potential value of our mission.

Peter's first sermon
This is the first recorded sermon of Peter, and, ex-fisherman as he was, unaccustomed to public speaking, it proved to be a show-stopper. But not every preacher has had such a dramatic build-up to their oration, nor have they had to begin by quelling what seemed likely to be mass panic. We are so used to a formal liturgical setting for our worship: how should we fare on a soapbox in Hyde Park, or a beach in Africa, or a cave in the Andes? The word of God that is in a Christian is there for every situation, every experience. Perhaps, in fact, the unpredictability of Galilee and its waters had done much to prepare the fishermen disciples for adaptability and quick thinking in mission.

Can we get excited about our post-Pentecost witness opportunities? They are waiting for us – and the time starts now.

Suggested hymns
Come, Holy Ghost, our souls inspire; Come, thou holy Paraclete; O joy, because the circling year; Spirit of the living God, fall afresh on me.

Trinity Sunday   22 May   *Principal Service*
Remember!   Isa. 40.12–17, 27–31; Ps. 8; 2 Cor. 13.11–13; Matt. 28.16–20

'[Jesus said] "Go therefore and make disciples of all nations, baptizing them in the name of the Father, and of the Son, and of the Holy Spirit, and teaching them to obey everything that I have commanded you. And remember, I am with you always, to the end of the age."' Matthew 28.19–20

When things are tough
Remember – when things are tough, and despair threatens to paralyse our spirits and bodies – Jesus is with us. Lord, why don't you do something to get me out of this mess? But he's waiting for *us* to do something, to lift our burdens over on to him; for he's

here, ready and waiting to take them, as soon as we'll let them go. But so often we cling to them for dear life, the sort of life that really is too dear, too expensive to afford. I am with you, *always*. This is a mega-helping of divine encouragement, designed to get us through to the completion of our worldwide commission, against all the odds.

GO – baptize – teach

It's a threefold commission: to GO, to BAPTIZE and to TEACH the gospel. But the 'going' comes first. We are not to wait for folk to come to us, for they will probably never come. Don't despair, Jesus is saying. Don't sit around and let the world's pressures get you down. Just get up and get out and do something to fight those ever-encroaching pressures: the media hype, the takeover of Sunday by business, the drive to have leisure and recreation at any cost; the obsession with wealth and insurance and long-range benefits. GO, and baptize, and teach. The kingdom of heaven is just as close to you in another house, another town, on another continent or island; because where I am, it is – and I am always with you.

And yet we cling to the familiar, and opt for praying for 'someone else' to go.

Go – BAPTIZE – teach

Anyone can legally baptize another in a life-threatening situation. One could argue that every second is such a situation. Jesus didn't go a bundle on the legalities. He kept his great commission simple. And baptism, at its simplest, is anointing with, or immersing in, water, symbolically washing away the sins of the former life and entering a new life with Christ, washed clean visibly by the water and invisibly (spiritually) by his blood.

Yet there are other ways of understanding baptism. We say, after a person has had a traumatic experience or conversion, that they've had a 'baptism by fire', meaning that their introduction to a new phase of life or occupation has been dramatic to the point of cataclysmic. The disciples' 'baptism by fire' could be said to have occurred at Pentecost, when the fiery tongues of the Spirit descended and alighted on everyone present. We may, indeed, have come to faith in a surprising, even startling way – or we may have had the privilege of seeing God deal in such a way with someone else.

Go – baptize – TEACH

A teacher to be worthy of the name needs instruction. Unless we have studied the word of God, we are not going to have much success in sharing it with others. The Church in China today is an example of this; in some of the country areas, where communication is still difficult and distances great, many (often young) Christians, still fairly new to the faith, are struggling to pastor house churches before they have read much of the Bible themselves: not because of arrogance or over-confidence, but simply because they have no access to more than a few verses of Scripture. There are areas where one Bible may have to be shared between fifteen thousand or more people. Cults and pagan teachings can infiltrate, and heresies weaken, these struggling congregations. We need to pray for more Bibles, more training for pastors and Christian teachers. And on our home ground, may we recognize all the wealth of teaching on our bookshelves at home and at church, so that it's not a case of the blind leading the blind.

Family service input

Encourage the young people to increase or implement an existing prayer/study programme of MISSION, MINISTRY and MENTORING, as part of the church's Trinity schedule.

Suggested hymns

Holy, holy, holy, Lord God Almighty; Lead us, heavenly Father, lead us; May the grace of Christ our Saviour; Three in One, and One in Three.

Trinity Sunday   *Second Service*   Woe Is Me?

Pss. 93, 150; Isa. 6.1–8; John 16.5–15

'The pivots on the thresholds shook at the voices of those who called, and the house filled with smoke. And I said, "Woe is me! I am lost, for I am a man of unclean lips, and I live among a people of unclean lips, yet my eyes have seen the King, the Lord of hosts!"' Isaiah 6.4–5

Cold feet

The vision was so dramatic that Isaiah, a mere mortal, got cold feet. We'd probably have done the same when the doorposts shook in their sockets, and the realization of our mortality hit us. On Trinity Sunday, however, we especially struggle to reach a better understanding of the divine. At best we fall short – often a long way short. And we can empathize not only with Isaiah, but also with the many other mortals in the Bible (and since) who have been nonplussed and terrified by such visions and revelations.

Yet God seems to expect us not to react so negatively. He has invested a lot of faith in us: can we not return it with interest – positively, not negatively? He's given us his Holy Spirit, which, in us, is equipped to respond to divine visions and revelations. We have a great advantage over Isaiah: we know Jesus as Saviour, we are children of the Spirit, empowered and emboldened to fight Satan. Should we be afriad of anything that God reveals to us?

God's investment
God quickly went to work on Isaiah's 'Woe is me!' protest, and the next words we hear from the prophet are a declaration of intent: 'Here am I. Send me!' (v. 8). That is a great sea-change. God is no respecter of persons; he can go to work on us equally dramatically. He's invested eternity in us, and he will see that we make good, if only we'll stand firm. And part of his investment is the capability of relating to the divine. The more we relate, the closer will come eternity.

Our investment
As members of the body of Christ, it's our privilege to relate his investment in us to others – to invest interest, love and concern, affirmation, encouragement and recognition of their talents. No one can live in isolation: we invest in others, however subconsciously, trust for heating, lighting, mail, water, food and social contact. But how much are we investing on the spiritual front? Those whom we trust as 'spiritual directors' in a more-or-less formal capacity are only a small proportion of our brothers and sisters in Christ. A Church that lives together as well as prays together is the strongest: living not literally under the same roof, but trusting one another, and able to share the many facets of spiritual as well as physical life. It is so sad when someone is able to say, 'I kept it to myself. I didn't feel I could share . . . a, b or c . . . with anyone else.'

That person's fellow Christians are as much to blame as he or she is. We may be longing to help another, but unless we give the other confidence that we can, we are not likely to be asked. Laryngitis is a far more common 'complaint' in practice than the medical text books would have us believe.

The right enthusiasm
We don't need a certificate of spiritual proficiency to hang on the living-room wall. Isaiah didn't wait for God to give him a full 'Job Specification' (or even an abbreviated one). He simply said, 'I'm here. Send me.'

> Send me forth, O blessed Master, where are souls in sorrow bowed;
> Send me forth to homes of want and homes of care;
> And with joy I will obey the call, and in thy blessed name
> I will take the blessed light of the gospel there!
>
> The Revd Elisha A. Hoffman

Once we've taken the first step of accepting God's invitation for service, he'll take care of the details, and will make each step known as and when we need to take it. If we end up floundering, it'll be because we've taken our eyes off God. The Lord will keep his side of the contract.

If there is an evil in the world today against which we, as Christians, need to make a concerted and immediate attack, that evil is spiritual unemployment. Too often it masquerades as 'sophistication' – which is one reason why it's often not recognized for what it really is.

Suggested hymns
Breathe on me, Breath of God; Bright the vision that delighted; Give me the faith that can remove; Inspired by love and anger.

Corpus Christi (Day of Thanksgiving for Holy Communion) 26 May *Principal Service*
True Living Gen. 14.18–20; Ps. 116.12–19; 1 Cor. 11.23–26; John 6.51–58

'[Jesus said] "Just as the living Father sent me, and I live because of the Father, so whoever eats me will live because of me. This is the bread

*that came down from heaven, not like that which your ancestors ate,
and they died. But the one who eats this bread will live for ever."'*
John 6.57–58

The long view

It was because Jesus could take the long view, his sights set on
eternity, that with perfect physical and spiritual poise and equilibrium he could meet the world's antagonism, unbelief and apathy.
He wept with the sisters at Bethany, he mourned over the arrogant
and scheming Jerusalem – but he knew that those dramas would
pass. The criteria governing his mission would continue for ever:
fruits of the Spirit, salvation of souls, and the love of God. These
indestructible things would see out the earth, and even the present
heaven; and they would still be operative to see in a new heaven
and a new earth. If our sights were more firmly set on eternity,
we would not get so strung up about the daily, *little* troubles.
Were we to realize more readily that small troubles are of Satan's
making, and larger ones of our own inflating, we should be less
willing to do the devil's work. Strong words? Yes – but Jesus gives
us the solution in three words: 'Do not fear.' Our fear magnifies
the devil's initial angst into mega-problems. We should focus on
the invitation of Jesus to believe in life, to feed on him who is the
life, to off-load the trouble *as soon as we get it* on to him, and to
leave it there. We need to recite this solution time and again, as
Jesus had to teach it to his disciples – not once, but many times.
It's a dastardly crime that Satan has conned so many into believing
that fear must be a part of life: the devil's idea of life is not
forty-second cousin to that of Jesus'.

Mute reminder

Every time we celebrate the Eucharist, the bread and wine are mute
reminders to Satan of the greatest battle ever fought – reminders to
him of the power he lost when Jesus claimed an everlasting victory.
Little wonder, then, that the devil works hard at blunting the
world's (and many Christians') understanding of the sacrament.
We come to the rail to show on whose side we are fighting; to
remember the great sacrifice of our Lord; to thank God for the life
that that sacrifice brought us; and to rededicate ourselves to his
service. There may be other reasons valid for individual communicants, but these are the prime reasons common to all.

In the Upper Room

In the Upper Room at the Last Supper, Jesus was not only fellow-shipping with his friends and preparing them for mission; he was looking down the years to come and anticipating the unifying and strengthening power of the sacrament, as it would feature in his Church. He saw you and me, joining at the altar rail on this Corpus Christi of 2005. We were on his mind, together with countless millions for whom he knew the sacrifice was worth it.

> *O Bread of heaven, beneath this veil,*
> *Thou dost my very God conceal;*
> *My Jesus, dearest treasure, Hail!*
> *I love thee, and adoring kneel.*
> *Each living soul by thee is fed,*
> *With thine own self, in form of bread.*

> *St Alphonsus, 1696–1787; tr.*
> *R. Vaughan, 1827–1908*

Christ's life

With Christ's life in us, we leave the eucharist as different people – stronger than when we came, more fully equipped to deal with Satan, more open to Jesus and to others by virtue of his life and light in us. Will others notice? Will it be God's fault if they do not? Let us reflect just what we are taking in: life, love, joy, peace, patience, kindness, generosity, faithfulness, gentleness, self-control, truth, the right way, the true vine, the Good Shepherd, the Son of God … No, we cannot fathom all that. But condense it into a wafer and a sip of wine, and there is hope. That was why Jesus made the Last Supper so simple.

Suggested hymns

Author of life divine; Be still, for the presence of the Lord; Strengthen for service, Lord; We hail thy presence glorious.

Corpus Christi *Evening Prayer* For Our Part

Pss. 23, 42, 43; Prov. 9.1–5; Luke 9.11–17

'But [Jesus] said to them, "You give them something to eat." They said, "We have no more than five loaves and two fish – unless we are to go and buy food for all these people." ' Luke 9.13

Jesus shows us the way

At the Last Supper, Jesus showed us the way to live: helping others by giving everything. He gave his body and his blood. No one could give more. But in the feeding of the multitude, earlier in his ministry, he showed us that giving is a corporate act: one person cannot and should not do all the giving. The disciples and the boy with the tuck-box had been involved; and, when their efforts were blessed by Jesus, the blessings could flow until all the assembled crowd had been fed. The Eucharist had a longer-term effect: in the Upper Room that night, Jesus ordered the disciples to re-enact the sacrament, again and again, each time observing it as a memorial and reminder of what he had done, suffered and provided. That is why we don't treat the Last Supper merely as a part of the Gospels (and also 1 Cor. 11.23–26), but as a command of Jesus, to be observed practically and as frequently as is appropriate. His is the gift, ours the participation. It has been 'communion by extension', centuries before the phrase was also given a modern, ministerial connotation – and the further we can extend it, the better. The bread may be white or brown, freshly baked or flattened into wafers impressed with sacred symbols or designs; the wine may be fermented or otherwise, red or white, depending on situation and availability. Since the institution, different churches have hedged the sacrament about with ritual and liturgical conventions, some of which have acquired the aura of 'tradition'. But at its simplest, it's there to remind us of what happened at Calvary. We may add to that, but we cannot take away this vital truth at the very centre of the observance.

Explaining the Eucharist

It is much easier to *know* the Eucharist, than to explain it – just as the disciples knew that a multitude had been fed from rations that were those of one boy's meal, but they couldn't explain how Jesus had multiplied the food. We can't explain how Christ can be in every Eucharist, or how his body and blood go to work in us. We believe it simply is so, and faith is built on this. If Jesus could be divinely implanted in Mary's womb, God is more than able when it comes to giving us his body and blood in the Eucharist. The exact hows and whys are not our problem.

A royal invitation

It is a royal invitation that he issues, for us to join in his feast; and while we come as his friends, he is nevertheless our King, and such invitations do not come lightly. With holy reverence and awe we kneel, for we are dealing in holy matters. It's possible to mess things up: 'Whoever ... eats the bread or drinks the cup of the Lord in an unworthy manner will be answerable for the body and blood of the Lord,' Paul warns (1 Cor. 11.27). If we are in strife with anyone, or if we believe anyone has a grievance against us, we need to get ourselves right with them, and right with God, so that the precious body and blood of Christ will not come up against harboured sin in our bodies, and so that we present them as a true 'living sacrifice', dedicated to God's service.

In some way that we cannot comprehend, Jesus left his body and blood on earth, for neither was needed by him after Calvary. Yet the resurrection body he now has still shows Calvary's scars. Can we bear to look on them? Yes, because they are real, yet glorified, capable of being felt by Thomas (John 20.27). The sight of them was sufficient to re-kindle faith in Thomas: 'My Lord and my God!' (John 20:28). Until then in the gospels, Jesus had not been called 'God'.

As the body and blood of Jesus spreads around the earth, in every Eucharist that is celebrated, like Thomas we come face to face with our Lord and our God, as honoured guests to his feast. And, as guests, we leave his table replete with the loving, generous provision of our host. 'We come with joy', as the hymn says. May we go back out into the world with his increased joy.

Suggested hymns

Bread of heaven, on thee we feed; O God unseen yet ever near; Once, only once, and once for all; We come with joy to meet the Lord.

First Sunday after Trinity (Proper 4)   29 May

Principal Service   **How Firm a Foundation?**

Gen. 6.9–22; 7.24; 8.14–19; Ps. 46; Rom. 1.16–17; 3.22b–28[29–31]; Matt. 7.21–29

'[*Jesus said*] *"Everyone who hears these words of mine and acts on them will be like a wise man who built his house on rock. The rain fell, the floods came, and the winds blew and beat upon that house, but it did not fall, because it had been founded upon rock."* ' Matthew 7.24–25

Our house of life

How is our house of life coming along? Its foundation is firm enough, for it is Jesus himself. But how have we built on this best of starts? Does prayer undergird every brick of mission, ministry and service? If so, the walls will stand. Do the windows in our house look out with the love and light of Christ? If so, they will shine. Does the fire burn with the flame of God's Holy Spirit? Then it will heat the house with a warmth great enough to be shared with others. We are building a house not made with hands, eternal in the heavens. Perhaps we shall actually see it when we get to glory – or perhaps we shall by then have other things on our minds.

Into action

We can listen to the words of Jesus until the cows come home, but listening is only the preliminary to the real work of life. Unless we translate the words we hear into action, we shall be of no use to anyone, least of all to God. Jesus placed such emphasis on his words that he told his disciples that one of the functions of the Holy Spirit would be to remind them of every word he had spoken. And, as John tantalizingly remarks, we know only an infinitesimal fraction in the Gospels of all that Jesus really taught in those three years of ministry; we can be absolutely confident that in that time he taught more than anyone else could have managed (John 21.25).

   We don't need to look far in any direction today for opportunities to put Jesus' words into action. Some Christians wear a cross and fix the 'fish' symbol to their cars; but the world is usually quick enough to spot a Christian by the way he or she lives, with or without the help of these outward signs. They can be, however, an advantage when we are away from home, often encouraging others to open up a conversation.

But, if we 'let down the side', then it's 'the Church' that gets the blame – which should surely be a sufficiently strong extra incentive for us to keep an eye on how we are building our spiritual house.

We can, in fact, go too far the other way, making such a virtue out of action (albeit Christian work) that we neglect our prayer and quiet times with God (called, in earlier times, 'waiting on God'). Every so often, Jesus retreated to a mountain or quiet place for quality time with God. We need these times just as much, if not more. 'Oh, I want to die in harness, not to be put out to grass!' is sometimes said by well-meaning, if rather hyperactive Christians. And God doesn't want slackers in his service, either; but let's take a leaf out of Jesus' book and see that our days include prayer as well as action. Some would, in fact, see prayer as action – and history may be seen to be peppered with outstanding prayer-athletes, such as Augustine of Hippo, Monica, Lancelot Andrewes, Madame Guyon, Brother Ramon. But prayer should undergird and precede Christian action, not be relegated to the ten minutes before bedtime.

> *Oh, what peace we often forfeit;*
> *Oh, what needless pain we bear!*
> *All because we do not carry*
> *Everything to God in prayer.*
>
> Joseph Scriven

The wobbly houses

In the topsy-turvy way that the world works, some of the most grandiose buildings are, spiritually speaking, wobbly. Some have been built on extortion, many on arrogance and not a few on credit. Their wealth is for their individual upkeep and magnificence – and yet, come disaster, they crack and crumble. In physical terms, they may have laid a heavy load on the land – but in God's eyes they have been built on the flimsiest of foundations, and trouble sorts them out sooner or later. Of such, may the Christian steer clear!

Family service input
Encourage the making of a collage/model showing Christ as the 'rock', and what the Church is doing in the parish as building-blocks. Add to these as the year progresses.

Suggested hymns
Christ is our cornerstone; Christ is made the sure foundation; How firm a foundation; Rock of ages.

First Sunday after Trinity   *Second Service*
Patient Endurance   Ps. 33; Ruth 2.1–20a; Luke 8.4–15

'[Jesus said] "But as for that [seed] in the good soil, these are the ones who, when they hear the word, hold it fast in an honest and good heart, and bear fruit with patient endurance."' Luke 8.15

Working for the harvest
Harvest doesn't come without effort, but the joy of cropping and eating good fruit is worth the time and energy spent in producing it. So is the work of Christ. We may seem to be labouring for very little return, but Jesus at the end of his ministry had no million-strong congregation to show for his work; yet his mission had been accomplished. Patient endurance has seen the Church continue and grow through nearly two millennia; there have been many trials and much persecution – but the effort has not been without joy. On the natural level, we can see this being like a strong, healthy plant which seemingly enjoys making the most of good soil, sunshine and rain, eventually opening its flowers to full view and then crowning its endeavours with seed of fruit, veg-etable or cereal. So we should grow in our Christian endeavours with joyful patience, joyful endurance. If we have no joy, folk are not going to be persuaded that God is a god of love and that Christ's way is worth following.

Long-lasting joy
The seed on the pathway sprang up with quick but ephemeral joy, losing it to the devil in the first encounter – and with the joy, faith too went out of the window. We need not run after this joy-of-the-moment: quickly received, it's just as quickly lost. The

144

seed on the rock also had an early surge of enthusiastic joy, but just as quickly lost it, because faith was not deeply rooted in the good soil of the gospel. We may avoid this sort of flash-in-the-pan joy by taking God's word as our daily medicine for good spiritual health. And the seed that landed among the thorns hardly saw any joy at all, being from the outset swamped with the world's distractions. They come a-plenty – fleeting pleasures, longer-lasting problems and pain-racked tragedies; the world well knows how to bank these up against a soul, for it has Satan at the back of them. Our stand against these distractions is ongoing; but the stronger we grow, the easier the work becomes.

A joy the world cannot understand
'You're just dumb! You can't see what trouble you're in!' come the sneers, when a Christian laughs and sings in great adversity. And sometimes, when our troubles have lessened, the mockers have forgotten their taunts, because they themselves are deep into anguish. The bad seed looks at the rain, and moans that it will be drowned and its growth will rot. The good seed opens its foliage and flowers to the 'showers of blessing', to make the most of the refreshment. The bad seed feels the hot sun, realizes its roots haven't any water, bewails an attack of sunstroke, and droops witheringly earthwards. The good seed grows visibly and greets the beautiful warmth by extra vigour, colour and natural grace. The bad seed finds itself at harvest-time dreading the cutting and pulling-up of its meagre stems. The good seed looks forward to becoming of even more use to the grower with whom it's had such a good working relationship.

It may be that we are not eagerly looking forward to our Harvester's arrival. If so, we'd do well to examine our lives and see where we can do some self-cultivating, so as to recover the full joy of growing in the faith as prime-quality seed.

Suggested hymns
A charge to keep I have; Fair waved the golden corn; Sow in the morn thy seed; The sower went forth sowing.

Second Sunday after Trinity (Proper 5)

5 June *Principal Service* Faith for Healing

Gen. 12.1–9; Ps. 33.1–12; Rom. 4.13–25;
Matt. 9.9–13, 18–26

'She said to herself, "If I only touch his cloak, I will be made well." Jesus turned, and seeing her he said, "Take heart, daughter; your faith has made you well." And instantly the woman was made well.' Matthew 9.21–22

A long wait

She had waited twelve years for healing (v. 20). That's a long time in anyone's book. Had she been too embarrassed to seek medical help? Or too poor? Or had no one been able to help? Had she been to the priests for healing? We don't know anything about her faith until she comes up to Jesus, and with full assurance touches his cloak. Who had persuaded her that that was all that was needed? We don't know. But after twelve years of misery, she was prepared to push through the crowds and get to Jesus, despite what anyone may say.

Healing today

While the Church is strong in affirming its right to preach and teach; to baptize, marry and bury; to operate mission outreach and evangelism, it doesn't appear to include healing at such a priority level. And though there are many Christian doctors and nurses, the medical profession is not exclusively Christian, and does not operate under the aegis of any denomination. There are healing services in a number of churches; and some parishes do operate a high-profile healing ministry – but it is not found in every church. At healing conventions and services, some people receive healing, yet others don't – and we don't know why. Is it because of individual lack of faith? Or that it's not God's will to heal that person at that time? Or is it because God is displeased about the relatively low profile that Christian healing has today? These are hard questions, and perhaps God is calling us to press him further for answers.

Jesus' healing

According to the Gospels, Jesus healed on a pandemic scale: 'curing every disease and every sickness among the people' (Matt. 4.23), and giving similar authority to his disciples 'to cure every disease and every sickness' (Matt. 10.1). You cannot get any more embracing than that. When he left his friends, he recommissioned them to 'lay ... hands on the sick, and they will recover' (Mark 16.18). Have we let the power to heal evaporate by default? We need, as a Church, to come before God with our heart-searchings and reasoned arguments (cf. Isa. 1.18), to discern his will on this, which should be a vital part of ministry.

God's will

As we read the Gospels, we can be sure that it is God's will for people to be well physically as well as spiritually – or Jesus would hardly have spent so much time healing people. And we can also be sure that sickness and disease come from Satan (Luke 13.16), because we have Jesus' word for it. These two premises can, therefore, surely form the basis of our prayers.

In faith, then, we may proceed with our healing ministry, certain that God will bless it, certain that he will make his will in it clearer and clearer to us as we go on. It should be possible for people to say, 'I'm going to church today; it's the place where folk get healed.' Is that daring? Of course it is – but it's faith built on what Jesus has already said and done. We need faith in what God can do – and God can do anything. It was the woman's faith that impressed Jesus, and called forth healing from him. Can we show a similar faith in him today? Or do we really believe that his power to heal isn't quite what it was?

Family service input

Encourage the young people to abstract from the Gospels all material relevant to the healing ministry of Jesus. If time and numbers permit, extend this into Acts and the early Church.

Suggested hymns

At even, ere the sun was set; She only touched the hem of his garment; Thine arm, O Lord, in days of old; Thou to whom the sick and dying.

147

Second Sunday after Trinity   *Second Service*
The Common Touch   Ps. [39] 41; 1 Sam. 18.1–16;
Luke 8.41–56

*'David had success in all his undertakings; for the Lord was with him.
When Saul saw that he had great success, he stood in awe of him. But
all Israel and Judah loved David; for it was he who marched out and
came in leading them.' 1 Samuel 18.14–16*

Success with feeling
David didn't let success go to his head. He had been a shepherd
lad, the youngest of a big family, and his brothers had certainly
not spoilt him (1 Sam. 17.28); but the experience of their short
temper had given him a valuable grounding in PR. When he was
elevated to great position in the army, he realized the importance
of going out to fight – and returning home – at the head of the
men who had also earned the name of 'soldier'. By contrast, Saul
appears to have been remote, distant, lacking the common touch.
It was no wonder the people acclaimed David. But their praise, far
from bringing Saul to his senses, made him jealous and vindictive –
and at the same time puzzled, for he couldn't understand why
David was fêted and he (even as king) was overlooked. It was not
that David was perfect (and in later life, far from perfect), but the
younger man had a sensitivity that was lacking in Saul.

Entrance for Satan
It was a lack that was to allow Satan the entrance he needed into
Saul's life, to convince the king that God was not in control, and
to seek instead 'advice' from the Witch of Endor, in calling up
Samuel from the dead. Coming at the end of a long-continued
suspicion and hatred of David, this was the sin that snapped God's
patience with Saul – just as today flirtation with the occult so often
heralds the point of no return for souls that are being lost to the
good. The life of Saul, as he slid further into Satan's power, is
replicated today with variations – sadly, sometimes inside the
Church as well as outside it.

God at our side
Keeping God at our side is the best antidote to giving Satan a
toe-hold; and maintaining good PR with fellow Christians is surely
a close second, for then we present a united front against the

devil's advances. There is safety in numbers, for he finds it harder then to gain a hearing. But the lonely, the depressed, those who like Saul withdraw to sulk or brood by themselves, these are fair game for Satan, and he is not short of ploys to distract their attention from God, or to convince them that God is not interested in them any more.

A good friend

David's friendship with Jonathan was doubly valuable, in that it mellowed David's pugilistic tendencies (few kings fought more wars than David), and it also saved Jonathan from being overwhelmed by his father's mood swings and hatred. Those who have not made such a friend, or been a friend to others, are less well adjusted to combat Satan's advances. Jesus knew the value of making and keeping friends, and his example was followed by the disciples in their ministries. It's of little use today to see someone who is short of friends, simply assume they are unfriendly folk, and leave them to get on with their solitary state. They may be alone for reasons beyond their control or not of their own making. Our extending of the hand of friendship may be what they most need. If we are rebuffed, at least we shall have tried. Certainly the feud between Saul and David could have been more serious had not Jonathan had the love of both.

Friends of Jesus

I call you servants no more, but friends, Jesus told his disciples in one of the most beautiful of Bible verses (John 15.15). And friends stick by each other, as David and Jonathan did. We can be sure that Jesus won't let us down – but are we showing our Best Friend to the world, in all we do, say, think, write, read and sing? What does Christ's friendship mean to us? Our friendship meant all of Calvary to him.

Suggested hymns

How sweet the name of Jesus sounds; I've found a Friend; O, for a thousand tongues to sing; What a Friend we have in Jesus.

Third Sunday after Trinity (Proper 6)
12 June *Principal Service* Giving Freely
Gen. 18.1–15; [21.1–7]; Ps. 116.1–2, 12–19; Rom. 5.1–8;
Matt. 9.35—10.8[9–23]

'[Jesus said] *"Cure the sick, raise the dead, cleanse the lepers, cast
out demons. You received without payment; give without payment."'*
Matthew 10.8

A tall order
Surely these were the most amazing recruitment instructions ever
given! The disciples' training had been watching and listening to
Jesus as he went from town to town healing and preaching – and,
we may reverently surmise, private tutorials when they were able
to escape from the crowds. In a land where sickness meant no
work, no pay and quite often a life of begging and an early
death, when news got round that the new healer was in the vicinity
Jesus would quickly be surrounded by people wanting to be
cured – especially as Jesus went further and raised the dead to
life. Yet he calmly tells his disciples to go and do the most amazing
things – curing, resurrecting, cleansing terminally afflicted lepers,
exorcising evil spirits – as if he were in a modern 'ops room',
sending out squadrons into battle, men and aircraft bristling with
armoury.

But Jesus' disciples are not even to take any cash for emergen-
cies, or spare clothing or footwear: not even a stick for the
occasional brush with a bandit. Wholly unprotected physically,
they must be wholly dependent on God. The provision was to
alter later, when they were to go further afield, but this early
mission was confined to the Jews, and as fellow countrymen they
were to travel light. Moreover, they were to be dependent on food
handouts: if their ministry was rejected, the inference was that
they would get no food until they happened on a more receptive
audience.

All the Twelve
Yet what is perhaps even more amazing is the fact that Judas the
betrayer apparently as calmly as the rest accepts these conditions,
and sets off with the others on the mission. He helped, it would
seem, towards its success, returned to enjoy the reciprocal joy of

Jesus, continued travelling in the team and learning from Jesus – and then betrayed his Master. And the capacity to renege on Christian loyalty did not die with Judas.

Service in the Church

The Church's work of mission goes on, and will go on until the End of the world. Some of it is financed by the sending churches, while other missionaries still go out depending in faith on God for everything. It's the same on the home front, some workers in the Church receiving salaries, many others giving their time and talents freely, like Paul supporting themselves with secular employment (Acts 20.34). Is there any difference or inequality in this work? No, it is all done for God, and is accepted as such by God. We have only to study how relatively unimportant money was to Jesus, to place it today in the context that he would have it. He is not recorded as ever carrying money himself. To illustrate the giving to Caesar of what belonged to Caesar, he had to ask for a coin to be shown to him (Matt. 22.19); when faced with the payment of toll for himself and Peter, he sent Peter fishing for the required cash (Matt. 17.27); and he very convincingly over-turned the tables of the money-changers in the Temple, sending their coins rolling in all directions (Matt. 21.12; Mark 11.15); one can imagine the children in the court (Matt. 21.15) coming out of that episode quite a bit richer! Jesus would hardly have subscribed to the preoccupation that so many have with money today. The cost of Calvary was not calculated in denarii or shekels: it was measured by human need, out of sheer love – freely given, so that we who have been bought so freely may in return give freely.

All to Jesus I surrender,
All to him I freely give;
I will ever love and trust him,
In his presence daily live . . .
All to Jesus I surrender,
Lord, I give myself to thee;
Fill me with thy love and power,
Let thy blessing fall on me.

Judson W. van de Venter, 1866–1939

So long as we are doing his work, God will see that we have all we need, which may not be either as much *or* as little as we think we need.

Family service input
Encourage the young people to list/discuss the things that can be done without money.

Suggested hymns
Firmly I believe and truly; Lord, her watch thy Church is keeping; My times are in thy hands; Take my life, and let it be.

Third Sunday after Trinity *Second Service*
When the Need Arises Ps. [42] 43; 1 Sam. 21.1–15; Luke 11.14–28

'So the priest gave [David] the holy bread; for there was no bread there except the bread of the Presence, which is removed from before the Lord to be replaced by hot bread on the day it is taken away.' 1 Samuel 21.6

Sabbath observance
Centuries after David, when Jesus took a walk through the corn-fields on the sabbath day and rubbed a few ears of grain between his hands to de-husk them, and then ate the kernels, the critics complained that he was violating the sabbath. In reply, he cited this occasion when David was given the holy bread (shewbread) of the tabernacle to eat (Matt. 12.4; Mark 2.26; Luke 6.4). Made fresh for the Lord each day, as successive batches were baked so the priests presented the new, still-hot leaves in the sanctuary and removed the previous day's baking for their own consumption. But David's need was great, and the wise (and somewhat nervous, v. 1) Ahimelech seems to have been only too glad to send David and his men away with the day's shewbread.

We can make a fetish of man-made rules. Ahimelech was not contravening the Ten Commandments by giving David the conse-crated bread; nor was Jesus endangering anyone's soul by eating grains of corn on the sabbath. God had made the sabbath for human beings, as a day of rest and refreshment; but human beings had taken the gift and hedged it round with so many caveats as to make the sabbath more of a burden than a delight.

God's provision
If we ever doubted the Lord's willingness to provide for our needs, we should remember the shewbread and the cornfields. The Jews were not the only people to amplify (and modify, where they thought fit) the God-given laws, until they were an encumbrance rather than an encouragement. We are still operating a similar policy – and not only outside the Church. Some of our liturgies and observances are well-nigh unintelligible to many non-believers. Is this the picture God wants us to give, the message he delights us to send? We have lived with these complicated practices so long that to us they have become not far removed from the minutiae of the sabbath as observed by the Jews of Jesus' day. The analogy is not perfect . . .

Many churches are using a combination of old and new worship forms: intricate and simple. And there will always be those people who would not be persuaded to come to worship, no matter what form was in operation. But for all of Christian history there has been a succession of new liturgy, new prayers and hymns, new ways of worship and witness. Are we to tread water, and to hand on nothing new from today to tomorrow – from this generation to the next? '[The Lord] put a new song in my mouth', sang the Psalmist (Ps. 40.3). Do we believe God has run out of new worship songs? When the need arises, surely he has a fund of new music at his command. Are we sure that no need for it has arisen today?

In extremis
When we go to minister to someone near death's door, don't we keep the gospel message simple? Those *in extremis* have (literally) no time for high-falutin' debate and argument, for longwinded semantics, however eloquent. They want to be assured of Jesus' love, forgiveness, compassion and salvation. They want a hand to hold, and a smile of love to show Jesus to them when words have come to an end.

But we don't need to leave these 'basics of faith' until the need is greatest. For *everyone* there is a need *now* for we never know when the call will come for them.

Laws can be wonderful aids to keep a nation functioning – and to keep the hierarchical structures of the Church itself in place.

But we need to remember that it was partly due to an unhealthy preoccupation with a plethora of man-made laws that those most programmed to expect the Messiah failed to recognize him when he came.

Suggested hymns
Colours of day; Meekness and majesty; Oh, the love of my Lord is the essence; We are marching.

Fourth Sunday after Trinity (Proper 7)
19 June   *Principal Service*   **For the Third Time . . .**
Gen. 21.8–21; Ps. 86.1–10, 16–17; Rom. 6.1b–11;
Matt. 10.24–39

'[Jesus said] "So have no fear . . . for nothing is covered up that is not to be uncovered . . . Do not fear those who kill the body but cannot kill the soul . . . Not one sparrow will fall to the ground unperceived by your Father . . . So do not be afraid; you are of more value than many sparrows."' Matthew 10.26–31

The solemnity of repetition
'This is for the third time of asking. If any of you know cause or just impediment why these persons may not be joined together . . .' The words are so familiar. As we make the solemn announcement, in the pews some heads may bow in embarrassment, others look covertly sideways, and, just occasionally, an objection is voiced and has to be discussed privately afterwards. It's often an awkward moment, but the words need to be spoken.

Why don't we give as much notice when Jesus, in the space not of three weeks but a few sentences warns us – commands us – three times not to fear? This is serious teaching and needs to be given full weight. In general, we've become so used to worrying over everything that were it not for the skill and strength God used to create us, and his Holy Spirit implanted and invested in us, we'd be in despair. It's a million times easier to say 'I believe in Jesus', than to obey Jesus and declare, '*Because* I believe in him, I do not fear.' Most of us would admit to welcoming a challenge.

Well, this is one of the greatest challenges going – and it's never too soon to tackle it.

A butterfly lives its vibrant, beautiful life for a few weeks of summer sunshine, and then dies. A bird sees life for a few years, a horse for a few more. Yet we love our fragile bodies so much that the prospect of going short on food or shelter throws us into trepidation, if not paroxysms of fear. Somehow, we think (if we don't shout it from the housetops) we need to make our existence here as comfortable as we possibly can. Nature implicitly relies on God for birth and death, and in between these two gets on with living in the conditions the Creator sends.

Go for it!

Jesus is telling us to go for it, to witness wholeheartedly, openly and with a spirited abandonment that trusts God for the essentials of life. Can we? Dare we? Aren't we already thinking up the first of a host of caveats? Lord, give me time and I'll make a convincing case! Since when did God give us time in order to argue *against* witnessing for Christ? Sure, Jesus knows we're timid by nature: so were the disciples, before he got to work on them. And we have a great incentive to fight fear: it's the devil's best weapon. Deprive him of using that in our lives, and we can surely meet the smaller fry in his armoury. 'I will not fear, for the Lord is on my side' (cf., e.g., Pss. 56 and 118) is a quality decision we need to pray the Holy Spirit to help us honour, time after time, every day, until it becomes as natural as breathing. And it's very difficult to think about our fears, while we're saying it. Jesus knew what he was about (and how well he knew human nature!), when he told the disciples: 'If you abide in me, and my words abide in you, ask for whatever you wish, and it will be done for you' (John 15.7). Lord, your words *are* abiding in me. You are on my side. I will not fear. If we *do* fear, the question arises: who *is* in us? Is it Jesus – or someone else? Let's get straight with God, and send fear back to where it belongs, with Satan.

Dark – and light

Fear stalks around in dark places, skulking in suspicion, foreboding and the darkness of dread. We can't pinpoint its beginning, because when we realize we've got it, usually it's pretty well developed. But the light of Christ can show fear up for what it is. And then we can deal with it, bringing our worry and anguish into the open, where God's light can go to work on it and show us the way out of the problem (cf. 1 Cor. 10.13). *And there is always a way out – with God.*

Family service input
Encourage the young people to share or learn about the trust that birds and animals show, and how this can be translated into our own lives.

Suggested hymns
I heard the voice of Jesus say; Put thou thy trust in God; Sing them over again to me, wonderful words of life; Tell out, my soul, the greatness of the Lord.

Fourth Sunday after Trinity *Second Service*
Magnanimity Ps. 46 [48]; 1 Sam. 24.1–17; Luke 14.12–24

'[David said] "See, my father, see the corner of your cloak in my hand; for by the fact that I cut off the corner of your cloak, and did not kill you, you may know for certain that there is no wrong or treason in my hands. I have not sinned against you, though you are hunting me to take my life."' 1 Samuel 24.11

The answer to hatred
Jealousy with Saul had grown into suspicion, and suspicion into hatred of David. And David's magnanimity was to bring about repentance in Saul – short-lived repentance, but a respite nevertheless. We, too, may feel that we can do little to effect a rapprochement with a modern-day Saul who has a grudge against us; but any lessening of hostility, however small, however fleeting, is worth the effort. We never know when God will call us, or the other party, and any time saved for peace is time denied to war.

Spiritual PR
Peacemaking is a good spiritual PR exercise, for it shows the Holy Spirit at work in us: forgiving, forgetting, refusing to harbour hatred or a grudge. It's a sobering thought, that by perpetuating differences we are instead showing Satan at work – in us. And

who in their right mind would want to do that? There can surely be few more counter-productive measures. David knew that for the good of the kingdom, Israel should not be seen by her many enemies to have her monarch and chief army officer at logger-heads. That alone would have been sufficient reason to mend fences; but the honour of Israel's God was also at stake, for every-one knew that Saul had been anointed king by the prophet Samuel, literally 'by divine appointment'. And so every weakness of the king could be seen as a weakness of the office itself. Similarly today, when we take on the name and office of 'Christian', we are the world's view of Christ. All (or most) of the good that we do may be taken as our duty; but when we fall down on our duty, the world takes notice. It may blame us, but Satan, being the dirty fighter he is, usually hits at Jesus. And, once Satan has found the chink in a person's armour, he knows where he can hit the mark again. Saul fell a vitim recurrently to the sins of suspicion, jealousy and hatred. Eventually it was the suspicion that God had not heard his prayer, that God had abandoned him, that God was no longer in control of his kingdom, that led Saul into the occult, to seek out the Witch of Endor. And that, for Saul, was the end – the end of God's patience with him.

Keeping the armour of God in place

To foil Satan's insidious advances, before they attain mega-proportions, we need to keep every piece of God's armour in place (Eph. 6); and particularly in this context, our feet shod with the gospel of peace – for, unless we take the initiative, as David did, the other party will probably not come to us.

Vigilance is all-important. Saul was not the first nor the last to attain high office and fall from grace. Office itself is no protection. Status and wealth are often sought with much energy and determi-nation – which could far better be directed towards God – for all the world as though they come with a lifelong guarantee. Neither of them guarantees exemption from misfortune or evil in this life, never mind eternity. Why do so many people settle for second-best? Partly the answer lies in our natural impatience for short-term benefits. 'Well, Lord, we can't see into the future; we'll concentrate on the here and now, and let you take care of what's to come.'

God will surely see to the future, but because he has the greatest heart of love, he is concerned about the short term as well. And his magnanimity exceeds David's by a fair margin. He comes looking for us, and when he finds us, instead of cutting off a bit of useless cloth, he *gives* – he gives his peace, his strength and his encouragement: picking us up, dusting us down and sending us back into the fray as newly energized Christians.

And, time and again, we congratulate ourselves on getting through by our own efforts.

Suggested hymns
Bind us together, Lord; In the cross of Christ I glory; Inspired by love and anger; Thy way, not mine, O Lord.

Fifth Sunday after Trinity (Proper 8)
26 June *Principal Service* **Beyond Endurance?**
Gen. 22.1–14; Ps. 13; Rom. 6.12–23; Matt. 10.40–42

'[God said] "Take your son, your only son Isaac, whom you love, and go to the land of Moriah, and offer him there as a burnt-offering on one of the mountains that I shall show you."' Genesis 22.2

One ask too much?
Was this one ask too much, after all that Abraham had been through? We can imagine that if a film was being made of Genesis 22, there would be poignant scenes of Abraham agonizing over whether or not to comply with this command; tender scenes of Sarah packing the men's lunch for their 'day out'; perhaps a series of shots of Isaac with his pet animals. It's the stuff of which films are made. But the biblical authors were not interested in such matters. And perhaps, indeed, Abraham did not go to hell and back; his faith may have been so strengthened in the 25 years of waiting for the promise of Isaac to come true, that he trusted God to do what was best, every time.

Yes, such faith may leave us speechless with awe. But what an example Abraham is to follow! When God seems to have deserted us in our time of greatest need, he really hasn't. We, like Abraham, must believe this, or we shall tear ourselves (spiritually speaking) to shreds.

Isaac's understanding

Isaac had not been told the true object of the journey – not that Abraham prevaricated, but he would not tell the lad what he believed would not happen. Yet as Isaac was bound to the wood, the young man must have wondered what his loving father was about, in much the same way that, implicitly if not aloud, we remind our Father that he too is supposed to love us and not to bring us into certain situations. Isaac's acceptance of the situation, like Abraham's, is a wonderful example of spiritual poise and faith.

So the biblical author may have omitted the agony! But agony, if any there was, would be expendable. Do we ever reflect on the energy we waste in agonizing over much that never comes to pass? And whatever does come to pass, does simply that: it does not remain for ever.

Life – and death

Life and death, God was reminding Abraham, are always in God's hands. He can give either, and withhold either; and the time between one and the other is equally under his control. He had given Isaac life, after Abraham and Sarah had nurtured the promise for 25 years; and he could, if and when he wished, take back that life. All life is God's: at best, we are temporary beneficiaries. Yet when Jesus came, he brought an extra dimension to life: eternity (if infinity can be termed a dimension). And, much more definitively than in Abraham's day, how we live this present life was suddenly seen to matter very much. Abraham's covenant had promised that he would be the father of many nations, and that in him families of the earth would be blessed. The coming of Jesus, in the new covenant, dotted the 'i's and crossed the 't's as his saving act was signed, sealed and delivered. Jesus killed death, so that life could continue. The animal sacrifices that had pertained from Abraham's day to his own were now obsolete; instead of the very young Isaac on the altar, the young Jesus had accomplished the fuller, greater sacrifice for the world: once, only once, and once for all.

Superfluous sacrifices

Yet those who don't acknowledge the sacrifice of Jesus, continue to make (or impose) superfluous sacrifices of their own. They are whistling in the dark – yet there's still time for Christ's light to shine in their darkness, if Christians will take it to them. But for the grace of God, we too might be in their gloom. The fact that we are where we are is not due to our wisdom, worthiness or any other virtue. 'You did not choose me, but I chose you,' Jesus is still reminding us (John 15.16). Likewise, Abraham had been chosen, for a very special purpose. And, as he and Isaac went back down the mountain, rejoined their servants and returned to Sarah, Abraham's thoughts must have been concentrated on that purpose, the foundations of which had been laid on such solid ground.

Family service input
Encourage the young people to draw the family tree of Jesus (Matt. 1.1–17 or Luke 3.23–38), and then to research as much data as possible about each person. The youngest members might illustrate the data, and the project could be spread over several weeks.

Suggested hymns
I come with joy to meet my Lord; Great is thy faithfulness; Lord of our life, and God of our salvation; The God of Abraham praise.

Fifth Sunday after Trinity   *Second Service*
Back from the Dead   Ps. 50; 1 Sam. 28.3–19;
Luke 17.20–37
'When Saul inquired of the Lord, the Lord did not answer him, not by dreams, nor by Urim, nor by prophets. Then Saul said to his servants, "Seek out for me a woman who is a medium, so that I may go to her and inquire of her." His servants said to him, "There is a medium at Endor."' 1 Samuel 28.6–7

Recognized methods
There were recognized methods of gaining access to God, such as repentance and prayerful confession; the dreams that God gave, the Urim (which seems, with the Thummim, to have been a type of priestly divination), and through the living prophets of the day. But Saul could not take these methods. Why? Because he had taken fear into his mind (v. 5). And nothing makes a more effectual block between a person and God than fear – Satan's prime weapon.
So Saul was in a spiritual limbo, and Satan had an easy task

160

persuading him to dabble in the occult. This episode with the Witch of Endor is a salutary lesson to any who feel inclined to take a short cut to safety. She proved to be a short cut, certainly – but to death.

Saul was not the first to be lured into bringing up spirits from the dead. The Witch of Endor appears to have been well established in her profession. And the episode needs to be taken seriously, for it shows that the dead can be recalled. Samuel appeared in a recognizable form, though his message was not what Saul wanted to hear; and his appearance was also the means of the Witch seeing through Saul's disguise.

Mediums of today

Today's world has more than its share of mediums, and the dead can still be called up. Many are dabbling in the occult, from fortune-telling to outright satanism. But it is as contrary to God's will as it was in the days of Saul. God is still telling us: 'It is possible, but don't do it. Spirits can be recalled – but outside of my will it is a sin to recall them.'

Yet forbidden fruit is as tempting as ever. The laws that made witchcraft illegal didn't succeed in wiping out the practice, though many witches (and not a few innocent women) were burned. It is a thousand pities that untold energies are spent in such a senseless, sinful pursuit, which could profitably be redirected in the cause of the gospel.

Starting with fear

Remember that it was fear: stark, paralysing fear, that sent Saul off the rails. Fear distorts our judgement, too, as well as blocking our lifeline to God. Why did the king need to fear the Philistines? God had defeated their champion Goliath, with a stripling of a lad who was now at the head of Israel's army and due to inherit the crown. But Saul, by his jealousy, suspicion and hatred, had boxed himself into a corner from which he could now only look out with eyes of fear. How had the mighty fallen! Saul was back, in spirit, to the days when Goliath was alive.

We may start out by being afraid of the silliest things, but if we can remember what fear did to Saul, it may help us to recover our spiritual equilibrium and to fix our eyes firmly back on Jesus.

Samuel's message
Apart from the initial rebuke at having been called up from the
dead, Samuel told Saul what he would no doubt have said, had
he still been alive. This at least tells us that those who have died
(for want of a better word) retain the mission that they have had
on earth. What *else* they may be doing in the spiritual realm, we
do not know. Nor are we yet supposed to know. Our brief is to
live this life as well as we can, as Christians, and the Lord will
lead us on to other things as and when he is ready.

Suggested hymns
Be thou my Guardian and my Guide; Jesus, still lead on; Jesus,
these eyes have never seen; Let saints on earth in concert sing.

Sixth Sunday after Trinity (Proper 9)
(or Thomas the Apostle; see p. 297) 3 July
Principal Service **Jesus' Yoke, Our Yoke**
Gen. 24.34–38, 42–49, 58–67; Ps. 45.10–17 or
Canticle: S. of Sol. 2.8–13; Rom. 7.15–25a;
Matt. 11.16–19, 25–30

*'For I do not the good I want, but the evil that I do not want is what I
do. Now if I do what I do not want, it is no longer I that do it, but sin
that dwells within me.' Romans 7.19–20*
*'We played the flute for you, and you did not dance; we wailed, and you
did not mourn.' Matthew 11.17*

How hooked are we on God?
If there's one thing that's certain in this often uncertain world, it
is that as soon as we take an interest in God, Satan homes in on
us. The folk Jesus was talking about, in the Gospel reading, had
not hooked up to God. They were so preoccupied with themselves
and their goings-on, that children could play at weddings or
funerals in front of them, and it was all the same: they took not
a scrap of notice.
    In the time of Jesus there were no Roman Catholics or Anglicans
or Pentecostals – but there was one Baptist! Yet people in general
didn't listen too much to him. They criticized him – for clean,

simple living – but they tuned out when John's preaching hit them where it hurt . . . for all the world, as if the salvation of their souls concerned anyone but themselves.

Paul's heart-searching
Paul, in his letter to the Romans, tried to grapple with the problem. And what he said, applies equally to Christians today. We know we have the Holy Spirit in us, urging us to will and to do, of God's good pleasure. We also know that God exists, and that his force for good, implanted in us, operates through us and guides us to do and say what is in line with the will of God. However a person comes to know the Spirit, there is an acceptance of the sheer love and might and power of the divine.

But as Paul had found, once he had locked on to the Holy Spirit, there was also another power to take into account. The ancient Hebrews had called it the 'Yetzer' – that gremlin that nowadays whispers to us, 'Go on, you've time to get across!' when the lights are on red. Or, 'You're not going back with that over-payment? Why bother? The shop will never miss it!' Or, 'Lie in today, and rest that headache – someone else will fill in at church for you.' The evil voice knows he needn't dangle murder or bigamy before us; we'll capitulate for something far more simple! 'What am I to do?' asks Paul. And he's not asking for himself alone; he knows every Christian in Rome will identify with the problem.

The challenge
If we shut our eyes to the things of God, Satan won't lose any sleep over us. But Christians should be committed to giving the devil a hard time; the fact that he will retaliate only adds to the challenge. Yet in today's Gospel, Jesus doesn't actually call it a challenge. He says, 'My yoke is easy, and my burden is light' (Matt. 11.30). Why, then, does the Christian way often seem so fraught, and far from being sweetness and light? Is the fault in us? Why, then, do we find Paul trying to come to terms with a problem that was giving him real pain?

Some of the problems may be of our making, but not all, surely. We know that the Archangel Michael fought against Satan and toppled him from heaven, since when the devil prowls around here on earth looking to cause trouble wherever he can. *Our* problem comes when we make compromise with him, and take his trouble on board. If only it came neatly wrapped and bearing the

163

name of the sender, wouldn't we make short work of sending it back to where it belongs?

The key
What is the key to the problem? There may in fact be several keys, but one is surely *encouragement*: the encouragement of Jesus, who is ready and waiting to stand between us and the problems, pleasures, pains and preoccupations of life. He has travelled our road, and he knows that with his Holy Spirit we can make it to journey's end.

But let us go around telling folk this, and it's guaranteed someone will soon turn round and say, 'Oh, I don't know! It's so *hard* to be a Christian in modern times!'

By way of encouragement, we can tell them something: Christians have always had to live in modern times.

Family service input
Involve the young people in modelling a large yoke from coloured card – the brighter the better. Choose suitable texts from the teaching of Jesus and write or stick them on to the yoke, which could then be positioned in the church and added to in successive weeks.

Suggested hymns
How sweet the name of Jesus sounds; Jesus, the name high over all; O Jesus, I have promised; What a Friend we have in Jesus.

Sixth Sunday after Trinity   *Second Service*
Loyalty Is Rewarded   Ps. 56 [57]; 2 Sam. 2.1–11; 3.1; Luke 18.3—19.10

'When they told David, "It was the people of Jabesh-Gilead who buried Saul", David said to them, "May you be blessed by the Lord, because you showed this loyalty to Saul your lord, and buried him."' 2 Samuel 2.4–5.

A beautiful gift
Loyalty is a beautiful gift at any time – but especially poignant when given to the body of someone who has died, for then the giver is looking for nothing in return. We may reflect on the loyalty

of Joseph of Arimathaea and Nicodemus, in anointing and entombing the body of Jesus, redeeming by their love some of the awfulness of that Friday. And David is touched by the loyalty of the people of Jabesh-Gilead, in giving Saul decent burial, when so many of his subjects had only scorn and disloyalty to voice. It's also noteworthy that the new king had to be told of the kindness by a third party: the Jabesh-Gileadites themselves had not made a song and dance about their virtue.

On our doorstep
In every parish this episode is replicated today, with many variations. In the care of our church, the participation in worship, the organization of events, visiting, counselling, helping ... the list goes on and on, with so many kindnesses never hitting the headlines, so much loving work loyally done in God's name for others. Let us not wait until the farewell speeches or the funeral orations before we look around and say 'Thank you' for these strands of loyalty that are continually interwoven to keep the parish and its mission alive. And – yes – there will be those who *know*, who can play the part of the 'third party' that brought the loyalty of the Jabesh-Gileadites to the notice of David.

Remember ...
Remember the centurion who asked Jesus to heal his slave. His faith in Jesus was so strong, he believed the Lord could effect the healing from a distance. Jesus marvelled at the faith of a non-Jew. Then a 'third party' of Jewish elders said, generously: 'He is worthy of having you do this for him, for he loves our people, and it is he who built our synagogue for us' (Luke 7.5). Jesus must have warmed not only to the centurion, but also to the charitableness and gratitude of these elders at the Capernaum synagogue.

Remember also Barnabas, who interceded for Paul at the outset of his ministry, when Peter and the other disciples (very naturally) were sceptical about the genuineness of Paul's conversion (Acts 9.27).

We may be the people doing the great, unseen work, or the third party which does some 'godly gossip' in making it known, or the person to whom it is made known. It matters not. There is so much bad news around today that anything we can do to broadcast encouragement is surely worthwhile. A candle is not purchased to be stashed away under a barrel, but to be set in full view where its light can be seen (e.g. Mark 4.21). If we cultivate an awareness of others' goodness, our community will be doubly benefited. True worth does not seek reward, but when recognition and reward follow, others are drawn into the action. Mother Teresa worked among the poor of Calcutta so quietly, but when folk began to spread 'godly gossip' of what she was doing, the work grew and grew. Christians have been noted throughout history for reticence in proclaiming their good works, and our Lord did teach that almsgiving should be done in secret (Matt. 6.2ff.); but he had also taught, a little earlier in the great sermon, 'Let your light shine before others, so that they may see your good works, and give glory to your Father in heaven' (Matt. 5.16).

Godly gossip glorifies God!

Suggested hymns
Christ is the world's true light; Help us to help each other, Lord; Make me a channel of your peace; To the God of our salvation.

Seventh Sunday after Trinity (Proper 10)
10 July   *Principal Service*   **Absolution**
Gen. 25.19–34; Ps. 119.105–112; Rom. 8.1–11;
Matt. 13.1–9, 18–23

'There is therefore now no condemnation for those who are in Christ Jesus. For the law of the Spirit of life in Christ Jesus has set you free from the law of sin and of death.' Romans 8.1–2

Peace with God
So, we have peace with God? Do we, really, or do we fret ourselves over one fear after another from breakfast to bedtime? Paul is saying, in effect: 'Don't worry, if you haven't got this or that, or you are not this or that; you've been justified by faith. You are what you are, and God loves you the way you are.' He made us, Jesus died for us, the Holy Spirit is living in us. Why can't we let go all those inner tensions, and rejoice? God has done his part. Let's now rejoice in whatever he calls us to meet; see it as a

challenge to be met with joy – because this is the only way we're going to have peace with God.

By faith
By faith, we have been justified. By faith, God is making us into what he knows we can be, into what he created us to be. And he's going to work on us so gently, most of the time we may not realize what he is up to. He's making something beautiful out of us for eternity. The artist John Ruskin once met a woman who was bemoaning the blot of ink she had accidentally spilt on a delicate and expensive handkerchief. Asking for the loan of the material, Ruskin returned it a few days later, with a beautiful design he had created on it, beginning with the blot and ending up with a work of art. In something of the same way, God is making of our bungles and blotches something beautiful. But the process at times may seem traumatic, even devastating. How can we rejoice when we're really in a time of turmoil?

The prayer of Jesus
Jesus never promised us an easy ride. 'I pray not that you would take my friends out of the owrld,' he said to his Father, on one occasion, 'but that you would keep them safe in the minefield of temptations and tribulations' (John 17.15, paraphrased!). If our faith is to mean anything for us, then we need constantly an awakened realization of the spiritual back-up that God has already given us to meet the daily challenge. We don't need to pray for it. He has given it already. We have been justified so that we can work for the Christ who has done the justifying. 'Because Jesus lives, I can face tomorrow'; and Gloria and William J. Gaither, the authors of this modern hymn, were so right. We can face tomorrow because Jesus lives, and because his Spirit lives in us.

We can – but many others can't. For them, when destruction, devastation, depression and despair get really bad, they reach a point where they can't face tomorrow. They're not just the people with no home or food, who launch out into the River Thames at night; nor just those who crash out at a drinks-and-drugs party. Some of them are the folk who pass us in the street, or stand next to us in the checkout queue at the supermarket. Some are the friends who wave as they pass the gate, or who ring when perhaps we're so busy there's no time for a word – or who don't ring, don't walk past the gate . . . because they don't want to bother us.

We are justified by faith. The theory of this is crystal clear, and we can rejoice in our salvation. But the practical meaning is that we have to work out what God has worked in.

When we rejoice in our faith, God notices and rejoices with us. But when we get cracking on using the power of the Holy Spirit in us, to implant something of our faith into someone else's life, that person can also rejoice – and God will rejoice even more.

Family service input
Provide each young person with an A4 sheet with a blot of ink on it. Encourage them to make something beautiful from it, and then to discuss how the illustration has been, is being or can be worked out in life.

Suggested hymns
For the beauty of the earth; Give me the faith that can remove; How firm a foundation; My faith, it is an oaken staff.

Seventh Sunday after Trinity   *Second Service*
Keeping Faith   Ps. 60 [63]; 2 Sam. 7.18–29;
Luke 19.41—20.8
'What more can David say to you? For you know your servant, O Lord God. Because of your promise, and according to your own heart, you have wrought all this greatness, so that your servant may know it.' 2 Samuel 7.20–21

God's faithfulness
God had proved his faithfulness to David, and the king was duly grateful. He had seen the success of Israel in battle after battle, and the future of the country was looking much brighter than when David had come to the throne. But he felt it necessary to remind God of his promise to keep a king of David's line on the Jerusalem throne, for David knew he had not been a perfect ruler. We, too, have our times when, conscious of our own shortcomings, we gain courage by focusing on the promises of God. Our feet may feel as though they're on shifting sand, but when we look to the solid rock that is God, some of his stability seems to steady us. Such is the lifeline of prayer.

Looking ahead

David, for his sins, was not to have the pleasure of building God's Temple in Jerusalem – just as Moses, who had had his times of doubt and mismanagement, was given sight of the Promised Land, but no foothold there. But David's disappointment was offset by God's promise that Solomon would build the Temple: the royal line would continue. God does not renege on his promises.

We may at times doubt others' ability to keep promises – at times may also fall down on the promises we make to others. But no promise made by God can ever be broken; he cannot be untrue to himself, for he is wholly good.

> *Yes, God is good! In earth and sky,*
> *In ocean wave and spreading wood,*
> *Ten thousand voices seem to cry:*
> *'God made us all, and God is good!'*
>
> *John Hampden Gurney, 1802–62*

David had proved the worth of a grateful heart; his focus on God's goodness and faithfulness had sustained him through Saul's long-continued jealousy, hatred and repeated battles; and not least was his gratitude for the friendship he had had with Jonathan. *In*gratitude had been one of the hallmarks of Saul, and David had learned many lessons from that.

Petitions and thankfulness

It must be wearying for God to receive prayers that are overloaded with petitions but short on thankfulness, especially if we have begged with much energy and persistence for something which, on its being granted, we have promptly forgotten, or have taken for granted. How ungrateful we must look to our Father if our only acknowledgement of his kindness is to start worrying about the next problem on the horizon! We would think our friends were singularly unappreciative if they treated us in a similar way.

Cultivating a grateful heart means that we become more aware of more goodness around us. That may seem self-evident, but it should be said. And the more that people, as well as God, feel valued, the better it is for the community at large. Throughout his life, David showed that he valued people – and not only those nearest to him, or whose status and opinions were high-profile. It was this quality that contributed so much to his greatness, and counter-balanced in some degree the unedifying episode with Uriah the Hittite.

We may not be called upon to rule a nation, nor yet to build a fine palace and make preparations for a grand temple; but we can show appreciation and gratitude for God's goodness and that of others; and we can, as James counsels, help to point others to God: 'You should know that whoever brings back a sinner from wandering will save the sinner's soul from death and will cover a multitude of sins' (James 5.20). For most of us, surely any work along these lines must be good news!

Suggested hymns
A debtor to mercy alone; Come, ye faithful, raise the anthem; Songs of thankfulness and praise; Yes, God is good! in earth and sky.

Eighth Sunday after Trinity (Proper 11)
17 July   *Principal Service*   **An Unwanted Takeover**
Gen. 28.10–19a; Ps. 139.1–12, 23–24; Rom. 8.12–25;
Matt. 13.24–30, 36–43

'[Jesus] put before them another parable: "The kingdom of heaven may be compared to someone who sowed good seed in his field . . . the good seed are the children of the kingdom; the weeds are the children of the evil one, and the enemy who sowed them is the devil; the harvest is the end of the age, and the reapers are angels."' Matthew 13.24, 38–39

In Satan's hands
The weed seeds have no option but to be sown as and when Satan decides. Thus Jesus portrays the absolute takeover of the devil of those who make compromise with him. They may not wish to be in a particular place, but once Satan has them in his hands he decides for them. They may feel that life and growth is theirs to make of it what they will, but the writing is already on the wall for them: come the harvest, these weeds will be rooted out as worthless material. From the time they put themselves in Satan's grasp, their fate has been sealed.

God's good seed

By contrast, the good seed, those who are destined for God's kingdom, are allowed by God to grow in their allotted place, even though that is cheek-by-jowl with the bad seed. The proximity of these seeds will not harm the good seed, which will grow to the best of its ability until the harvest, when at last it will be separated from the weeds and can then be seen, without competition, for the high-value crop that it is.

Point of no return

Does this mean that the outcome of the good and bad seed is predestined? That we are what we are from birth, and whatever we do we cannot be converted either from bad to good or vice versa? How could this be, if God is a good, loving and compassionate Father?

Jesus came to warn people that such is the case for those who don't acknowledge him. He made the difference. He came to give his all, so that all may have the chance to make good. He came to call sinners to repentance, in reality to make possible the impossible, by change – transformation – from bad to good, from weeds to fruitful grain. His whole ministry was bent towards saving sinners from the error of their ways, calling them to a realization of who he was, and of who they could be in him. He told the penitent thief that he would be with him that very day in Paradise (Luke 23.43); even at that last hour, the thief repented, and the power of Jesus converted him from bad seed to good. That is why it's so vital that as long as we have opportunity, we need to help as many people as possible to come to Jesus. 'Woe betide me if I do not proclaim the gospel!' said Paul on one occasion (1 Cor. 9.16), and probably on many other days as well.

Proclaiming Jesus

'Proclaiming the gospel' can take many forms, from straightforward exposition from the pulpit, to mowing an elderly neighbour's lawn or giving someone a lift to church. It means showing Jesus to others and making a difference for him in their lives; reaching out in his love to others, even though we may be hurting dreadfully with worry, pain or trouble of one kind or another. It was said by an Anglican dean bereaved of his wife that extending the love of Jesus to those in need brought him through grief; it 'works' with whatever trouble we are in. In the darkness of withdrawal,

171

trouble only grows, until it swamps us in a paralysing grasp and makes us unfit (often physically as well as spiritually) for service. Reaching out in Jesus' name to others proves often to be a lifeline for us as well as for them. God has not called us into his army for us to operate a policy of self-destruction, but of growth in whatever service to which he has called us. He's after spiritual athletes, not couch potatoes or chronic invalids. And as we grow he'll give us enough strength to share; God is a giver, and he never stops enlarging on his blessings.

Family service input
Encourage the young people to grow or illustrate flowers, salads or herbs, to bring later to the Harvest Festival, as a reminder of today's reading. The project could be extended to wildflower or 'weed' seeds.

Suggested hymns
All things bright and beautiful; Lord for the years; Praise to the holiest in the height; We are marching.

Eighth Sunday after Trinity   *Second Service*
Boldness in Faith   Ps. 67 [70]; 1 Kings 2.10–12; 3.16–28; Acts 4.1–22 [or Mark 6.30–34, 53–56]
'Now when they saw the boldness of Peter and John and realized that they were uneducated and ordinary men, they were amazed and recognized them as companions of Jesus.' Acts 4.13

Extraordinary courage
It wasn't the cross round their necks – folk had not begun wearing crosses at this time; it wasn't even the fact that they operated a successful healing ministry, nor yet that they were eloquent preachers. It was the simple fact that they were preaching and healing at all. They were unlearned and ignorant men! What sort of extraordinary, supernatural boldness had taken hold of them, that they could go around acting like doctors and priests all rolled into one? That was what grabbed people's attention; and after due investigation and cogitation, folk decided that these two ex-fishermen of Galilee *must have been with Jesus.*

Is this how folk outside the Church see us? Do we puzzle them by living above their expectations, by laughing at difficulties, over-coming setbacks, smiling when by (human) rights we should be wallowing in the depths of despair? Yes, it may be hard to laugh and smile at such times, but why should we give Satan the satis-faction of other folk seeing he is getting us down? When cir-cumstances are bad, and the devil seems literally 'hell-bent' on destroying us, that is the time when we need to work at our spiritual hardest, in order to show Jesus, not Satan, to the world. Folk see quite enough of the devil, without Christians adding to his publicity.

No cakewalk

Peter's and John's Jerusalem ministry was no cakewalk. The city was as volatile as ever, the religious hierarchy now even more suspicious of known followers of Jesus after the resurrection. Yet the disciples boldly witnessed, and people were being converted. The power of Christ seemed unstoppable and Jerusalem found itself at a religious crossroads, the 'old guard' trying to preserve the status quo, while others – among them Joseph of Arimathaea and Nicodemus – were arguing that the resurrection was true and that the disciples of Jesus should be given a fair hearing. It was an exciting stage on which to preach, with audiences divided between the two opinions. Confusion was rife, as those seemingly best qualified to pontificate on religious matters were in opposition to the religious message being preached by men who so obviously had been with Jesus.

The message today

The gospel message today has an equally exciting setting, though the opponents are not the religious hierarchy but the plethora of distractions that the world has been accumulating and is still increasing. In what we like to term 'civilization', we proclaim Jesus largely against a battery of apathy and antipathy. Only when the gospel is taken to new ground, where people and communities have not yet heard of Jesus, can we experience more nearly the situation of, say, Paul, when he preached in the cities far from Jerusalem, where pagan cults and rituals were the main, if not the only, competitors for people's attention. Paul was in his element there: in fact, at one point he admitted that he wanted to proclaim the gospel where it had not before been aired (2 Cor. 10.14ff.).

On the home ground

Probably few of us have broken new ground in this way. Yet when we welcome someone to our church who has not been there before, don't we look eagerly for the things that strike them first? Don't we share our love of the place that means so much, with the longing that they too will be blessed by the sharing? Don't we often see the familiar things in a new light, just because we are sharing them with someone else for the first time? Ministry on the home ground is a wonderful opportunity for showing others that we are 'companions of Jesus' – as Peter and John found in Jerusalem that day.

Suggested hymns

Blest are the pure in heart; Jesus shall reign, where'er the sun; The Church's one foundation; We love the place, O God.

Ninth Sunday after Trinity (Proper 12) 24 July
Principal Service **Old and New** Gen. 29.15–28;
Ps. 105.1–11, 45b or Ps. 128; Rom. 8.26–39;
Matt. 13.31–33, 44–52

'And [Jesus] said to them, "Therefore every scribe who has been trained for the kingdom of heaven is like the master of a household who brings out of his treasure what is new and what is old."' Matthew 13.52

The kingdom of heaven

No wonder Jesus could captivate an audience with his teaching, for he put these words into eloquent yet simple practice. What shall we say the kingdom of heaven is like? Well now, think of mustard seed, growing from a tiny speck into a big plant; think of treasure, hidden, but just waiting to be discovered and brought to light; or what about a beautiful pearl, the sight of which almost takes your breath away? Or a net, thrown into the sea empty but drawn up heavy with fish of many sorts, shapes and sizes?

'Have you understood all this?'

And the hopeful disciples, inspired with the confidence infused into Jesus' teaching, cried: 'Yes!'

> *'Are ye able'* still the Master
> Whispers down eternity.
> And heroic spirits answer,
> Now, as then in Galilee.

> Earl Marlatt, b. 1892

For two thousand years

And for two thousand years teachers of the gospel have followed in the footsteps of Jesus, illustrating the gospel with old and new material. Old prophecies and promises are interpreted as history provides new learning and new insights. God has safeguarded his word, often against severe odds; and in his wisdom has given us more and more examples of how his love is being worked out here, for the hereafter. He provides more and more opportunities for witness, as we show him we care.

'The one who believes in me ... will do greater works than these, because I am going to the Father,' Jesus told his friends (John 14.12). What would he have made of all the material on offer today, to illustrate his gospel? Probably far more than all Christians put together – but, please God, we'll make a difference.

Defying explanation?

'The kingdom of heaven defies explanation.' Who has not heard this declared, usually by a non-believer? Does it, really? Is this what Jesus was really saying? That a little mustard seed does not grow into a tree: so the kingdom is unknowable? That treasure is not treasure when it is brought to light: so the kingdom is not to be revealed? That the most exotic, extravagant and expensive pearl must for security be kept under wraps: so the kingdom must be locked away from view? That a net is usually cast in a certain place for a certain type of fish: so the kingdom will be restricted to a certain type of person?

Yes, all these are possible explanations, or at least construction, on what Jesus said. None of them negates the kingdom. Who would dare to do that, anyway? But they all *limit* it, in ways to which Jesus did not subscribe. He would not be limited, particularly by man-made laws of the sabbath. God himself is limitless – though folk still try to do it, and we may have been guilty of that as well. The kingdom of heaven is not to be limited. It's as though Jesus is saying: 'I'm dealing with ideas and things with

175

which you are familiar – but I want you to stretch your understanding of each, to the *un*familiar: go beyond what you know – the seed growing more than normal; the treasure greater than you've ever seen; the pearl outshining and larger than any you know; the fishing net with a catch more cosmopolitan than Galilee could ever match . . . and then you will be closer in spirit to the kingdom of heaven. The best *is* yet to be!'

Family service input
Encourage the young people to illustrate the reading, and then to suggest further examples.

Suggested hymns
Praise, my soul, the King of heaven; The Church of God a kingdom is; The kingdom of God is justice; The spacious firmament on high.

Ninth Sunday after Trinity   *Second Service*
Prayer Marathon   Ps. 75 [76]; 1 Kings 6.11–14, 23–38; Acts 12.1–17 [or John 6.1–21]
'While Peter was kept in prison, the church prayed fervently to God for him . . . he went to the house of Mary, the mother of John whose other name was Mark, where many had gathered and were praying.' Acts 12.5, 12

Too hard for God?
Is anything too hard for God? We may answer 'No' to that – partly because we think it's the right thing to say. But do we really believe it? When something is too much for us, do we ask God to do something about it, and then shrug if nothing seems to happen, and think of something else rather than admit God has us baffled? God is able. And surely, as Christians, we know that, deep down. Nothing is beyond God – even if, at times, we don't understand.

Peter is in prison, but so confident that God is able to work out that problem that while the people down at the church are praying round the clock, Peter can settle down for such a good sleep that the angel has to kick him in the ribs to wake him. That was sheer trust – in a man who not so very long before had denied Jesus three times, but who has come to believe that, come what may,

Jesus will stick with him. He goes with the angel out of the prison, to freedom, and then the realization hits him and he 'came to himself' (v. 11). Can we not see Luke smiling as he wrote that! 'The Lord has sent his angel' – and Peter comes to himself as the truth hits him.

Slow to believe

The people praying in the house church of John Mark were even slower to believe that their prayers had been answered. They'd been fervently keeping up the prayer marathon for Peter. But then, when God gave them the miracle, they were so shocked that it took Peter some time to get the message through to them.

It's part and parcel of the Christian life that God continues to surprise us. Yet it's also apparently part of our human psyche that we feel obliged to bend over backwards to explain everything.

God's children

It's as though God in these miracles is saying: 'My little children, just accept that I know what I am about. I work with absolute power and authority, not with explanations and reasons!' If we insist on looking for explanations and reasons for all of life, we're going to miss out on a lot. It was not explanation or reason that got Jesus out of the tomb on Easter morning, but absolute love that absolutely defies explanation.

God is limitless

God can do anything, and any day, in any number of ways at his disposal, he shows us a bit more of himself. It's there, if we'll only look for it. But there are still those who go around in a spiritual fog. We need to guard against the preoccupation of those gathered in John Mark's house – worthily concentrated in prayer, yet taken unprepared when the answer came. Do we ever pray without expecting an answer? Perhaps those people had determined to 'pray through' to the morning. We, too, determine on a timetable that God may disregard. The Almighty will not be scheduled. An all-night prayer marathon may look good when reported in the parish magazine, but are we polishing our pedestal of virtue, or asking God to show us more of himself?

But we should not criticize those all-night petitioners: we'd have probably been caught equally off-guard. They were praying – while God went to work. At times we may tell ourselves that we can do both. Yet the experience would no doubt be a powerful incentive to pursue the power of prayer in the coming days and months.

Suggested hymns
Give thanks with a grateful heart; Lord, teach us how to pray aright; Pray when the morn is breaking; Prayer is the soul's sincere desire.

Tenth Sunday after Trinity (Proper 13)
31 July   *Principal Service*   Antidote to Grief
Gen. 32.22–31; Ps. 17.1–7, 15; Rom. 9.1–5;
Matt. 14.13–21

'Now when Jesus heard this, he withdrew from here in a boat to a deserted place by himself. But when the crowds heard it, they followed him on foot from the towns. When he went ashore, he saw a great crowd, and he had compassion for them and cured their sick.' Matthew 14.13–14

Grief's reaction
John had been his cousin, his forerunner, the man who had baptized him. News of his death made Jesus react as many others in a similar position would: he sought privacy, to mourn away from noise and crowds. But the crowds and the noise followed him. Where a lesser man might have snapped, in misery and frustration, Jesus showed only compassion and undertook a loving healing ministry.

How short is our own fuse – with or without grief? Perhaps we don't expect patience from others, and don't practise it ourselves; or perhaps we are long-suffering, without looking for it in others. Or perhaps life runs on smooth wheels, and we give and receive patience in good measure! Let's give God the glory!

The friends of Jesus
The disciples were not so pleased to see the crowd. They might have felt a little protective towards Jesus, but probably they simply wanted to be alone with him for a while, to try to make sense of what had happened in Machaerus, and to discuss what John's

disciples may do now. Would they, for example, join forces with the Twelve? But the crowd's appearance put paid to any quiet words with Jesus – and the disciples, perhaps naturally, seem to have felt aggrieved. Yet the healings, followed by the miraculous feeding, would in themselves deflect attention from their grief. Helping others is still as effective in bereavement today. It takes a lot of effort to pull away from the suffocating stranglehold of grief (which itself is a type of fear); but someone else's need can help to achieve it. And wherever we are, there is always within easy reach at least one person in need. Jesus accentuated the need, throwing the ball into the disciples' court: '[The people] need not go away; you give them something to eat!' (v. 16). It was also a rebuke, for they had pressed him to send the people away. Jesus reprimands their unfeeling and selfish attitude, and tells them to solve the problem themselves.

Using available resources
They had access only to the smallest of rations – but Jesus responded to their attempt, and multiplied the food beyond all expectations. It's a lesson in making good use of all that we have; because we are usually too proficient in protesting about the paucity of our resources. God is at his most loving when we ask him to show us how to use what he has given us. 'But, Lord, I haven't enough for what I need!' Do we really believe we know better than God what we need? Did Jesus need a pantechnicon of groceries for the crowd? If we feel badly treated, may we remember those loaves and fishes – and imagine, if we can, the five thousand men, *plus* the women and children.

Respect for the dead
A fairly conventional set of traditions has grown up around bereavement. We've come some way since the suffocating black crepe, drawn curtains and seclusion of Victorian grief; but if the newly bereaved are seen going about their normal work immediately, the feeling is often expressed (or implied) that proper respect for the dead is not being shown. What is 'proper' in this context? Surely the work of Jesus and the disciples, in healing, feeding and serving the crowd, did a lot of folk a lot of good and did not damage John's memory in any way? The Baptist was beyond human help. Wouldn't John himself have approved more of their ministry than if they had insisted on going into seclusion? Our

commission from Christ is to the living within reach; the departed are convincingly in God's hands already.

Family service input
Encourage an explanation by the young people of the volume of food needed to feed, say, ten thousand people – with perhaps a contest among the whole congregation as to who can most accurately estimate the weight and/or cost.

Suggested hymns
Can I see another's woe; Jesu, lover of my soul; Jesus, stand among us; Oft in danger, oft in woe.

Tenth Sunday after Trinity   *Second Service*
The Problem of Pride   Ps. 80; 1 Kings 10.1–13;
Acts 13.1–13 [or John 6.24–35]
'When the queen of Sheba heard of the fame of Solomon (fame due to the name of the Lord) she came to test him with hard questions.' 1 Kings 10.1
'When the proconsul saw what had happened, he believed, for he was astonished at the teaching about the Lord.' Acts 13.12

A very modern problem
In the readings from both 1 Kings and Acts, we have a very modern problem, one which the Church has to combat today, as hitherto: PRIDE. Solomon was so full of his importance and wealth, he couldn't resist showing off in front of the Queen of Sheba. He took all the credit, instead of giving the glory to God. In fact, the only person we are told who mentioned God was the Queen of Sheba herself (v. 9). And Solomon went on to take more foreign wives, and to flirt with the occult, in his dalliance with the cults of Ashtoreth of the Zidonians, and Milcom of the Ammonites (ch. 11).

Paul, at Paphos in Cyprus, came up against Elymas, the magician so proud of his spells and incantations that he faced up to Paul, causing a scene in the governor's house as Sergius Paulus, having invited Paul and Barnabas to tell him of Jesus, was listening to Paul's sermon. Paul, justifiably angry at the intrusion, turned on Elymas and struck him down with blindness. And if anyone knew how Elymas would feel after such treatment, it was Paul, for hadn't Jesus done the same to him on the Damascus road?

Pride no respecter

Sergius Paulus was duly impressed: 'he was astonished at the teaching about the Lord' (v. 12). Probably Paul had had no intention of the governor's introduction to Christianity being quite so astonishing, but that's how it happened.

Today, those who live in luxury have to guard against pride more than most – although, of course, pride is no respecter of persons. It can be found in a cottage as well as in a castle. We are usually quick to spot it – in others, if not so quickly in ourselves. And it's so common that in small doses it can often be taken for granted, masquerading under euphemisms such as confidence, ambition, and their ilk.

An old gospel hymn runs:

> The world is a stage of excitement,
> There's DANGER wherever you go.
> But if you'd be true to your manhood,
> Have courage, my boy, to say 'No!'

> H. R. Palmer and Ira D. Sankey

The more we stand up and stand out for God, the more we find that this is true. The devil is trying to entice us away from focusing on God, trying to lure us into taking up with the occult, in every place and by every means he can: by fortune-telling, ouija boards, tarot cards, witchcraft, demonology, magic and outright satanism. Christians need to go on a real prayer offensive if these pernicious practices are to be dealt with.

What can we do?

One meets a sadly large number of people who are in, or near to, despair. And not only over personal problems. They often ask: what can we do about the state that the world, or our church, is in today? What can a voice in the wilderness achieve?

Well, one voice in the wilderness achieved a lot: John the Baptist made a pretty good fist of preparing people for the ministry of Jesus. And soon afterwards there was another lone voice in the wilderness – and he made an even better job of slamming Satan down, time after time, with the word of God.

One voice can make a difference against pride and evil of any kind. But only if it speaks out, loud and clear.

Suggested hymns
Come and see the shining hope; Come ye that love the Lord; Stand up, stand up for Jesus; Tell out, my soul, the greatness of the Lord.

Eleventh Sunday after Trinity (Proper 14)
7 August   *Principal Service*   **Little Faith**
Gen. 37.1–4, 12–28; Ps. 105.1–6, 16–22, 45b;
Rom. 10.5–15; Matt. 14.22–33

'Jesus immediately reached out his hand and caught [Peter], saying to him: "You of little faith, why did you doubt?" When they got into the boat, the wind ceased. And those in the boat worshipped him, saying, "Truly you are the Son of God."' Matthew 14.31–33

High tension
The disciples would surely not be at their best, at the time when Jesus caught up with them. News of John the Baptist's death had been followed by Jesus setting out with them for a quiet time of prayer. This had been abandoned when the crowds followed them; and Jesus had conducted a healing ministry among the people. Then the disciples had acted as catering staff, serving five thousand men and their families with food. Jesus had sent the crowds away after the meal, and had eventually retired to the mountains for solitary peace and prayer. The disciples had gone fishing, and as night had fallen they had been caught in a storm.

It had been a very long day. And they were at a low ebb – physically, mentally, spiritually.

Defying gravity
Then out of the darkness they see someone defying gravity and walking on the water. Matthew tells us they 'were far from the land' (v. 24). The water would be deep. Stalwart fishermen as some of them were – and in their home waters – they succumbed

not to mere fear, but stark terror. 'Take heart,' said Jesus. 'Don't be afraid.'

Peter's willingness

Peter started off well enough, with faith that if Jesus thought he could walk on water he really could. And he did – until he took his eyes off Jesus and thought about the storm. Is our attention span equally short when praying or listening-out for God? 'Yes, Lord, I believe you'll help me through this . . . but, ooh! what a mess I'm in!' It only takes the first thought, and our attention is right back on to our problem, and off God. 'You of little faith . . . Joe . . . Janice . . . Jim . . . Jane . . .' And we wonder why God has left us to work out a trouble that's more his size than ours.

He hasn't left us. But we're looking in the wrong place. God is not in the problem. Jesus wasn't in the storm-tossed boat. He was in the last place anyone would have expected: walking on deep water.

Using our minds

From birth, we are taught to relate to others – our parents, friends . . . gradually the circle widens. Then come the first words, and slowly our minds take in more and more knowledge. But the knowledge of operating with freedom from fear seems to come way down the list of priorities – if it figures there at all. Yet God appears to expect us to live without fear. Jesus repeats the command with almost monotonous regularity in the Gospels; repeatedly before the resurrection the disciples worry their way from one situation to the next. Just as many of us do today.

After the resurrection of Jesus, those same disciples are new people, operating without fear. Why can't we be post-resurrection disciples too? Jesus is Lord! He is alive! What have we to fear? Faith diminishes when fear takes over, so the more we agonize, the quicker our reserves of faith are depleted. Do we leave ourselves time to get back to the operational norm, between our times of fear? Put like this, doesn't fear sound too dangerous a game with which to tangle? Peter's fears had so depleted his faith that on the night of Jesus' arrest there was only a flicker left when he attacked the servant Malchus in Gethsemane. After that, it was all downhill until the three denials in the high priest's house.

It took a resurrection to restore his faith – but the restoration proved to be permanent.

183

Using concordances etc., eacourage the young people to abstract
as much data on 'faith' from the Gospels as they can. In subsequent
weeks this can (1) be collated into a parish project, (2) be illustrated
by new hymns, or form the basis of a Flower Festival or Workshop.

Suggested hymns
Jesus calls us, o'er the tumult; Lead, kindly light; Master, let me
walk with thee; Will your anchor hold.

The Eleventh Sunday after Trinity
Second Service **One Man's Faith** Ps. 86;
1 Kings 11.41—12.20; Acts 14.8–20 [or John 6.35, 41–51]

*'He listened to Paul as he was speaking. And Paul, looking at him
intently, and seeing that he had faith to be healed, said in a loud voice,
"Stand upright on your feet." And the man sprang up and began to
walk.' Acts 14.9–10*

Overlooked
The man had been in that sorry state from birth. He was a cripple
whom hundreds, even thousands, of people must have walked
past for years without a second glance. Yet as soon as Paul had
healed him, things started to happen: Paul and Barnabas were
treated like gods, then attacked as trouble-mongers; finally, Paul
was stoned and left for dead. In an age when stoning was very
convincingly carried out, this revival could in itself have been a
miracle. The man whose healing had sparked off all the action
seems to have kept a low profile; but one hopes that he went on to
witness on his own account. Certainly his days of being overlooked
were at an end.

Faith to be healed
Paul had looked at him eyeball to eyeball, and had recognized the
man's belief that he could be healed. So Paul healed him. But
we're not told that he healed in the name of Jesus, which is strange.
Did Luke omit this information? Or, were the disciples treated

like gods because it was thought that 'Zeus' had done the miracle? Usually Paul was very careful to give the credit to Jesus. In the shock of sacrifice being done to them, Paul was quick to preach God. It was a salutary lesson; in future, he and Barnabas were careful to proclaim Jesus, especially in an area where the gospel was being aired for the first time.

May we not store up trouble for ourselves by omitting to give God the credit; to preach Christ, and him crucified; to point others to God, and not to ourselves; to recognize that we are not God's greatest gift to all humankind, but witnesses to that gift. Then God will honour our witness.

Volatility

The Lycaonians may have been more volatile than the average British person today; but we can still be a pretty fickle race, applauding one minute and heckling the next. From sacrificing to stoning seems to have been accomplished pretty quickly – yet Paul survived, to carry on his mission work elsewhere. If our witnessing for Christ runs into problems, do we pull out and go to another place? Or do we stay and try to win over the opposition, or (perish the thought) retreat into our shell and embrace the unsatisfactory and unsavoury title of 'mediocre'? Satan loves mediocrity! He'll leave us alone – for a while, at least – to get used to being ordinary; but we probably won't even notice, because it's so ordinary being ordinary.

The old saint who once prayed, 'Lord, make me an uncommon Christian!' must have been far from ordinary. Isn't it a prayer that Paul himself might have used?

If one doesn't want to stand up and stand out in a crowd, the simple solution is to keep one's head down. It's a surprisingly common way of living, and not one to which Paul or Barnabas would have subscribed.

If we're going to be uncommon Christians, let's make sure we're uncommonly good.

Suggested hymns

A charge to keep I have; As the hart pants for the water; I bind unto myself today; I feel the winds of God today.

Twelfth Sunday after Trinity (Proper 15)

14 August   *Principal Service*   **Humble Determination**   Gen. 45.1–15; Ps. 133; Rom. 11.1–2a, 29–32; Matt. 15. [10–20]21–28

'She said, "Yes, Lord, yet even the dogs eat the crumbs that fall from their masters' table." Then Jesus answered her, "Woman, great is your faith! Let it be done for you as you wish." And her daughter was healed instantly.' Matthew 15.27–28

So God made mothers

'He couldn't be there himself, so God made mothers,' runs the beautiful saying. And didn't he do well! Even in nature, we can see the mother-love and concern of a blackbird for her fledgelings, as they hop the first few steps from the nest and then totteringly take to the air. Mother squawks and flutters, clucks and bobs, attracting everyone's attention, but not caring so long as she encourages and guards her children. And mother-love is seen in even more strength and beauty in our human mothers. It's so precious that God in his love arranged for Jesus to have Mary's mothering from conception to the grave. The troubled mother in our reading was determined, with gentle but persistent humility, to do and dare all for her little girl. At first, she received no encouragement – from Jesus, or the disciples; the latter were frankly rude, but Jesus was drawing out more and more of the faith which he knew was there, and which he also knew would prove a salutary lesson for his disciples.

When we are in great trouble today, we don't always pause to reflect that God may be using our anguish, as he draws out more of our faith, to help others. Usually we're so blinded by our personal struggle. It was probably also far from the woman's thoughts that her trial would benefit the disciples and others within earshot. Her mind was concentrated on her daughter's need, and the ability of Jesus to meet it. Once having brought those two things together, she *knew* – she had complete faith – that he would be willing as well as able.

A woman's pleading

We sometimes call it woman's intuition. Whether it is that, or simply faith, is probably not important. Mary had a similar faith when, after Jesus' apparent rebuff, she calmly went ahead with her order to the servants at the Cana wedding feast – and her Son acknowledged his mother's faith with immediate, miraculous effect (John 2.5ff.)!

Wholehearted pleading

It's a lesson in spiritual exercise. Jesus is asking us – even demanding – that we show as much energy as we can in our prayers and petitions. That means, as a rough guide, considerably more than we usually show. The intensity of our faith should be on a par with the energy expended in *winning* (as against merely competing in) a race. Until the woman's plea reached that pitch, her request was not granted. Isn't it, after all, discourteous to God to ask with a casualness which virtually takes his accession for granted? Order your case, he tells us. Prepare your arguments. Let's reason it out together . . . (cf. Isa. 1.18). He is urging us to take trouble over our prayers. We can imagine the 'psyching-up' of this woman, even to come near to the crowds around Jesus; but that led her to elbow her way through them, getting more determined with every push. With all that preamble, she wasn't in a mood for turning back when eventually she got to his side! Her little girl's life hung in the balance. Mother was at the point of no return!

How athletic are we in our praying? Progress not being dependent on climate, availability or finance, we can go into training at any time, in the confidence that our enabler, trainer, encourager and rewarder is One and the Same. May we pray with courage, gaiety and a sound mind, for it is our loving Father to whom we are talking.

Family service input

Begin plans with the young people for this year's Harvest cards, prayers, produce and publicity, to involve the whole parish – including, if possible, other congregations.

Suggested hymns

A safe stronghold our God is still; Forth in thy name, O Lord, I go; O Lord, all the world belongs to you; Thine arm, O Lord, in days of old.

Twelfth Sunday after Trinity *Second Service*
Directed by the Spirit Ps. 90; 2 Kings 4.1–37;
Acts 16.1–15 [or John 6.51–58]

'When [Paul] had seen the vision, we immediately tried to cross over to
Macedonia, being convinced that God had called us to proclaim the good
news to them.' Acts 16.10

A new team member
Luke is now with Paul, as the 'we passages' of Acts begin. That
he proved his worth from day one is evident, in that he implicitly
includes himself in the preaching work (v. 14)! It's a fair assumption that Luke by now has had the advantage of gaining material
for the Gospel that bears his name, from Mary and some of the
disciples. He is obviously a believer, and may have joined forces
with Paul in a preaching capacity, or partly also as a medical
companion. Paul's constitution must have been tough, but he had
been through a lot of rough handling as well as natural rigours;
a resident team doctor would be a distinct advantage. Paul would
not be too proud to accept Luke's professional help if it meant he
could continue his mission.

   Today, God continues to send us helps for our ministry – friends,
food, finance – the aid comes in so many ways. Let us never take
it for granted, or be too proud to accept it with grateful hearts;
but let us use it to the full in his service – and to him be all the
glory. And, as much as lies within our power, may he lead us to
help others in their various ministries, in a reciprocal building up
of the body of Christ. It may be a telephone call, a visit, a card;
we may never know how much that word of encouragement has
meant to the person God brought to our mind.

Come and help!
In response to Paul's vision, the missionaries set out for Macedonia. Quite possibly Luke, the Greek, was already familiar with
the area. He may even have interpreted for Paul if they ran into
language problems. And the mission was blessed. Lydia proved
to be a useful contact to carry on the good work after the disciples
left.

   In the days before the vision, we had heard that the Lord had
forbidden them to go into Asia and Bithynia. Paul seems to have
been conscious of directions not of his own choosing. But as soon

as he'd been joined by the Greek doctor, the green light came for them to enter Macedonia. God was firmly in the driving-seat, and Paul was willing for him to lead. Are we as amenable, or do we seek to push our plans through, whether we hear that little voice inside or not? 'Saving face' is not as important as spiritual integrity. Paul's active, eager mind would encourage him to go here, there and everywhere – but he tempered his enthusiasm in accordance with God's will.

And God helped him, by making progress into certain areas impossible (vv. 6–7)! It is an advantage when the Lord convincingly takes over, though we may not appreciate it as such at the time.

Doors and windows
'When the Lord closes a door, somewhere he opens a window.' Sure he does, because God never leaves us in total darkness. We may keep our spiritual eyes tightly closed against the light he is letting in on our problem – then it really *is* our problem. But his light is always there, if we'll have the courage to look. We may feel that the window he has opened is too high, and way beyond our reach. He has thought of the answer to that one, too! When the time is right, we shall be able to take advantage even of that high window.

It's not a cake-walk, but a faith-walk, this trusting in God for every step. Only faith can make it – one step at a time.

Suggested hymns
New every morning is the love; One more step along the world I go; Put thou thy trust in God; When morning gilds the skies.

Thirteenth Sunday after Trinity (Proper 16)
21 August   *Principal Service*   **Divine Revelation**
Ex. 1.8—2.10; Ps. 124; Rom. 12.1–8; Matt. 16.13–20

'Simon Peter answered, "You are the Messiah, the Son of the living God." And Jesus answered him, "Blessed are you, Simon, son of Jonah! For flesh and blood has not revealed this to you, but my Father in heaven."' Matthew 16.16–17

Looking out for God

To wake every day in the sure trust that God has us on his mind is only half the story. We should have God on our mind, be looking out for him, earnestly expecting revelation, guidance and love at every step. 'But that's not possible, Lord, with all that I've got on!' No, it may be impossible, but God urges us to try. He has to work harder to gain our attention if it's divided between other interests. Peter had been spending quality time with Jesus, and he had been brought by God to the stage where the truth of Jesus' messiahship had dawned. The other disciples in the mission team had also been with Jesus – but undeniably Peter had been his closest friend; and this shows us the value of getting close *and staying close* to God. We are then in a position to receive grace upon grace, grace abounding.

> I will not let thee go
> Unless thou tell thy Name to me.
>
> Charles Wesley

Stand firm

As the joy of Peter's revelation 'You are the Messiah!' resounds, Jesus comes back immediately with a magnificent, loving, trusting response: 'You are Peter!' You are the rock, Peter. You must stand firm, be worthy of this precious name I have given you. Oh, Peter, you will tremble; like a rock in an earthquake, you will tremble before the storm of my Passion! But you will regain stability and will go forward in faith.

Were thoughts like these passing through Jesus' mind as he looked lovingly at his right-hand disciple? He knew – Peter did not. Yet the Lord did not hold the near future against Peter, for he also saw the more distant future – the belief, the triple affirmation, the mission, the martyrdom, and glory. But Peter did not. Living for the moment, he accepted Jesus' trust and the promise of the keys of the kingdom of heaven.

For the moment

We, too, live for the moment. We agonize in trouble, and we blossom in joy; we try to do our best for those presently in need. Yes, we know there is a future – but it rarely keeps us awake at night. God in his wisdom has hidden it from us and bids us live for the moment. This moment is ours. What, then, are we doing with it, we who stand in direct line from Peter, as the Peters of today? Are we overwhelmed with the moment? Anxious? Serene? Joyful? Apprehensive? In pain, doubt or fear? It is our moment – every agonizing, joyful part of it; unless and until we share it with God.

Jesus didn't selfishly bask in the joy of Peter's 'You are the Messiah!' – sweet though it must have sounded after the indifference and antipathy of so many other people. He forthwith applauded and rewarded his dearly loved friend.

How can we respond, as Peter responded so long ago? How can we show Christ to the world, and not ourselves? How can we bend all our considerable energies into giving God the glory?

> Lord, let this work be all of you,
> and none of me.
> The voice may be mine,
> but let the message be yours.
> And whatever you want to change, Lord,
> it's yours to change;
> So long as I show your glory,
> and not mine!

A prayer like this, made before any undertaking, will surely bend the Lord's ear. And may Christians pray it and practise it, until the song goes round the earth, that Jesus *is* the Messiah!

Family service input
Explore with the young people how the Church is growing in one or more far-flung corners of the earth. Discuss (1) how our home church can help, and be helped by, these other congregations; and (2) open up links wherever possible between the churches.

Suggested hymns
Far round the world; Hills of the north, rejoice; Thou art the Christ, O God; To God be the glory.

Thirteenth Sunday after Trinity
Second Service   **Resurrection Doctrine**   Ps. 95;
2 Kings 6.8–23; Acts 17.15–34 [or John 6.56–69]

'Others said, "He seems to be a proclaimer of foreign divinities." (This was because he was telling the good news about Jesus and the resurrection.) . . . "Since we are God's offspring we ought not to think that the deity is like gold, or silver, or stone, an image formed by the art and imagination of mortals."' Acts 17.18, 29

Brilliant rhetoric
It was a masterpiece of rhetoric, this sermon that Paul gave before the sophisticated gathering in the Athenian Areopagus. He was following in the footsteps of the greatest orators of the day, and much prayer must have gone into the preparation of his speeh. He could hold the people's attention on matters of pantheism and the universe; but when he got to particulars, and in particular the resurrection of the dead . . . he didn't even on this occasion mention Jesus (though he had earlier, in the synagogue and marketplace), before his audience took umbrage and, with great restraint and cold politeness, terminated the address.

Paul would not mind overmuch. He sensed his crowd: intellectual curiosity would give him another hearing. But for today he had laid the foundation.

We are God's offspring
This would be a novel concept to his listeners, particularly the Stoic philosophers. Gods of stone or marble were pretty cold and lifeless deities, but they'd been around long enough for the Greeks to invest them with something approaching character if not feeling. Paul was now saying that their lump of stone, 'To an unknown God' (v. 23), was a mute reminder of a God who has a heart of love, who's given us life and everything else we have, and who asks of us *more* than respect and sacrifice – he wants love and joyful service.

A God who is almost human? Heads would shake, eyebrows lift, and rather superior smiles quirk at the corners of classic lips. But they would be intrigued to hear more.

Life from the dead
Did Paul take a deep breath, did he clench his hands under his robe, did he flash a quick arrow prayer heavenwards, as he got

to the main point of the speech? 'Of [all] this, he has given assurance to all by raising him from the dead' (v. 31). This was too much even for intellectuals to take on board at one sitting. But they would talk behind closed doors; of that, Paul could be certain.

When we are sharing the gospel with others, doesn't there come a time when we, too, know our listeners have reached saturation-point? Can we hear God saying, in effect, Here ends the first lesson? The seed has been sown. It may lie dormant for a while in its new soil – or it may begin to grow quite quickly. That is now in God's hands.

We find the same in our church projects – perhaps an initial surge of enthusiasm, then a setback or hiatus, followed by a resurgence of progress. God knows best the capacity and capabilities of every one of us. Let's be open to his guidance. But when he has cleared the way to go forward, may we not look for an excuse to do otherwise.

A famous site

Who can visit the site of Athens' Areopagus today without recalling Paul's visit? He may, in fact, have spoken only this once on its famous stones. But if that was the case, once would be enough. We may witness for God only once in any place or to any person; but if God so limits it, that once will be enough. It's surely a powerful incentive to make our witnessing always the best we can.

Who cannot say that Paul made the most of his Areopagus opportunity?

Suggested hymns

Inspired by love and anger; Jesu, our hope, our heart's desire; Sing of the Lord's greatness; Spirit of God, as strong as the wind.

Fourteenth Sunday after Trinity (Proper 17)
28 August   *Principal Service*   **God Will Repay**
Ex. 3.1–15; Ps. 105.1–6, 23–26, 45b; Rom. 12.9–21; Matt. 16.21–28

'[Jesus said] "For the Son of Man is to come with his angels in the glory of his Father, and then he will repay everyone for what has been done.

193

Truly I tell you, there are some standing here who will not taste death before they see the Son of Man coming in his kingdom." ' Matthew 16.27–28

Investment honoured
God will repay our investment in him. The Bank of the Holy and Undivided Trinity does not default on its payments. It operates on love: God has invested life and love in us, from whom he looks for service and love. As the divine wheel of love turns, he returns our love with eternal life. Who in their right mind would refuse to invest with such a caring bank? Who would reject such loving reciprocity? God loves, so that we love, so that he can love more. The world doesn't understand this sort of business, in an age where trust, honour and love are increasingly hard to come by.

When Jesus comes
When Jesus comes again, no one on earth will be able or allowed to miss the event. It is to be 'Repayment Day', when the accounts are made up and settlements made. Where shall we stand? That's God's business – and we may be surprised when the time comes. The Master of Ceremonies will not hurry or dawdle over the business, but he will be thorough. It's pretty certain that we shall have forgotten much of the good we have done in his name. And the blessing is that we have not been required to keep a record: the Master is taking care of that as well.

Shall we regret leaving anything behind? No – not by that time, for there is so much to look forward to. And if we have been busy for God here, we shall probably be even busier there.

'Some standing here'
Theologians have covered a lot of mileage over these words of our Lord; but surely he was referring to his post-resurrection appearances, in his glorified body, as a foretaste of the kingdom to come – though, in a way, the kingdom had already come near, in his person (e.g. Matt. 12.28). Of course, there will be others on the Great Day who will not yet have died when the Lord comes. We may be among them, if the Church in our lifetime has completed worldwide evangelism. It's a sobering thought, that if this was given international and interdenominational priority, the work could be completed before the year is out – by a fair margin.

Surely this is an indication of the patience of God, that after

194

nearly two Christian millennia he is still waiting for our mission to be accomplished. If anyone is delaying the business, it's not God.

Business before pleasure?
The business needs to come first: not of converting everyone, but of giving them a chance to hear or read the gospel. Just that, only that. Nothing else matters. If Jesus had not kept his mind set on the business of his mission, the crucifixion might have been long delayed. If the Church today could only be as single-minded, the Great Day would not be so long delayed.

Fervour – zeal – enthusiasm. If we work on these, they will grow in us, and in others. The fact that we underestimate our capabilities (and not only in this age, but from the time of the disciples on) can be deduced from the oft-repeated command of the Lord: 'Don't fear, don't be afraid!' He has obviously calculated that, with the equipment (physical, mental and spiritual) he has given us, we should be able to live in freedom from fear.

Instead of trying so hard to prove him wrong, why can't we do just that – concentrating, for starters, on getting the gospel right round the world?

Family service input
Encourage the young people (1) to illustrate, or (2) compose new hymns for, the Great Day.

Suggested hymns
Awake, my soul, and with the sun; Firmly I believe and truly; King of glory, King of peace; Take my life, and let it be.

Fourteenth Sunday after Trinity
Second Service   **Green Light for Ministry**
Ps. 105.1–15; 2 Kings 6.24–25; 7.3–20; Acts 8.1–16 [or Mark 7.1–8, 14–15, 21–23]
'One night the Lord said to Paul in a vision, "Do not be afraid, but speak and do not be silent; for I am with you, and no one will lay a hand on you to harm you, for there are many in this city who are my people."

He stayed there for a year and six months, teaching the word of God among them.' Acts 18.9–11

The way forward

Did Paul recollect any of the Twelve telling him of how Jesus had taught that, if the mission was opposed in any place, the disciples were to leave and move on to another town? Or perhaps no one had shared this with him. At any rate, the early opposition of the Corinthian Jews was countered by God telling Paul to stay where he was and continue his ministry – if not in the synagogue, then next door in the house of Titius Justus, a believer. And Paul would be encouraged that not all the Jews were against him: Crispus, the synagogue official (no less), became a believer.

This 18-month ministry augured well for Corinth, and at the same time gave Paul a couple of staunch allies in Priscilla and Aquila, Jews having left the Claudian persecution in Rome.

But Paul was told in his vision not to fear the antipathy shown in Corinth, but to speak up and speak out bravely for Jesus. The inference is that he had been considering moving on. But God had plans for Corinth: many hearts had already been stirred, and needed nurturing in the faith. Right there in Corinth was the place where God wanted his man, regardless of any opposition, or attraction of other mission fields.

Right here

And 'right here' is where God has placed us, with ministry on our doorstep – and perhaps some opposition. And we stay, until we are certain that God has work for us somewhere else. Right here is where he has considered our ministry to be his will. Perhaps our work, our family, our friends will move, or point towards a move in the future – and then another place, another opportunity will be God's will for us. Paul was infinitely adaptable to God, with this extended ministry in Corinth, an even longer one in Ephesus, and much travelling in between many other places. He would work (at Corinth with Priscilla and Aquila) to maintain himself, and yet give all the energy and time he could to the ministry.

While he would no doubt have the Christians in other places on his mind, and would pray for them (e.g. 2 Thess. 1.3ff.), Paul did the work that was nearest, faithfully and well. The people next door, or across the road, who are in trouble or doubt will not gain much comfort from us as neighbours if our minds are preoccupied with mission (however laudable) half a world away – or if we are concentrating so much on heavenly matters, that we are of no practical earthly use. Paul's tent-making in itself would ground him in Corinth, and would endear him to his new neighbours as a man who put his teaching into practice.

Melting the opposition
Fear of opposition usually brings the heavy tanks rolling in against us. Conquer the fear by God's grace, and very often the opposition melts away. We may even forget we were afraid – 'out of sight is out of mind' – but if possible, recall and thank God for doing what seemed impossible. It's a fair assumption that Paul's tent-making and preaching at Corinth left him little time to fear. Work – especially for God – is the best antidote going. If we take fear into our bodies, it can often be because we've spent time in thinking about it, time that could more profitably be spent in work for God.

Paul would be glad for the opportunity to work, to support himself, and to be seen to be doing so; but he tried hard not to be boastful about it (Acts 20.34). Those who have work today should be similarly thankful, and understanding towards those who for one reason or another have not.

Suggested hymns
Beneath the cross of Jesus; Father, hear the prayer we offer; The God of Abraham praise; The head that once was crowned with thorns.

Fifteenth Sunday after Trinity (Proper 18)
4 September *Principal Service* **Agreeing as Best We Can** Ex. 12.1–14; Ps. 149; Rom. 13.8–14; Matt. 18.15–20

'[Jesus said] "Truly I tell you, whatever you bind on earth will be bound in heaven, and whatever you loose on earth will be loosed in heaven. Again, truly I tell you, if two of you agree on earth about anything you ask, it will be done for you by my Father in heaven. For where two or three are gathered in my name, I am there among them." ' Matthew 18.18–20

Full agreement?
The author of the little first-century work entitled 'Teaching of
the Twelve Apostles' (*Didache*) was one honest man: 'Do all the
commandments of the Lord,' he wrote, 'but if you can't be perfect,
do the best you can.' And Christians are still trying – getting it
right some of the time. In today's Gospel, Jesus discusses dissension among believers, and this is still a hot potato, not least because
of the negativity it broadcasts to those outside the Church.

With the best intentions, we don't 'hit it off' all the time with
all the folk, in even our own church – although, to be fair, we are
probably quicker to seek a rapprochement here than in the wider
field. Can we ever hope to attain unity with different denominations when we can't agree among ourselves? Is it possible, this
side of eternity? Perhaps not, but, Lord, keep us trying!

History's page
History's page has shown that religion can bring great tension
and strife to the cold, clear light of day, and there are those in this
modern world overloaded with anaesthetics and placebos, who
would say that it's healthier for disagreements to be aired rather
than bottled up. Jesus is not saying that we should allow them to
simmer away till they have sapped our strength, but that if they
do come to the boil then the Church should contain the damage
rather than let it spill out into the world where it could be miscon-
strued with dangerous ease.

Jesus is here
Jesus is here, in our struggles as well as when life is running
smoothly. Even where two or three are together in spirit (as well
as in a physical sense), he is there, too. The Holy Spirit came at
Pentecost, where folk were together 'with one accord' (Acts 2.1,
AV). If we are in discord, God can bring about a miracle of agreement; but if we are already in agreement, can we not expect even
greater things to happen? Possibly if our expectations were greater,
our disunity would be less.

These words of Jesus are a measure of how he values the individual. It is wonderful, on 'state' occasions, to see a church packed
to the doors. But our Lord tells us here that he values the worship
of a very few, and is there with them ever as lovingly as with a
great congregation in a vast cathedral. Each of us matters to him,
not just for what we do for him, but for who we are in him. Every

so often, can we jettison what we are experiencing from the outside and try to see our *selves* for what we are in Jesus? How many others see their inner self, rather than the image that a mirror shows? How does the real 'me' differ from the 'me' that I allow the world to see? To 'see ourselves as others see us' may, in reality, be far from the true picture; for we've become so used to seeing the world as a stage that our acting ability has made great progress (one way or another).

The more open we are to Jesus, the truer will be the 'self' that we show to the world. A minister in the north of England used to walk into town on a Saturday morning, looking especially into the eyes of the people he met. There were eyes clouded with worry, grief, suspicion – he came across these much more frequently than bright, shining happy eyes. We may say what we believe others want to hear, whether or not our thoughts are in line with our words, but our eyes present a truer picture.

When we've lined up our eyes, hearts and words, we'll be closer to that perfection to which Jesus is still pointing.

Family service input
Encourage the young people to illustrate the various ways in which our eyes show others what we are thinking or feeling. Discuss how this can help or hinder Christian ministry.

Suggested hymns
Brother, sister, let me serve you; Here, O my Lord, I see thee face to face; Jesus, stand among us, at the meeting; O perfect love! all human thought.

Fifteenth Sunday after Trinity *Second Service*
Extraordinary Miracles Ps. 108 [115];
Ezek. 12.21—13.16; Acts 19.1–20 [or Mark 7.24–37]

'God did extraordinary miracles through Paul, so that when the handker-chiefs or aprons that had touched his skin were brought to the sick, their diseases left them, and the evil spirits came out of them . . . A number of those who practised magic collected their books and burned them publicly; when the value of these books was calculated, it was found to

199

come to fifty thousand silver coins. So the word of the Lord grew mightily and prevailed.' Acts 19.11, 19–20

Miracles v magic, then

God was fighting magic with miracles – and the miracles won. (When, after all, has God ever lost a fight?) The simple act of touching Paul with material belonging to the sick, cleansed the invalids from disease, so full was Paul of the Holy Spirit. The magicians, whose spells were almost certainly more complicated than this, couldn't replicate such healing – and, in frustration or conversion, or a mixture of the two, burnt their books to the tune of 50,000 silver coins. Paul's three-year ministry in Ephesus (Acts 20.31) bore much fruit. This, coming after a good ministry in Corinth, would give great encouragement to the by-now ageing apostle, for these were two of the most influential cities of his travels.

Miracles v magic, now

Today we still have magicians and their art to contend with – from the stage conjurors which many would regard as pretty harmless, to those heavily into occult practices such as ouija boards and tarot cards, black magic and satanism. At whatever level, this magic is dealing with a spiritual dimension which is not of God, and we, as Christians, need to oppose it in Christ's name; it's too close to Satan for comfort.

God is fighting magic today in no less determined ways than he used at Ephesus so long ago. Through the touch of our hands, he brings healing; through prayers, exorcisms and even replication of the touching by materials. That we don't give these miracles more broadcasting, is not the Lord's fault. We should, and we must, in the twenty-first century's onslaught against Satan and his magic; in an age when drugs make headlines, magic needs to be recognized as being just as harmful to the spirit as drugs are to the physical body. Both are a form of escapism – though both in reality ensnare their practitioners in an ever-downward spiral of restriction.

Getting rid of magic

And the effects of magic, unless confessed and repented of, can stay for a long time. If there has been a known involvement with any magical practices, these need to be brought out into the open and broken convincingly by cleansing in Jesus' name.

> He breaks the power of cancelled sin,
> And sets the prisoner free;
> His blood can make the foulest clean,
> His blood availed for me.

Charles Wesley

With the prevailing power of Jesus, we can move Satan off the ground – *God's* ground – that he is trying to pinch as his own. We can pitch against magic in all its forms, because 'the one who is in [us] is greater than the one who is in the world' (1 John 4.4). We can launch out with the energy of the Holy Spirit within us, against the magical infiltration of secret societies and Internet usage by questionable practitioners. We need never be ashamed of taking Jesus *anywhere*, so long as his light can replace spiritual darkness and intrigue.

One day, perhaps many years hence, people will thank us for the stand we take today. But if they don't notice the difference we are making, God will.

Suggested hymns
Forgive our sins as we forgive; Soldiers of Christ, arise; Thine arm, O Lord, in days of old; Thou art the Way; by thee alone.

Sixteenth Sunday after Trinity (Proper 19)
11 September *Principal Service* **Ad Infinitum**
Ex. 14.19–31; Ps. 114 or Canticle: Ex. 15.1b–11, 20–21; Rom. 14.1–12; Matt. 18.21–35

'Then Peter came and said to him, "Lord, if another member of the church sins against me, how often should I forgive? As many as seven times?" Jesus said to him, "Not seven times, but, I tell you, seventy-seven times."' Matthew 18.21–22

From the heart
'But another member of the church should know better than to sin against me!' If we don't say it, the thought is often there. It's harder to forgive someone who is close, someone of whom we expect a high moral, Christian standard; harder than a

non-believer half a world away whom we know merely as an acquaintance. But Jesus says, forgiveness needs to begin at home, within God's family – and it must be 'from the heart' (v. 35), thoroughgoing and absolute. Forgiving but not forgetting (as some try to do, by way of compromise) is not forgiving.

Again and again
We may need to forgive seventy-seven, seventy times seven, or a lot more; whatever it takes, we must do it. We ask for grace to forgive daily in the Lord's Prayer: to be forgiven, as we forgive; so if our forgiveness is half-hearted, what more can we justifiably expect from God? If he was not a God of love, and magnificently unfair into the bargain, we'd be in a sorry state.

Not bearing a grudge
If we can be magnanimous enough not to bear a grudge against anyone, we are on the way to forgiving from the heart. We have only to look at the world today, to see the wars and *non*-entente cordiales that are being perpetuated by grudge-bearers, long after the initial reason for the disagreement has died a natural death. Disputes are maintained, year after year, generation after generation. It is humanity at its most childish, but still it goes on; and not only at the international level, for there are innumerable replications on the home front. Let us pray for grace not to begin to bear a grudge against anyone. There will still be those whom we find difficult to meet, much less love. But God loves them. Can we not begin to see them through his eyes?

Letting go
It's a conscious letting-go of what we feel is our right to justice, our right to be vindicated. We can get along all right without this right. Let it go! Jesus is saying. Be reconciled to people, and so to God. It's good for the other party, and also for us: it will help to keep the colour of our hair, our nerves will respond positively the length and breadth of our body – and our heart will approve as well. Folk may even notice the difference before we do. There's every reason one can think of for letting go a grievance.

Kinder to ourselves
It is kinder to ourselves when we forgive others. At times we become so tensed up, our performance suffers – at work, at home,

at church. We literally haven't the physical or spiritual energy to give of our best, because we're wasting that effort in angst. Let it go, and forgive! says Jesus – and proceeds to follow up his command by the parable of the unjust servant who came to a sticky end through unforgiveness.

The prime example
The prime example of forgiveness came from our Lord himself, on the cross.

> *Forgive them, O my Father,*
> *They know not what they do!*
> *The Saviour spoke in anguish*
> *As the sharp nails went through.*
> *No word of anger spake he,*
> *To them that shed his blood.*
> *But prayer and tenderest pity,*
> *Large as the love of God.*

> *Mrs C. F. Alexander*

Family service input
Discuss with the young folk how holding on to a little grudge can escalate. Illustrate the hymn cited above.

Suggested hymns
Amazing Grace!; And can it be; Forgive our sins, as we forgive; Forgive them, O my Father.

Sixteenth Sunday after Trinity   *Second Service*
Message of Grace   Ps. 119.41–48[49–64]; Ezek. 20.1–8, 33–44; Acts 20.17–38 [or Mark 8.27–38]
'And now I commend you to God and to the message of his grace, a message that is able to build you up and to give you the inheritance among all who are sanctified.' Acts 20.32

A poignant encounter
This last meeting of Paul with his Ephesian friends is a poignant encounter. For three years, he has given them teaching, healing

and encouragement. And yet he has something more to give: I've got a message for you from God, that you need to hang on to, Paul is saying. It's GRACE!

Grace – that indefinable, unmerited mercy of God, by which we are made aware of God's love. Grace – that loved us before we loved him. Grace – that stands between us and the evil foe. Grace abounding – that gets us through crises and trials which humanly speaking are impossible. Grace upon grace – that will see us across the divide into eternity. Just hang on to this grace, Paul says, because it's able to build you up!

> *Each trial will make you the stronger,*
> *If you in the Name of the Lord*
> *Fight manfully under your Leader,*
> *Obeying the voice of his word.*
>
> Rian A. Dykes

Every new trial safely through builds up our spiritual athleticism. Sometimes it may seem as though God is never satisfied, for, with a gruelling trial only just behind us, he causes us to meet an even greater time of testing. 'No, Lord! I can't take any more!' we protest – and that still, small voice reminds us that God will be the judge of our strength.

Hard though it was for Paul to leave these Christians who had shown him such kindness and responded so well to his ministry, he knew the time had come to return to Jerusalem for the next stage of mission. He knew only too well that it would be fraught, but perhaps at this point he had not envisaged Rome.

If anyone could justifiably feel that he was being tested more than most, it was surely Paul. Yet he is prepared to meet the trials still to come with a spiritual equilibrium that leaves us gasping. When our own trials have equalled those of Paul, may we still be as eager for what may be yet to come!

> *Long as our fiery trials last,*
> *Long as the cross we bear,*
> *O, let our souls on thee be cast,*
> *In never-ceasing prayer.*

> The Spirit's interceding grace
> Give us in faith to claim;
> To wrestle till we see thy face,
> And know thy hidden name.

Charles Wesley

Life's journey
The further we travel on life's journey, the more spiritual athletes we find: some of them have endured trials that we would not wish to have to face in our own lives. Some appear at first sight to have been blessed by an easy ride, but as we come to know them better we find this is not the case. The woman whose serene smile cheers all whom she meets has been nursing a war-wounded husband for nearly forty years. The young man who is always so ready to help and whose house is always open for church meetings and functions lost his wife in childbirth less than a year after their marriage. The couple who keep the churchyard in immaculate condition, and each year plant colourful flowers to edge the church paths, have two autistic children.

By contrast, there are some with good health, a lovely home, a good job, children doing well at university, who always seem to be grumbling about something or other. There, but for the *grace* of God . . .

May we resolve to share this grace, that we don't build ourselves up at anyone else's expense. And to God be all the glory.

Suggested hymns
All for Jesus; God of mercy, God of grace; Grace! 'tis a charming sound; How can we sing this wondrous grace.

Seventeenth Sunday after Trinity (Proper 20)
18 September   *Principal Service*   **God's Generosity**
Ex. 16.2–15; Ps. 105.1–6, 37–45; Phil. 1.21–30; Matt. 20.1–16

'"Friend, I am doing you no wrong; did you not agree with me for the usual daily wage? Take what belongs to you, and go. I choose to give to this last the same as I give to you. Am I not allowed to do what I choose

with what belongs to me? Or are you envious because I am generous?"'
Matthew 20.13–15

God's choice

God reserves to himself the right to do as he will with what is his, and, since he made everything, all is his. We cannot dictate how he deals with us, especially if we have agreed the terms of our employment. When we came to belief in Jesus, those terms were understood as a prerequisite: we obey what Jesus commands, and God sees to the spiritual finance.

The employer in Jesus' parable did not allow any of his workers to work either for nothing or for less than their due. The sticking point for some came when others who had started late seemed to be paid for work they had not done. But that was the mere human evaluation, which employs logic, reason and common sense. God doesn't measure our labour in purely physical terms, nor does the Master of time need to time us with a stop-watch, or demand that we 'clock in' or 'clock out'.

'Whatever is right' – in God's judgement, not ours – he will pay us. In eternity, there will be some who have toiled through seven, eight, nine or even ten decades on earth, while others may have lived only a few days, or even have died while still in their mother's womb. Are we to believe the latter will be eternal paupers, while the nonagenarians bid fair to be the millionaries of infinity? Put like this, is it any wonder that God doesn't allow us to oversee the eternal rewards? We'd make a really unholy mess of the work.

'Whatever is right.' He is asking us to trust him. If we can't, are we heading for the wrong place to spend eternity?

God's generosity

God's generosity leaves ours far behind. He knows what we do not. We look on the outward appearance, which only gives us a fraction of the data relevant to any person's life. But we make our judgements on this inadequate material, partly because it's all we have and partly because we seem to need an opinion on everything.

By contrast, God looks on the heart – the inner thoughts, intentions, hopes, fears, strengths and weaknesses – and bases his judgement on the whole person: physical, mental and spiritual. And he pays us the reward he knows is right. He makes it look simple (every worker received the same wage, in the parable) – and so, in a way, it is: eternal life for whoever believes in Jesus (John 3.16). It is so simple that we need help to misunderstand it. Eternal life – all of it, not a part. How, after all, could one apportion eternity? As we reflect on this truth, don't our daily worries over trifles drop into a healthier, spiritual, godly perspective? How God must sigh, as we tie ourselves in knots over matters that will disappear a long, long way on this side of eternity! Only one precious thing will accompany us across the line between here and the hereafter: the words of Jesus, which are spirit and life. Let's hang on to these, committing as many as possible to memory, sharing them as often as possible with others, and putting as many of them as possible into action.

Calvary – the costliest sacrifice of all time – paid for as many believers as possible to receive full board and accommodation for all eternity. That's a very long time – and generous beyond comprehension, in anyone's book.

Family service input
Discuss generosity – human and divine – with the young people, and if possible ground the discussion in parochial priorities.

Suggested hymns
Great is thy faithfulness; In full and glad surrender; Put thou thy trust in God; What a Friend we have in Jesus.

Seventeenth Sunday after Trinity   *Second Service*
Out of Mind?   Ps. 119.113–136; Ezek. 33.23, 30—34.10; Acts 26.1, 9–25 [or Mark 9.30–37]
'While [Paul] was making his defence, Festus exclaimed, "You are out of your mind, Paul! Too much learning is driving you insane!" But Paul said, "I am not out of my mind, most excellent Festus, but I am speaking the sober truth."' Acts 26.24–25

Intellectual put-downs
Festus' reaction was typical of the intellectual put-downs of history before and since: when we meet the unexpected, the unknown, our first reaction is so often, 'It cannot be true!' We may dress it

up a little less rudely, but the message is the same: 'You must be out of your mind (because I don't know what you're talking about)!' We get a similar reaction when we share with others the miracles that God has been working, either in our lives or in the lives of those around us. 'Things like that don't happen today! There must be a *logical* explanation!' And the scoffers either do their best to come up with an explanation of sorts, or walk away from the inexplicable.

What the brain can take
It is true that 'much learning can make one mad', but such learning is not of God. Since the Lord created our brains, he is never going to work towards their failure. Satan has no such scruples, and employs fear as his number one weapon, backed up with drugs, alcohol and pressures of time, ambition, greed and their ilk. But the things of God *feed* the mind, strengthen the spirit and enable us really to live.

> *My strength will I ascribe unto thee;*
> *for thou art my refuge.*
>
> Ps. 59.9, Book of Common Prayer

The sober truth
The charge had quickly been levelled at the fired-up disciples on Pentecost morning, that they were drunk (Acts 2.13); and Peter, in his first Spirit-filled sermon, had been quick to refute this with the sober truth. So now, Paul stands before Festus, similarly witnessing to this truth. The saying 'Tell the truth, and shame the devil' is always the best policy. Always, even though some folk will go to great lengths in arguing that 'black is white, and blue is no colour at all'.

The sober truth is that the gospel is to be preached/published at every opportunity, regardless of whether the time is right or wrong, the preacher/publisher feels well or ill, or whether people want to hear it or not. This is the complete freedom given by God to every Christian, and we are to use it to the full. If we are killed in the process, we shall stand in an honourable line of martyrs of the calibre of Paul, Peter and thousands of others who have stood up and stood out for God.

But as we shall probably come nowhere near to testing of such rigour, can't we take the risk? Today, although Christians are being martyred by the bomb or the bullet in too many parts of the world, in so-called 'civilized' areas Satan concentrates more on indifference and ridicule, which can inflict quite as much spiritual hurt as a bullet can harm the body. Whichever opposition we face, God has given us the stamina we need, to tell the sober truth without fear or favour.

In high circles
Paul's appeal to Caesar had already been made, and had been accepted (as by law it had to be) by Festus (Acts 25.12). But the apostle knew that what he had told Festus, and now also Agrippa and Bernice, he would tell Caesar, should a hearing be granted, without any deviation from the truth. Truth will stand in the highest circles of society, as in the lowest. May we always guard against the temptation to be or say one thing to one person, and something different to someone else. Life is complicated enough without such additional deviation.

Suggested hymns
Father, I place into your hands; O Holy Ghost, thy people bless; Stand up, stand up for Jesus; Take my life and let it be.

Eighteenth Sunday after Trinity (Proper 21)
25 September *Principal Service* **Ungodly Intransigence** Ex. 17.1–7; Ps. 78.1–4, 12–16; Phil. 2.1–13; Matt. 21.23–32

'[Jesus said] "John came to you in the way of righteousness, and you did not believe him, but the tax-collectors and the prostitutes believed him; and even after you saw it, you did not change your minds and believe him."' Matthew 21.32

Intellectual snobbery
These 'chief priests and elders of the people' (v. 23) had been too proud to bow intellectually before the rough man of the desert. Would anyone consign a present-day John the Baptist to a ghetto? Would we want to tidy him up a bit, even if we considered offering

him our pulpit for a Sunday morning? Or perhaps we'd allow him an Evensong slot? God did not finish surprising and shocking the established Church in the first century AD. He's still at it! And the more intransigence he sees, the more he surprises and shocks. It is this divine, magnificent 'unstuffiness' of God that goes towards making our Christian life so exciting. When we've stopped being shocked and surprised by God, we may seriously question whether we are living. Let's take our spiritual pulse at regular and frequent intervals.

The unexpected

The unexpected folk are sometimes those who respond most positively to the word of God. Uninhibited by the suffocating aura of formal erudition, or the effort of maintaining their position in society, they are free to listen, to accept and believe. And sometimes they go on to live out and give out the gospel in new, surprising and even shockingly good and beautiful ways. It's a bit like reading the latest translation or version of the Bible for the first time: some verses surprise and even shock us, while others show us immediately new insights and revelations. 'Lord, I've read this passage thousands of times – but you've never shown me that before!' Even here we feel on safer ground if we can 'blame' the Lord for delaying a revelation! And a truth like this may indeed hit us with such freshness that it's easier to believe it was written for us in 2005 than 200 or more years ago. Such is the ongoing newness and vitality of the gospel.

Keeping up with God

And we need to keep up with God, who is constantly moving us into new truths, new revelations, new situations. The tragedy of the chief priests and elders of Jesus' day, was that they would not move forward. They had hedged themselves around with what they saw as the security of their traditions; and when first John and then Jesus cut through those traditions, the ecclesiastical hierarchy was wrong-footed.

Yet each of the hierarchs still had freedom of choice. Nicodemus and Joseph of Arimathaea used their freedom to good advantage; Caiaphas and Annas were among those who chose the easier, but tragic way, sticking to the paths they thought they knew, the guide-posts they believed would direct them aright.

---✂-----

**Pax Travel Ltd
Freepost LON 12342
LONDON
NW1 4YD**

✂ ---

ORDER FORM: **CHURCH PULPIT YEAR BOOK 2006**

**Please supply .... copy/copies at the pre-publication price of £15.50
plus £1.50 to cover post and packing to any UK or RoI address.** (Ask
for details of overseas carriage). On publication, a cover price of £16.50
(plus p&p) will apply.

I wish to pay by cheque for £......... made payable to **G. J. Palmer &
Sons Ltd or by Credit Card** (Visa and MasterCard accepted: Please
delete as appropriate)

Number: .... **Expiry:** ___/___

Signature: ....   *VISA* MasterCard

Name: ....

Address: ....

....

....

Post Code: .... **Telephone:** ....

Send this order form with your payment or credit card details to

G. J. Palmer & Sons Ltd, 16 Blyburgate, Beccles, Suffolk NR34 9TB

Right influences
The grandees could influence and be influenced by each other, but they did not consider the lower classes capable of teaching them anything. This attitude didn't die out in the first century, either. Today, a professor can enjoy a tramp's company on the boundary of a village cricket field, but let the man of the road wax eloquent on the don's pet subject and there is the likelihood of a sea-change in attitude. Today, clothing styles have changed so much from even a century ago that different styles now cause fewer social problems than intellectual standards. When shall we see the wood as well as the trees?

Family service input
Encourage the young people to discuss/list different types of work and trade; fashion and clothing; speech; houses, cars, holidays; the areas in which we live ... and how all these affect the way we live, and how we interrelate with 'different' people.

Suggested hymns
Bind us together, Lord; Brother, sister, let me serve you; Make me a channel of your peace; We are one in the Spirit.

Eighteenth Sunday after Trinity   *Second Service*
Only through Jesus   Ps. [120, 123] 124; Ezek. 37.15–28; 1 John 2.22–29 [or Mark 9.38–50]

'Who is the liar but the one who denies that Jesus is the Christ? This is the antichrist, the one who denies the Father and the Son. No one who denies the Son has the Father; everyone who confesses the Son has the Father also.' 1 John 2.22–23

The one and only way
John presents the simple, unvarnished truth, that the only way to God the Father is through God the Son. This is all of a piece with the teaching of Peter: 'There is salvation in no one else, for there is no other name under heaven given among mortals by which we must be saved' (Acts 4.12). We surely need help to misunderstand such clarity.

Jesus is the Way, the only way to God. He came to tell us and to show us, that there will be one fold and only one Shepherd. There are those who try to tell us that 'all roads lead to God', but this is not biblical. Some may argue that in the multi-faith world of today, these words of Jesus need reinterpretation. Quite apart from the serious warning in Revelation 22.18–19, we need to remember that since the Fall we have always lived in a multifaith world. Mystery religions and pagan cults abounded at the precise time that Peter was preaching and John was penning his first letter. Both men, filled with the Holy Spirit and eye-witnesses of the ministry of Jesus, were able to say with godly conviction: there is one way and one way only to God and salvation – and that way is Jesus.

The one God
It's made clear here that the Father and Son are one; and the negation of one is the negation of the other. Conversely, when we believe in Jesus, we are also taking on board full belief in God.

As the Proper Preface for Trinity Sunday puts it:

Who art one God, one Lord; not one only Person, but three Persons in one Substance. For that which we believe of the glory of the Father, the same we believe of the Son, and of the Holy Ghost, without any difference or inequality.

Book of Common Prayer

Jesus the Gate
'I am the gate. Whoever enters by me will be saved, and will come in and go out and find pasture,' promised Jesus (John 10.9). And the sheepfold (= the Church) had only one gate, one entrance. Intruders could gain entrance by climbing up some other way, but they had no *bona fide*. If anyone tries to claim Church membership and at the same time denies belief in Jesus, they too have forfeited the right of being called a 'Christian'. They have also, according to John, denied themselves access to God.

The 'rock of offence', or 'stumbling block', that Jesus proves to be to non-believers is for Christians the stepping-stone to salvation. 'This is our faith', as we affirm in the baptism service. We didn't invent it. God gave it to us, and we believed and accepted it.

Tripartite strength
God underlines the strength of the faith that is being built in us: it's the gift of God, the name of Jesus, the power of the Holy Spirit.

It enables us to say (as did the Psalmist with faith, albeit less revelation): 'With the Lord on my side, I do not fear . . . The Lord is on my side to help me' (Ps. 118.6–7). Freed from fear, the Lord will help us to stand up for Jesus.

It's the last thing Satan wants us to do – but God is not giving us new life each day to please the devil.

Suggested hymns
I'm not ashamed to own my Lord; Judge eternal, throned in splendour; Shepherd Divine, our wants relieve; Thou art the Way.

Nineteenth Sunday after Trinity (Proper 22)
2 October   *Principal Service*   Arresting Fear
Ex. 20.1–4, 7–9, 12–20; Ps. 19; Phil. 3.4b–14; Matt. 21.33–46

'[Jesus said] "Therefore I tell you, the kingdom of God will be taken away from you and given to a people that produces the fruits of the kingdom. The one who falls on this stone will be broken to pieces, and it will crush anyone on whom it falls." When the chief priests and the Pharisees heard his parables, they realized that he was speaking about them. They wanted to arrest him, but they feared the crowds, because they regarded him as a prophet.' Matthew 21.43–46

Inability to act
Fear blocked the ability of the chief priests and Pharisees to arrest Jesus: fear of crowd reprisal and backlash. Their position was dearer to them than anything else, for it fed their pride and gave them prestige. The parameters that governed their behaviour were set according to how they looked in the sight of others. The irony is that they really cut a pathetic spectacle that attracted only time-servers and sycophants.

Yet even if fear had not inhibited them, the arrest of Jesus would not have taken place until God willed it: and the time was not yet ripe. We don't need to accept fear into our lives to make us do *this*, or to stop us from doing *that*; once we make compromise with fear, we have taken up with the wrong master. It would be the undoing of the chief priests and Pharisees.

Weighty matters
The cornerstone – Christ himself – is a weighty matter. It's taking the whole weight, the total strain, of the Church. Who are mere mortals to tangle with it? Those who fall on it, trying to do their own thing, to follow inclinations and commands that are not of Jesus, will be broken up – cut into little pieces and served to the devil. Those who try to undermine Jesus and the gospel with false teaching, heresies, religious subversion, dalliance with occultic powers, will find the stone falls on them. Its weight is so great, nothing of value will be left, only the crushed remains of what was once a candidate for eternal life.

Yet how many refuse to see the serious difference between deciding for Jesus and deciding against him? How many blithely try to live as though he doesn't exist? And how many might be saved if we take the gospel to them?

Judgement, with mercy
The owner of the vineyard exacted retribution, but only after he had offered chance after chance to the wicked tenants. Judgement was certain, as certain as that it will come at the End of time; but only after the mercy of God has allowed enough time for us to make good.

There was an urgency about the early Church, as the disciples and their congregations, convinced that the Judgement would not long delay, worked with fervent zeal to evangelize – and to some effect, for 'day by day the Lord added to their number those who were being saved' (Acts 2.47). Then, as the centuries passed, the Day delayed, and the Church established firmer and firmer parochial structures and hierarchy, and the urgency diminished.

Today is not too soon for it to be regained, for we are much much closer to the gospel being published in all nations (Matt. 24.14; Mark 13.10). God has given his Church nearly two thousand years of opportunity. With the recent tremendous advances in technology, could he not be saying, 'I'm increasing your capabilities, because I want the job done quickly'? But do we have to delay until we actually hear him saying it?

A thought for the week: have we enough zeal to get anyone else fired up?

Family service input
Discuss with the young people multi-language Christmas cards for the parish, which can be used as aids to praying for evangelism.

Christ is made the sure foundation; Christ is our cornerstone; How firm a foundation; We have a gospel to proclaim.

Nineteenth Sunday after Trinity   *Second Service*
Old and New   Ps. 136; Prov. 2.1–11; 1 John 2.1–17 [or Mark 10.2–16]

'Beloved, I am writing you no new commandment, but an old commandment that you have had from the beginning; the old commandment is the word that you have heard. Yet I am writing you a new commandment that is true in him and in you, because the darkness is passing away and the true light is already shining.' 1 John 2.7–8

Past, present and future
The word of God spoken before Jesus came is precious and not to be discarded as obsolete, for much of it pointed to Jesus. Yet it also referred to the past and the future – from the Beginning to the End of time. Therefore, we should treasure it and continue to learn from it, even as Jesus valued it and used it in his teaching. It grounds our faith on the rock that is Jesus, and in it we can become one with giants of faith such as Abraham, Moses and Elijah. In that word, we have a cloud of witnesses in glory gunning for us.

We have the Gospels and the other New Testament writings as our *vade mecum* for living here and now: our basic material, with the revelations given us by Jesus as we progress to God, for sharing our Christian faith. There is nothing more valuable than the words of Jesus recorded here; we are not sharing merely our understanding and interpretation with others: we can say in all sincerity, 'Jesus said this, so you can believe it, because it is Truth itself speaking' (John 14.6).

And we have the visionary material, the New Testament revelations, to encourage us in our eternal expectations. The old and the new fuse together, coalesce in the person of Jesus who made salvation possible. 'The true light', John says, in wonderment yet absolute certainty, *'is already shining.'* Our eternal expectation has already, in a marvellous way, begun to be fulfilled; faith is already being overtaken by sight. If you doubt it, take a look at how the light of Christ is pushing back the darkness of unbelief around the world – by the grace of God shining at its brightest in some areas where the darkness of persecution, pagan cults and indifference has been greatest. That light is unstoppable; if it had not been so, Satan would have made a better fist of overcoming it before now. And, no matter how many folk he cons into helping him from today onwards, he will not stop the gospel light advancing. Because, since Calvary, Satan has no real power. Only the guile to con us into thinking he has.

Looking for the light

Remember how the disciples gazed heavenwards, as Jesus ascended (Acts 1.11). We don't need to look up for the light of Jesus, because at Pentecost he sent his life- and light-giving Spirit into the hearts of all believers. We can see it shining out of others – and, please God, may they see it in us. May they be able to say that they can see we have been with Jesus. There is no more beautiful compliment that can be paid.

'Let your light shine before others,' Jesus ordered his listeners (Matt. 5.16). It was far from an impossible command, because he gave us the necessary equipment.

> *Say, is your lamp burning, my brother?*
> *I pray you, look quickly, and see,*
> *For, if it were burning, then surely*
> *Some beams would fall bright upon me.*
> *Straight, straight is the road, but I falter,*
> *And oft I fall out by the way.*
> *Then lift your lamp higher, my brother,*
> *Lest I should make fatal delay.*

> *Ellen H. Gates*

Our responsibility is not only to save our souls – Jesus has already accomplished that for us – but to shine his light on others, that they may also be saved. How can they come to him if no one lights the way?

Suggested hymns

A new commandment I give unto you; Christ, whose glory fills the skies; Jesus, the very thought of thee; To him we come.

Twentieth Sunday after Trinity (Proper 23)

9 October   *Principal Service*   Divine Expediency

Ex. 32.1–14; Ps. 106.1–6, 19–23; Phil. 4.1–9;
Matt. 22.1–14

'[Jesus said] "The king was enraged. He sent his troops, destroyed those murderers, and burned their city. Then he said to his slaves, 'The wedding is ready, but those invited were not worthy. Go therefore into the main streets, and invite everyone you find to the wedding banquet.'"'
Matthew 22.7–9

No empty seats

God will tolerate no empty seats at the celebration he has planned, when heaven and earth have served their purpose and the new order is ushered in. If those for whom preparations have been made are found wanting, God will not change his plans: he will find others to inherit glory. Already, two thousand years ago, when the Jews in general rejected Jesus, the gospel was taken to Gentiles, who were given equal status in the new order, without the need for circumcision and the formal laws previously deemed essential for Jews. But Gentiles may not assume a *right* to glory: the criteria remain – belief in Jesus, and adherence to his commandments. These combine to form our 'wedding garment'. If we get to glory without the garment, our stay there will not be long, and our departure ignominious.

At the eleventh hour

In the acceptance of the penitent thief (Luke 23.43), and the eleventh-hour labourers in the vineyard (Mat. 20.8ff.), God has shown that his mercy extends to late conversions. There are 'cradle Christians', whose faith continues to grow and expand, and who just go from strength to strength until, their lives full of sheaves of fruitful corn, their harvest is gathered in. But there are others who become lax in their faith (or lose it altogether), who come to the end of their lives sapped not only of physical but of spiritual stamina as well, their 'wedding garment' threadbare and in tatters. Tennyson may have said that it is

> *Better to have loved and lost,*
> *than never to have loved at all.*
>
> *In Memoriam*

But these 'have-been' Christians are, according to this parable of Jesus, in no fit state for glory. Once having known Christ, they have now shown that love for him has been replaced by something else in their lives. They will be denied the glory banquet, in favour of those who, like the penitent thief, respond to God's call and by his grace keep their zeal white-hot until seated at the banquet table. They may have a chequered history on earth – but God has work for their zeal and for their particular capabilities.

The call
'Many are called, but few are chosen' (v. 14). Yet among the 'few' who answer God's call, the variety is great: surely an indication of the excitement and breadth of eternity. With the God of the Infinite at work, the prospects tease the imagination out of thought. We think this earth, with its wide horizons, its natural and varied beauty, and the range of colours and cultures among its people, is exciting enough – but the best is yet to be. If the prospect doesn't thrill us into going out and sharing Jesus and the chance of salvation he made possible, then whatever will?

Accepting invitations
On a less cosmic scale are the invitations we receive every day. How many do we accept with joy? How many from a sense of duty? And how many do we find an excuse to decline? May we, with today's parable in mind, take a little more thought about these lesser invitations: each one may be more important than we think. If at any time we are not found in the place where God wants us to be, it will not be his fault.

Family service input
Discuss with the young people the various strands (love, joy, peace . . .) which would comprise a 'wedding garment' in glory, illustrating them pictorially or diagrammatically. A 'real' garment could be woven, as further illustration, with coloured threads, keyed or labelled.

Suggested hymns
Bread of heaven, on thee we feed; Come, risen Lord, and deign to be our guest; I come with joy to meet my Lord; We come as guests invited.

Twentieth Sunday after Trinity *Second Service*
No Half Measures Ps. 139.1–18; Prov. 3.1–18;
1 John 3.1–15; [or Mark 10.17–31]

'For this is the message you have heard from the beginning, that we should love one another ... We know that we have passed from death to life because we love one another. Whoever does not love abides in death. All who hate a brother or sister are murderers, and you know that murderers do not have eternal life abiding in them.' 1 John 3.11

Black – or white

There is no grey area left in this argument of John: if we are walking in love, we are in the light, and we have the life of Jesus in us. If we are in strife with anyone, we are in self-inflicted darkness, and are walking with Satan. Ouch! That's tough talking. Examine yourselves, John is saying. Sort out those areas of hatred, mistrust, suspicion, jealousy, unforgiveness and the rest. Send them packing, and start over. They are bad news, and it's dicing with death to hang on to them. If we believe the work is too difficult to handle on our own, let's pray God into the situation – because, in his magnanimity, he finds something to love even in the person we find it the hardest to love. And even if we cannot *like* that person very much, we should at least be able to love them through God.

An essential command?

Just as we tend to break Jesus' command, 'Do not fear', with impunity, so we often harbour negative thoughts about certain people with far less weight than our Lord puts on such thinking. 'We've nothing in common!' is an oft-repeated excuse. Jesus died for both of you – isn't that sufficient reason to get together? 'They're not Christians!' Jesus came to save the down-and-outs, the prostitutes, the sinners. And, is it *our* fault if someone we know is not yet a Christian?

'They've gossiped about me, misrepresented me, been jealous . . .' Well, this is just a case of unforgiveness on our part, isn't it?

No matter the excuse, John's teaching still stands. To hate, for any cause, is tantamount to murder. Double murder, too – for we're not only damning their souls, but ours as well, while the hatred is perpetuated. So long as we are in strife, we're alienated from Jesus, and alienation from him means death – present spiritual death, ahead of the physical sort.

Double murder, double death. Isn't it a powerful incentive to get quickly back into the way of love! 'So that', says John, 'when [Jesus] is revealed we may have confidence and not be put to shame before him at his coming' (1 John 2.28).

From earliest times
If God's patience were not superhuman and divine, wouldn't he have given up on humankind before now? For, from the time of Cain, we have been told repeatedly of the tragedy and loss brought about by hatred. Until we have learned the lesson, shall we – can we – be entrusted with an eternity where there is no hatred, and where death is not an option? Have we realized what a different way of life this will be? Are we ready for it, for continued love? Are we spiritually strong enough? No, not yet: that's why we're still here, struggling to work out the love that Jesus has worked in; because the more we love, the more love we are given. That's God's divine law – not of averages, but of magnificent unfairness and generosity. It's a foretaste of glory, because that's how God operates. We take a little more of it on board each day. If we want others to recognize Jesus in us, love is the best way of showing him.

Surely it's the only way? No – he is primarily love; but he is also 'joy, peace, patience, kindness, generosity, faithfulness, gentleness and self-control' (Gal. 5.22–23). When we go to work on all these, there won't be too much time left for tangling with less positive things like hatred.

Suggested hymns
Faithful Shepherd, feed me; From glory to glory advancing; Like a mighty river flowing; Love is his word.

Twenty-First Sunday after Trinity (Proper 24)
16 October   *Principal Service*   **Fair Division**
Ex. 33.12–23; Ps. 99; 1 Thess. 1.1–10; Matt. 22.15–22

'But Jesus, aware of their malice, said, "Why are you putting me to the test, you hypocrites? . . . Give . . . to the emperor the things that are the emperor's, and to God the things that are God's." ' Matthew 22.18, 21

Sacred and secular – then

Jesus here very carefully divides the sacred from the secular. Coinage minted by humans is of no use to God: Jesus apparently had no coin on his person, and asked for one to be shown to him, to illustrate his teaching. Of course he would not handle money, for it bore Caesar's likeness, contravening the second Commandment (Ex. 20.4). The Jews would not argue with him over that: their own compromise with Rome would be evident in their ability to produce one of the hated coins, and a reminder of the ignominy of being under an alien army of occupation that they could have done without.

But to God belong worship and service. If these are given to anyone else, God is being robbed of his due. It is some measure of just how far down the road of compromise the Jews had gone that, their judgement blinded by hatred of Jesus, their grandees were trapped into assuring Pilate, on the morning of the trial, 'We have no king but the emperor' (John 19.12).

Sacred and secular – now

How clearly do we see the division between sacred and secular today? Or is there a grey area of compromise that we hesitate to bring under too close a scrutiny? We certainly put more value on currency than did Jesus. The shortage of it causes problems of hunger, homelessness and the denial of what we term the essentials of life. The abundance of it solves these problems, but often also brings corruption, greed and indifference. We spend a lot of time gaining money, and the rest of the time letting it go. Billions of pounds, dollars and yen change hands on screen and paper every day, without a coin in sight. It has never been more true that, in a secular sense, 'money makes the world go round'.

Where is faith?

Where is faith, in this merry-go-round of currency? It's surely no accident that the Church so often grows strongest in the less affluent countries, among people who have not made a god out of their bank accounts. Do we need an international stock market crash to bring the rich nations back in revival to God? Jesus did not say it was impossible for rich people to gain the kingdom of heaven; but for those who trusted in riches it would be pretty unlikely.

> *From those forever shackled to what their wealth can buy,*
> *the fear of lost advantage provokes the bitter cry:*
> *'Don't query our position! Don't criticize our wealth!*
> *Don't mention those exploited by poverty and stealth!'*

> *John L. Bell and Graham Maule*

While there are people who trust in securities of finance, there will be greed and oppression. But, come the end of this life, who will equate the security of Messrs Barclay or Lloyd, with that of the Holy and Undivided Trinity? Why can't we live as those who may one day die? Why can't we raise our sights to eternity? It has everything to do with us, and nothing at all to do with currency.

God as security
Jesus' teaching on security was very simple, so basic that it has proved too simple for most people: 'Do not worry, saying, "What will we eat?" or, "What will we drink?", or, "What will we wear?" ... Strive first for the kingdom of God and his righteousness, and all these things will be given to you as well' (Matt. 6.31, 33).

With God as our security, our priorities slowly but surely will get into line with his way of working – which seems to turn the secular world of commerce upside-down: for the most precious, costliest gem of eternity comes absolutely free; salvation is something that money cannot buy.

Family service input
Encourage the young people to design a poster/collage, for display in the church, of God's treasures that our money cannot buy. Use recent religious journals and newspapers for materials.

Suggested hymns
All my hope on God is founded; Firmly I believe and truly; The kingdom of God is justice and joy; Ye that know the Lord is gracious.

Twenty-First Sunday after Trinity

Second Service   **Infallible Test**   Ps. 142 [143.1–11];
Prov. 4.1–18; 1 John 3.16—4.6 [or Mark 10.35–45]

*'By this you know the Spirit of God: every spirit that confesses that Jesus
Christ has come in the flesh is of God . . . for the one who is in you is
greater than the one who is in the world.' 1 John 4.2, 4*

Litmus test

It's the ultimate litmus test: the power and truth that reveals to
us that Jesus Christ has come in the flesh gives us the faith to
declare it. They will haggle and debate, and wriggle one way and
another, those who have no faith and who cannot declare it; but
their lack of faith stops them from passing the test. They may
bluster and affect faith for a while; but they cannot sustain it,
because they do not have the power and truth of the Holy Spirit
inside them – that power that is greater than anything else on this
planet. The Spirit doesn't testify of itself, but Jesus, for it is his
Holy Spirit.

It's enough to make Satan wild with anger, to know that we
have a greater power than the devil himself. But he's not the prince
of sin for nothing, and so he doesn't (often) lose his cool. Instead,
he banks on us not realizing the power inside us. He banks on
non-believers persuading us to desert God for the world's love of
wealth and luxury. He banks on discrediting the name of Jesus,
so that we'll be too ashamed to stand up and stand out for him.

The devil's banking system is as full of holes as a colander, but
he relies on most folk not seeing all the faults in his system. What
a shaky ground Satan operates on! But he banks on most folk not
noticing the quagmire until they've sunk beyond the point of no
return.

Lord, give us discernment

We may imagine that on retreat, or sequestered behind convent
or monastery walls, our spiritual perception would be heightened.
Relieved of the cares and pressures of the rat-race of modern life,
we should be quicker to discern the advances of Satan, and quicker
still to defeat the old devil. Many men and women have thought
along similar lines – and have discovered that spiritual discernment can be ever as hard to practice in solitary confinement as in
the bustle of business. God is there, wherever we are – but so is

223

Satan: and by the law of averages (if nothing else), solitude gives us more opportunity to listen to both.

We need to pray for discernment where we are, not where we are not; and if much of our waking life is taken up with busyness, then we need discernment there: discernment to look into the eyes of the people we meet, to read behind the lines of the papers and screens we study, to listen to the voice beyond the voice on the telephone, to ask God constantly for his wisdom (for we have a negligible amount of our own), for his love (for ours is always in need of a top-up), for his confidence, to keep fear and doubt out of our hearts.

It's a full-time job, keeping one step ahead of the devil; but it's possible because we have this Holy Spirit dynamo inside us. He wants us to win. Satan wants us to lose. Our only safety lies in training our minds to listen to the greater of these two powers, keeping faith with the power within us, and keeping the lesser power as far from us as possible.

If God didn't think we could make it, he would never have sent Jesus to do the hardest work for us.

Suggested hymns
Come down, O Love Divine; O Holy Ghost, thy people bless; Spirit of God, as strong as the wind; Spirit of the living God, fall afresh on me.

Last Sunday after Trinity (Bible Sunday)
23 October   *Principal Service*   **People of the Book**
Neh. 8.1–4a [5–6] 8–12; Ps. 119.9–16; Col. 3.12–17;
Matt. 24.30–35

'Let the word of Christ dwell in you richly: teach and admonish one another in all wisdom; and with gratitude in your hearts sing psalms, hymns and spiritual songs to God. And whatever you do, in word or deed, do everything in the name of the Lord Jesus, giving thanks to God the Father through him.' Colossians 3.15–17

A cloud of witnesses
On this Bible Sunday, it's fitting that we should focus (a) on the value of God's word, and (b) on those men and women who have

given their lives to translating the Bible into new languages, or to new versions of existing languages.

Jesus lived by the book: he was the direct fulfilment of its prophecies, and his teaching was grounded in the scrolls of what we now call the Old Testament. His interpretation of it sometimes shocked the religious dons of the day – primarily because they had blurred their view of the scrolls by the encrustation of a plethora of man-made laws and regulations. Jesus cut through the obfuscation, and taught simply and directly from the original scrolls. The importance of the whole Bible for us today can be rooted in the value that Jesus gave to the 'Bible' of his time.

Spreading the word

Through the Christian centuries, giants of the faith have devoted their lives (and sometimes lost them) in the work of Bible transcribing, translating and publishing. Jerome, writing long hours in a cave near Bethlehem, gave us the first major Latin translation, the Vulgate. It was far from perfect, but was widely used for many centuries. William Tyndale, however, was resolved to give his countrymen and -women the Bible in their English language. He taught himself Greek and Hebrew, so that he could produce the finest translation possible – not based on the Vulgate, but on the ancient texts behind it. He lost his life on the Continent, when a sixteenth-century Judas shopped him. Within a year or two of his execution, the English Bible was authorized in this country; even today 90 per cent of Tyndale's translation survives in the Authorized Version of the New Testament.

Overseas

Robert Morison gave the Lisu people in China the Bible in their newly transcribed language. William Carey spent twenty years in India learning the language and translating the whole Bible. James Evans – against all odds – gave the Cree Indians on the banks of Lake Winnipeg St John's Gospel in a language he devised for them, using birch-bark for paper and sooty fishoil for ink. Frances Siewert studied Hebrew and Greek, and produced *The Amplified Bible*, comprising a wide variety of texts, which is deservedly popular in her native America, and now gaining ground also in Britain.

These, and so many more, have greatly furthered the spreading of God's word, in line with the Great Commission, and today we pay especial tribute to them.

Our own Bible work

We may not be called to work as translators, printers or publishers, but each of us has Bible work to do: studying, memorizing, sharing, interpreting, witnessing – doing whatever we can to see that as many people as possible can hear or read God's word, making it so familiar that, when we go from here into eternity, it will really feel like 'coming home'. Jesus has promised that this will be the one thing that will make the transition to glory with us (Mark 13.31; Luke 21.33).

> Carry your Bible with you,
> Let all its message outpour;
> It will sustain you each moment,
> Take it wherever you go!
>
> Fred P. Morris, alt.

In the Bible is comfort for every sorrow, help for every need, guidance for every step, and sheer encouragement for every minute. May God continue to open its truths to us.

Family service input

Teach the young people the best-known Bible verse – John 3.16 – in a foreign language, perhaps Cree, and encourage them to illustrate it.

John 3.16 in the Cree language

Ke-sa-ma-ne-to	God
sa-keh-tat	loved
as-ye-yew	the world
as-peh-che	so
ke-oh-che-maket	He gave
O-pa-ya-ko-sa-na	His only Son
As-peh-che-ke-che	so that
A-e-yak-ka-ta-pa-ya-ye-ma-ka	whoever believes on Him
Ne-se-a-na-te-set-a-ka	will perish not
Ma-ka-a-yat	but he has
Ka-ke-ka Pe-ma-te-sa-en	everlasting life

Suggested hymns
Father of mercies, in thy word; I heard the voice of Jesus say;
Lord, thy word abideth; Tell out, my soul, the greatness of the
Lord.

Last Sunday after Trinity *Second Service*
Word of Trust Ps. 119.89–104; Isa. 55.1–11;
Luke 4.14–30

*'For as the rain and the snow come down from heaven, and do not return
there until they have watered the earth, making it bring forth and sprout,
giving seed to the sower and bread to the eater, so shall my word be that
goes out from my mouth; it shall not return to me empty, but it shall
accomplish that which I purpose, and succeed in the thing for which I
sent it.' Isaiah 55.10–11*

Successful accomplishment
This is a promise, an encouragement, an empowering and a challenge, all rolled into one. God is saying, in effect: 'I've given you
my word, I've made it known to you. I have faith in you, that you
will return my investment with a good rate of interest.' And that's
very fair, isn't it? God has given us the gift of life – here, and
hereafter – and his word to keep us going in the meantime. He's
done his part, investing life in us, and he's trusting us to make
something of it. We hear plenty about 'trust' in the world today,
but too often it's of the negative kind: the breakdown of trust, as
seen in scandal, mismanagement and misappropriation of one sort
or another. Ripples of mistrust run through society, as people
wonder just who they can believe, or who may be the next to let
them down.

How great is trust?
A couple of homeopaths were discussing tension, and one said to
the other: 'I'll show you how to get rid of tension. Sit on this chair,
the wrong way round, and let yourself fall back into my arms.
Try it five or six times. Don't worry, I won't let you fall. Trust me!'
Her companion did trust – and felt better afterwards. But how
many would have trusted a near stranger or even a friend, thus
far? That makes it all the more wonderful, that God trusts us –

trusts us with his precious word, to put it to good use and to make it grow. As his trust in us grows, so he asks for us to trust him more.

Our trust to date
We probably don't often pause to reflect on how much we trust God already. The promise of God, in Isaiah 55, where it talks about the rain and the snow watering the earth, reminds us of the promise God gave to Noah, that 'As long as the earth endures, seedtime and harvest, cold and heat, summer and winter, day and night, shall not cease' (Gen. 8.22). However subconsciously, each day we take these things from God *on trust*. We've done so since the days of Noah, who repaid God's investment in him, with interest.

The Very Revd Fenton Morley, a former Dean of Salisbury, once remarked that there had been a relation between investment and religion ever since the time of Noah, who 'was the only man able to float a company, when the rest of the world was in liquidation'. And why? Because Noah knew that God was on his side. He trusted that God would see him through.

Noah had that precious thing called 'trust', in abundance. Just imagine how folk would laugh, when they saw the ark being built, far inland, and not a cloud in the sky!

Our growth in trust
When we were born, among all the delight and celebrations, we were pretty small and a fair way from turning the world upside-down with the gospel. Yet God had infinite trust in the squalling, wriggling human thing. How is his trust being repaid, as we focus on the gospel, this Bible Sunday?

Suggested hymns
Give me oil in my lamp; Go, tell it on the mountain; Inspired by love and anger; Meekness and majesty.

Fourth Sunday before Advent (or All Saints' Day, if transferred from 1 Nov.; see p. 323)

30 October   *Principal Service*   **Enduring with Joy**

Micah 3.5–12; Ps. 43; 1 Thess. 2.9–13; Matt. 24.1–14

'[Jesus said] "And because of the increase of lawlessness, the love of many will grow cold. But anyone who endures to the end will be saved. And this good news of the kingdom will be proclaimed throughout the world, as a testimony to all the nations; and then the end will come."'
Matthew 24.12–14

How can we?

How can we possibly endure the test of life on earth? Well, it's hard, but God calls us to do it. He goes further, and tells us to endure it with joy (e.g. Acts 20.24; Rom. 15.13; Heb. 13.17): 'as sorrowful, yet *always rejoicing*', Paul says, encouragingly (2 Cor. 6.10). If he could do it, so can we. We can attempt the test in our own strength, and buckle under the strain; or we can accept the gift of God's strength, and surprise ourselves. The 'love of money will grow cold', and unless our love for God and his word is at white heat, we shall not be able to rekindle the fire in many others.

> *O let it freely burn,*
> *Till earthly passions turn*
> *To dust and ashes in its heat consuming.*
>
> Bianco da Siena, tr. R. F. Littledale

This thing called 'joy'

This thing called 'joy' (which the world translates into a fleeting experience called 'happiness') is a fruit of the Holy Spirit. Therefore we don't need to go looking for it. We have it implanted in us already. It's a strange animal, for it makes a nonsense of trouble, sorrow, pain and worry, that otherwise have a habit of grinding a person into the ground. It means that we can endure whatever comes, we can go forward proclaiming the good news of the kingdom. Not to put too fine a point on it, if we didn't have God's joy, the work would not get done, and the 'end' would be delayed ad infinitum. 'The joy of the Lord is your strength' – Nehemiah had discovered this, long before Christ came to underline it (Neh. 8.10). There was no way the walls of Jerusalem could be rebuilt without God giving the builders under Nehemiah extra strength, because they were under severe pressure from enemies, as well as facing a tremendous physical task.

Our weakness, God's enabling

This is why God sends so many sheep into the wolf-infested world with his gospel. It has always been so, since eleven unlettered men were entrusted with the start of worldwide evangelism. As vulnerable as we can be, with no great wealth, pomp or ceremony, we take his word and share its worth. Ridiculed, ignored or persecuted, Christians keep on keeping on; and the end of the mission is now two millennia nearer than when it began.

The great world courtroom

The world is like a giant courtroom, in which we are presenting the testimony of the gospel. God, the Judge, is eminently fair: how can people expect a fair judgement at the Great Assize if the testimony has not been presented? That is why it is so imperative for us as a Church to get the gospel testimony published in every nation. There are still over three thousand minority languages which have not yet so much as heard of the gospel. Don't we care about the millions of unsaved souls this means?

Of course we do. That's why we're doing something about it. And when this life is translated into glory, please God we shall meet many friends whom our testimony has helped to save from the darkness of unknowing.

God's joy is inexhaustible. When we've taken it all round the world, there will still be a superabundance left for the hereafter. So there's no reason for us to be penny-pinching about using and sharing it here.

Family service input

Encourage the young people to discuss, say, the Indian subcontinent, with its 1,700-plus languages and dialects, and how, as a parish, prayer can be focused throughout the year on evangelistic and Bible outreach.

Suggested hymns

Awake, my soul, and with the sun; I come with joy to meet my Lord; Rejoice! the Lord is king; Jesus, sprinkle many nations.

Fourth Sunday before Advent *Second Service*
World Service Pss. 111, 117; Dan. 7.1–18;
Luke 6.17–31

'I saw one like a human being, coming with the clouds of heaven. And he ame to the Ancient One, and was presented before him. To him was given dominion and glory and kingship, that all people, nations, and languages should serve him.' Daniel 7.13–14

All nations

This is why the gospel needs to be published in 'all the nations' (Matt. 24.14; cf. Mark 13.10). All peoples, all languages (even the least spoken, minority languages) are included here. God values equally every single person he has made. In our world today, where so often 'biggest is best', the minorities are increasingly being overlooked; the twenty-first century Goliaths are still scornfully arrogant towards the Davids.

Yet even with visions such as Daniel's, the Jewish hierarchs down to Jesus' time were closing their minds to the prospect of world evangelization where Gentiles would have equal rights with Jews. They despatched proselytizers as far afield as they could from Jerusalem – but with instructions to make Jews out of their converts, Jews who would need to be circumcised and to keep the Torah to every jot and tittle.

We, too, can read God's word and interpret it only as far as is comfortable. Jesus may have had this selective process in mind when he told his disciples that if they were to forget (conveniently or otherwise) any of his words after he had returned to the Father, the Holy Spirit whom he was sending to them would remind them – of every word: *'all* that I have said' (John 14.26). The same Spirit is with us – just in case.

God's inventiveness

God is infinitely inventive. The beasts in Daniel's vision tease the imagination out of thought – but give these verses to children, and they have little problem in illustrating them. Perhaps we need to revive our childhood imagination to get the most from this vision. As with many in Revelation, its breadth is immense, drawing the past, present and future together. Of course, we read it as Christians, with the hindsight that Christ's incarnation brought, knowledge that Daniel did not have. King after king would rise to power, and fall from power; but the son of man would reign for ever, over every language and nation.

The vision was for many days. Faith and patient endurance would be needed – as they still are today. Yet these visions are given to us, to thrill, encourage and enable us to persevere in working out Christ's commission. God is saying, 'I want you to get excited not only about my work here, but also about what is in store.'

We have only to read such books as Daniel and Revelation to see God at his most creative and inventive: sizes, colours, images, lights – glory itself – of much greater variety, brilliance and beauty than we experience at present, is somewhere out there, in God's providence for our eternity. It's difficult to understand why anyone should not want to have a part in all this glory; the negativity of millions among his children must be a source of great sadness to the loving Father-heart of God.

> When comes the promised time,
> That war shall be no more,
> And lust, oppression, crime
> Shall flee thy face before?
> We pray thee, Lord, arise,
> And come in thy great might.
> Revive our longing eyes
> Which languish for thy sight.
>
> L. Hensley, 1824–1905

We are not to sit with folded hands, idly waiting till kingdom come! We have work to do, and the quicker it is done the sooner will come the kingdom.

And after that, we'll probably have even more and greater work to do.

Suggested hymns
Far round the world; Round the Lord in glory seated; The Church of God a kingdom is; Thy kingdom come, O God.

Third Sunday before Advent (Remembrance Sunday; see p. 328) 6 November
Principal Service **The Day Will Come**
Wisd. 6.12–16; Canticle: Wisd. 6.17–20;
1 Thess. 4.13–18; Matt. 25.1–13

'Later the other bridesmaids came also, saying, "Lord, Lord, open to us."
But he replied, "Truly I tell you, I do not know you." Keep awake,
therefore, for you know neither the day nor the hour.' Matthew 25.11–13
'For the Lord himself, with a cry of command, with the archangel's call
and with the sound of God's trumpet, will descend from heaven, and the
dead in Christ will rise first.' 1 Thessalonians 4.16

Resurrection day
It is coming, this day so long awaited – but when, God alone
knows. Only when every nation has heard the gospel. How many
will be aware of it? Everyone on earth, and in glory. No one will
miss it, because the glory of God will see that everyone he has
ever created will be judged, to identify the value of the time they
have lived. The noise will be tremendous – but we shall have
exchanged physical for spiritual hearing. The light will be brighter
than anything we have known – but we shall be seeing with the
spirit rather than with mere eyesight. The sheer size of the multitude will be staggering – but God will be doing the counting; and
the work we are doing now will determine our fate on that day.
Are we working for Christ? Almost certainly. Are we working as
hard as we can for him? Probably not, but there's still time to
remedy that, or we'd not be here.

Making time for God
Time is God's gift to us, to increase for him. It works like this (and
divine alchemy is at work, which defies a logical explanation): the
time we deny to God and his work is wasted, and slips away
faster than we know how; we rush from one thing to the next,
and find ourselves always short of time, persuading ourselves and
anyone else within earshot that we're terribly busy. And we're in
company: the number of mobile phones and laptops that accompany most business folk everywhere they go is phenomenal.
   But, begin to save time *for* God: share the gospel, go to Bible
groups, help a housebound friend with shopping or gardening,

write a letter of encouragement to a missionary half a world away
. . . and the miracle starts happening: time is saved, and inexplicably
we find we have more time for more work for God. It's his way of
showing appreciation, and no one but God knows how it's done.

It doesn't mean that the End time will be longer delayed, either:
in fact, the folk who do more work for God will probably be
helping that day to arrive sooner – and that in itself should be an
incentive. Why, after all, should we waste so much of God's precious time doing things that don't help anyone else, that don't
spread God's word, and that won't be likely to be needed in
eternity? There were no doubt wonderful places to visit, in the
sophisticated world of Jesus' day (like the treasures of China and
South America), but the last thing on Jesus' agenda would appear
to have been the 'Grand Tour'. Among the great sights of India,
and the fabulous wealth of the country's gems, Mother Teresa
contented herself with ministering to the poor of Calcutta. As a
new Church year approaches, and the celebration of our Lord's
nativity, can we reflect on how our priorities may tie in with
God's? Will the oil in our lamps light us along the royal Way? Or
have we thought up so many excursions en route that we will run
our lamps dry before journey's end?

> If once all the lamps that are lighted
> Should steadily blaze in a line,
> Wide over the land and the ocean,
> What a girdle of glory would shine!
> How all the dark places would brighten,
> How the mist would roll up and away!
> How the earth would laugh out in her gladness,
> To hail the millennial day!

> *Ellen H. Gates*

Family service input
Encourage the young people to trawl through copies of the current
religious newspapers and abstract material for an Advent Prayer
Diary.

Suggested hymns
Give me oil in my lamp; Let the song go round the earth; Shine,
Jesus, shine; When I needed a neighbour.

Third Sunday before Advent *Second Service*
Every One Counts Ps. [20] 82; Judg. 7.2–22;
John 15.9–17

*'So Gideon and the hundred who were with him came to the outskirts
of the camp at the beginning of the middle watch, when they had just
set the watch, and they blew the trumpets and smashed the jars that
were in their hands.' Judges 7.19*

Reinforcements needed?
'It's beyond me!' 'We'll be swamped!' 'Get busy and order
reinforcements!' These and similar cries can be heard whenever
there's a major work or engagement looming. Unless we can actually see the scales tipped in our favour from the start, it's natural
to hesitate. Jesus knew exactly how the human mind works, and
how commanders delve deeply into logistics before committing
their armies to a battle (Luke 14.31). Like the unprofitable servant
(Luke 16.1ff.), the practices of the world will continue, but they
are not God's way of operating. The Lord showed Gideon that
while any great army can defeat a smaller one by sheer numbers
and no faith except that which they place in their own strength,
the best way – the divine, royal Way – is to look in faith to God:
God can multiply the efficacy of a few, a very few, to defeat far
greater numbers.

Giving the glory to God
The outcome is so surprising, it's obvious that human prowess
has not been the cause of success and victory – the glory goes to
God, and must be seen to go to him. So faith is increased, and we
can go forward in his strength to do greater things. It may be
macho to try to go it alone – but God is more interested in our
becoming macho in faith. As we grow older, or if sickness and
trouble hit us, our physical strength may decrease dramatically;
but faith built on God's word continues to grow, for God operates
by laws of increase, not decrease, and the best is yet to be.

Get up!
'Get up!' Gideon, full of faith in the God who could speak to him
through another man's dream, told the Israelites. 'Get up, for the
Lord has given the army of Midian into your hand!' His men
would probably raise their eyebrows, at being told to 'fight' with

trumpets, torches and empty jars – and maybe the Lord also smiled at Gideon's unusual preparations. But when we realize that God does deal with his children in ways that the world still calls 'unusual', we are improving in faith. Many men and women have felt the call to preach, teach, baptize or heal, and have answered in faith, without finance, formal qualifications or security as the world evaluates it.

After all, that's exactly how the first disciples answered the call of Christ.

Faith in the commander

The hundred chosen men had faith in the faith of their commander, Gideon. However many questions they may have had, they still obeyed his instructions. We are fortunate if we have a godly, Spirit-filled friend, priest or mentor, with whom we can share our faith and to whom we can turn for Christian fellowship, advice, or just a listening ear. And we are privileged if we can be such a friend to others. It's not a case of 'putting one's trust in princes' (Ps. 146.3, AV), over against God, but of recognizing the value of 'two or three' kindred souls meeting together for mutual encouragement, affirmation and edification.

'I will not go out free'

> *I'm the property of Jesus,*
> *Satan has no right to me,*
> *For to free me from his bondage,*
> *Jesus died on Calvary.*
> *Oh, I love, I love my Master,*
> *And I will not go out free.*
> *I am his, today, for ever,*
> *His for all eternity.*

> J. H. Watson

When we hear God's call, no matter how unusual the mission, or how inadequate we feel, we are – like Gideon – called to go out in faith: it may be with two or three others, or a hundred, or simply on our own with God. But not to go may be to miss an opportunity to give glory to God.

Christian, dost thou see them; Christian, seek not yet repose; Go
forth and tell; To God be the glory.

Second Sunday before Advent

13 November   *Principal Service*   **You Should Be
Prepared**   Zeph. 1:7, 12–18; Ps. 90.1–8[9–11]12;
1 Thess. 5.1–11; Matt. 25.14–30

*'But you, beloved, are not in darkness, for that day to surprise you like
a thief; for you are all children of light and children of the day; we are
not of the night nor of darkness. So then, let us not fall asleep as others
do, but let us keep awake and be sober.'* 1 Thessalonians 5.4–6

Readiness

Paul is telling us that, even though only God knows the day and
time, we are not to be unprepared for the End. As 'children of
light', we have the advantage of Christ's teaching, guidance and
presence. At every stage of his ministry, when the disciples' first
reaction seems to have been fear, Jesus was quick to tell them *not*
to be afraid – the inference being that they *should not* have feared
in the first place. Nor are we to be fearful about the End: it will
come, anyway. If each day we have done the best we can for God,
then the Day may surprise us, but it should not take us unawares.

Before a new year

In the wisdom of the lectionary compilers, we have these texts of
awareness in the run-up to Advent, to prepare us for the start of
a new Church year: a foretaste, in a way, of the infinitely greater
'New Year' that will be ushered in at the End of time. And therefore how we prepare for Advent is in a small measure an indication
of our preparedness for the Day. It's a time for new resolutions,
for examining the road we have travelled in the past year. What
has happened over these past weeks and months? The first things
that God brings to mind are probably those which have mattered
most to him. If we have placed ourselves prayerfully before him,
may we allow these thoughts that surface first to be our guide as
to where we stand spiritually.

It may have been a year of upheaval, or calm – or one which has seen great joy, or sadness, good health, or long-continued sickness. We shall no doubt have temporarily lost to glory some dear friends, but certainly we shall have made new ones. Perhaps we have moved house or changed our job; perhaps we have rejoiced at new birth in our family, exam successes, university degrees.

Or perhaps it will be surprisingly *little* things that God brings first to mind: the smile of a stranger, that day we'd just received bad news, or felt like death warmed up ... the first snow-drop, way back in the January frosts ... a gorgeous sunset, after we left the church at Evensong, that summer evening when the roses in the churchyard were in full bloom and their scent filled the air.

What is God telling us in these remembrances? We may even want to write them down, to pray over in the coming days.

Taking time
Taking time to take stock of our spiritual life is never wasted when it's seen as an aid to preparation and readiness for the End. We've only to read the Gospels to see how Jesus was constantly preparing not only himself but his disciples for the culmination of his mission. At times it seemed as though they were being abysmally slow to understand, but the groundwork laid in their lives by Christ during those three busy years bore fruit in the end.

We are not to get downhearted if our spiritual check seems to show very little progress; there are plateaux as well as mountains and valleys along our way to God; let's offer our lives to him, and ask him to make clear to us, at this time of year end and year beginning, what he is expecting of us in the coming months.

God only allows us to rest on a plateau for a while – and then he prods us to be up and doing again.

> *Sitting still and wishing*
> *Never made a person great;*
> *The good Lord sends the fishing,*
> *But we've to dig the bait.*

Anon.

Family service input
Encourage the young people to run spiritual checks of their own, discussing/listing/illustrating memories of the past year.

238

A charge to keep I have; For my sake and the gospel's, go; In full and glad surrender; Take my life, and let it be.

Second Sunday before Advent   *Second Service*
I, John   Ps. 89.19–37; 1 Kings 1.15–40 (or 1–40);
Rev. 1.4–18 [or Luke 9.1–6]

'I, John, your brother who shares with you in Jesus the persecution and the kingdom and the patient endurance, was on the island called Patmos because of the word of God and the testimony of Jesus. I was in the spirit on the Lord's day' Revelation 1.9–10a

The present three
John makes no distinction in time between the three experiences: persecution, kingdom and patient endurance. For him, they coalesce: the 'persecution' had, under Domitian, seen him exiled to Patmos, a bleak little island some 35 miles off Miletus on the coast of Asia Minor. It's likely that John was one of a group of exiles set to work either quarrying stone or carrying it down to the shore for shipping to the mainland where no doubt it would be used in the building schemes dreamt up with ever more extravagance by the emperor.

The 'kingdom', however, was also with John. It had come near him with Jesus – and, since Jesus had promised to be always with his disciples, it had stayed with him, to comfort and strengthen him in his trials. It is the experiencing of God in our lives that makes the kingdom not only one for which to look forward, but also a present reality.

And the 'patient endurance' that John had shown, not least in refusing to worship the emperor, was now to be rewarded by this series of revelations, which still today give every reader of the book a great spiritual uplift, and must also have worked wonders for the aged disciple who was bidden to write them down (v. 11).

On the Lord's day
It's interesting to note that John (perhaps because of his age) had had some free time on the Lord's day. Perhaps he went to one of the many island caves overlooking the sea, and was actually

gazing across to where the horizon hid the 'Seven Churches of Asia', when he received the visions. Already (the year would be around AD 95) the day we call 'Sunday' was, in remembrance of the resurrection, being called 'the Lord's day', in contradistinction to the Jewish sabbath (Saturday).

And John was open to receiving the revelations. With 'patient endurance' he was keeping his mind on God and the kingdom, and had not allowed his persecutions to get him down. It's note-worthy that God gave him these precious visions, not at a time of relative ease, but when John was in exile, undergoing forced labour. Sometimes when we are under trial, God will similarly come. It's as though he is *signalling* (NRSV) or *hissing* (AV) to attract our attention (Zech. 10.8) – saying, 'Pssst! I've something for you, something I want to tell you! Are you listening out, or are you taken up with your problems of the moment?'

If John had been wallowing in deep despair, too preoccupied to hear the divine 'Psst!', just think what we might have missed!

Keeping alert – on the Lord's day and every day – for what God is wanting to tell us, not only stops us from allowing problems to get us down, but also keeps us in touch with God's kingdom. It means the invisible umbilical cord linking us to our Lord is firmly in place, so that Satan has first to tangle with that in order to get to us. He can manage it, because he's cute; but it means he has to work harder to get our attention – and anything that gives Satan extra hassle must be good news.

Suggested hymns
I hunger and I thirst; Lord, speak to me that I may speak; Master, speak! Thy servant heareth; Shepherd divine, our wants relieve.

Christ the King (Sunday next before Advent)
20 November *Principal Service* **Head of the Family** Ezek. 34.11–16, 20–24; Ps. 95.1–7a; Eph. 1.15–23; Matt. 25.31–46

'[Jesus said] "And the king will answer them, 'Truly I tell you, just as you did it to one of the least of these who are members of my family, you did it to me.'"' *Matthew 25.40*

Head of the house

In Victorian and early Edwardian times, many Christian houses had this text on their walls, in tooled leather or sampler embroidery:

> *Christ is the Head of this house,*
> *The unseen Guest at every meal,*
> *The silent Listener to every conversation.*

And it's still possible to find it, in modern print form, in Christian bookshops and on church literature stalls. It gives Christ his rightful place, as head of the house: a place that Jesus emphasized, in today's Gospel reading: 'Members of *my family*' reminds us that in whatever good we do (or fail to do) we're not dealing with strangers. We should treat everyone with similar love and respect, as brothers and sisters with us in the great house, or family, of God. It's so simple, we often ignore or forget it – but can we pray these relationships into our hearts, until they become an integral part of us? 'There is no longer Jew or Greek, there is no longer slave or free, there is no longer male or female; for all of you are one in Christ Jesus', Paul told the Galatians (Gal. 3.28). We should concentrate on our shared relationship as members of Christ's family, until we don't notice these non-essentials: at the intersection, allowing another vehicle into our line of slow-moving traffic, whether the driver's at the wheel of a stretch limo or a clapped-out mini; holding the train door open for a pink-haired, bejewelled youngster, or for a frail octogenarian; giving as genuine a smile of welcome at worship to a 'gentleman of the road' as to the lord of the manor – and making all this such a natural part of our lives that we don't notice the difference.

Christ the King

Christ the King is ruler over all his family, irrespective of colour, sex, age or beauty. The world, by contrast, has become obsessed with status and qualification. Christ simplifies these, in the best-known verse of the Bible: 'God so loved the world, that he gave his only Son, so that *everyone who believes* in him may not perish but may have eternal life' (John 3.16). The only difference he acknowledges is belief or non-belief. Whoever is not for him is against him. There is no recognition of 'half-and-halfers'. Christ operates his monarchy on this single law of difference.

Yet it's a law that does admit change! We can have faith, and then lose it; and non-belief, even after many years, can see (or be shown) the light. Prime examples of each of these positions, were Judas Iscariot and the penitent thief. The former, called and chosen, threw away his privilege as a member of the King's family, while the penitent thief, after presumably a lifetime of crime, came good at Calvary.

He is the head
It's good to remember this headship of Christ as King, on this last Sunday of the Church's year, if at no other time, because it carries an implicit caveat. Many folk still don't believe, and not a few of those who do are fairly 'laid back' about their faith. Just a few Christians go 'all out' for Christ, and if these are not labelled 'eccentric', there's a danger of making them into saints before their time. Our place is not to bolster our own image, but Christ's – to point people to him, not to our wonderful selves and marvellous work. A vice-admiral turned high-church cleric, half-a-century or so ago, gave the latter part of his life after ordination to parochial work in London's East End. At his death, though his church was packed, there was a scarcity of high-sounding panegyric; instead, the consensus of opinion was, 'Well, you know, he was a good man; just a very good man; one feels better for having known him.' He had been Christ in so many ways to so many people, his identity had been hidden behind the glory of his King. That is the message that Christ is giving us on this his 'Kingship Sunday'. Can we meet his challenge, and lose our *selves* in him?

Family service input
Encourage the young people to construct a collage of 'Parish Life and Work, Advent 2004 to Advent 2005'. Include, if possible, projects also for the coming year.

Suggested hymns
Christ is the King, O Friends, rejoice; King of glory, King of peace; Rejoice, the Lord is King; The King of love my Shepherd is.

Christic the King *Second Service* **Ruling in the Light** Ps. 93 [97]; 2 Sam. 23.1–7 or 1 Macc. 2.15–29; Matt. 28.16–20

'The God of Israel has spoken, the Rock of Israel has said to me: One who rules over people justly, ruling in the fear of God, is like the light of morning, like the sun rising on a cloudless morning, gleaming from the rain on the grassy land.' 2 Samuel 23.3–4

God is light

'God is light, and in him is no darkness at all' (1 John 1.5), and in this great light he rules with all-seeing, all-knowing, all-revealing. In glory, he permits no darkness, sin, sorrow or sickness; no subterfuge, confusion or conniving; therefore, the more we excise these dark spots from our own lives, and the more we try to eliminate them from the lives of others, the more 'at home' we shall be when we eventually get to glory.

Centuries before Christ, David had been pondering to good effect the brightness of the divine monarchy. He had proved God's light could bring him safely through the dangers of Saul's mercurial mood swings, convincingly through the traumas of Goliath and subsequent military engagements – and that it could heal, even after David had fallen from grace over the Bathsheba episode and the callous murder of Uriah the Hittite. For David, the Sun of Righteousness had risen on Israel; and now near the end of his life David could appreciate the light that God's grace had brought.

Thankful for the light

David could have resorted to self-pity, that his biggest project, the great Temple, was not to be his but his son's. But he acknowledged the sovereignty of God, and gave thanks for all the blessings he had been given. We, too, can get so bogged down by what we imagine is hard or unfair treatment – or simply by the pressures of life – that we fail to appreciate what God has done, or the blessings he is currently giving us. Let us resolve to look for his light, rather than stumble along in the darkness of fear or foreboding; to make a quality decision – 'I am going to walk in the light of Christ' – and then to stick to it, come what may.

The past year

How much of God's light have we been given in the past year? Without doubt, all that we have needed. How much have we *received*? Probably only a fraction. God's mercy and grace are lighting every step of our way, yet we rarely receive the light as coming from him; we're usually pretty good at giving ourselves the credit – and occasionally others. But God doesn't get the kudos too often. May we pray for a greater discernment of our King's light in the coming year.

But his light is for the *world*; and we, as Christians, receive it on the world's behalf, to be used for those whom God gives us opportunity to meet. We may never know the number of people we light up with Christ's brilliance – nor how many they, in turn, light up. Let's just set the ball of brightness rolling as fast and as far as we can, and leave the recording of it to God.

King of our hearts

With Christ's brightness in our hearts, there shouldn't be room for anything Satan tries to bring along; prince of darkness as he is, he doesn't like bright conditions that show him up. The brighter Jesus shines in us, the harder Satan will need to work to gain a hearing.

Whatever new-year resolutions we make, as another year ends, may we resolve to 'look out' for Christ's light, not only in what is happening in our home-ground area, but around the world. The same sun that warms us is warming every other nation; the same spiritual brilliance and warmth of Christ that cheers us is good news also for millions of others. May we resolve to be more open to what Christ the King is doing in and for other nations, as his kingdom comes close.

Suggested hymns

Christ is the world's true light; Lead, kindly light, amid the encircling gloom; Thy kingdom come, O God; Thy kingdom come, on bended knee.

SERMONS FOR SAINTS' DAYS AND SPECIAL OCCASIONS

The readings in this section are taken from Brother Tristam SSF, *Exciting Holiness* (Canterbury Press, 1997); Robert Atwell, *Celebrating the Saints* (Canterbury Press, 1998).

St Andrew, Apostle   30 November   Fisher of Men   Isa. 52.7–10; Ps. 19.1–6; Rom. 10.12–18; Matt. 4.18–22

'So faith comes from what is heard, and what is heard comes through the word of Christ. But I ask, have they not heard? Indeed they have; for "Their voice has gone out to all the earth, and their words to the end of the world."' Romans 10.17–18

From Galilee to foreign fields

Andrew answered the call of Jesus when busy on his fishingnets at Galilee (John 1.41) – and, immediately going to tell Peter about Jesus, can probably be seen as the first Christian missionary. He was one of the 'inner four' of the Twelve, and after Jesus' ascension is thought to have travelled through Greece, eventually being martyred on an X-shaped cross at Patras, in or around AD 60.

His faith had grown 'from what [he] heard', in the three years of Jesus' ministry, and he was obedient to the Lord's prompting to go out from Jerusalem, after the Holy Spirit had been given.

How we listen

It's often not so much that we hear but how we listen to what is being said that counts. At prayer, we can be so busy telling God everything we think he should hear that we forget to listen out for what he may be saying to us. Even in church, we can drift into thinking of other things, and suddenly realize that the reading or the sermon has come to an end, while we've been otherwise engaged. We can switch on the news, and be so preoccupied with family matters that we don't hear a word of what the newscaster is saying. And how often do we read the newspaper from cover to cover, or the parish magazine, or even the weekly information sheet? If our church has a print-out of each Sunday's lessons and/or sermon, how often as the week advances do we freshen up on the Sunday news? God is showering us with opportunities for prayer, outreach, revelation and insight – and we're passing them up with amazing nonchalance.

A fine example
Andrew, for all we know so little about him, is a fine example of someone who took the trouble to get involved. Called from the local fishing fleet, for early mission, travelling with Jesus, helping at the feeding of the multitude, and finally mission to foreign fields, Andrew was constantly learning new skills, in new situations and with a variety of people such as a Galilean fisherman would not have imagined he would ever meet.

He would never forget his Galilean home – but had he stayed with the family fishing business how many souls now in Paradise would be in another place? And Scotland would have had to find another patron saint! In faith, Andrew went out – and made a difference for the Christ who had loved him and called him to service.

If, to date, our ministry has been fairly localized, can we be sure that the Lord is not calling us to take Christian light further afield? While we have our minds on 101 mundane matters, God still has his sights on worldwide evangelism. He calls, and if we don't respond, he may call again – or he may wait quite a time, or he may never repeat the call. Andrew didn't wait for 'the next time'. And his quick response was rewarded by Jesus. He may never have returned to Galilee after the ascension: but no one is tied by an eternal cord to any place or anyone but God.

Suggested hymns
I hear thy welcome voice; Follow me (leave your fishing nets and boats); Jesus calls us, o'er the tumult; Put thou thy trust in God.

St Ambrose, Bishop of Milan, Teacher of the Faith 397   7 December   Work of Reconciliation

Isa. 41.9b–13; Ps. 20; 2 Cor. 5.16–21; Luke 22.24–30

'So we are ambassadors for Christ, since God is making his appeal through us; we entreat you on behalf of Christ, be reconciled to God.' 2 Corinthians 5.20

Growing up in the law

Born *c.* 340, the son of Aurelius Ambrosianus, a Christian noble-man and praetorian prefect in Trier, Ambrose was trained as a lawyer, until the office of Bishop of Milan became vacant, and he was one of two candidates nominated for the office. By public acclaim, he won the vote: perhaps surprisingly, as he was not yet baptized. The Church, however, quickly resolved this problem, and Ambrose progressed from neophyte to bishop in eight days. He was 34, skilled in administration and diplomacy, and became Milan's best-loved and most respected bishop.

Between court and community

Ambrose used his episcopal power to the full, yet with a humility and charm that won over court and community. He began by distributing his appreciable wealth among the poor, and revising the ecclesiastical liturgy that had become ponderous and out-moded. He firmly believed that the Church should lead not only in matters of religion, but also of politics; and it's a measure of his diplomacy that he was able to influence the emperors Gratian, Valentinian II and Theodosius. In 390, Ambrose even excommuni-cated Theodosius for causing a massacre of seven thousand people in the circus at Thessalonica following the death of an army captain – forcing the emperor to do penance before being readmitted to the sacrament.

Fearing neither friend nor foe

It was this fearless policy that gave Ambrose the platform from where he could influence the life of his day, in a manner that his contemporary, John Chrysostom at Constantinople, could not. John was too close to the court and the vindictive empress Eudoxia for comfort, and was sent several times into exile for his plain speaking. Ambrose was able to dictate stronger terms to Justina,

247

the widow of Valentinian I, largely because he proved an able intermediary between her and Magnus Maximus who was threatening her heretical court.

Hymn-writer of note

While John Chrysostom was uneasily moving from vehement preaching to exile and back, Ambrose at Milan had an easier ride which favoured the exercise of his gift for poetry and the writing of hymns. His best-known is probably the basis of the hymn we now sing as 'O strength and stay', but a trawl through the hymnals of the last century provides us with many more, including those listed below:

Come, Holy Ghost, who ever one
Come, thou Redeemer of the earth
Creator of the earth and sky
O God of truth, O Lord of might
O God, the world's sustaining force
O splendour of God's glory bright
O Trinity, most blessed Light

Ambassadors for Christ

When Ambrose was studying for a career in law, the bishopric of Milan would not be in his thoughts. We, too, are not privy as to what the future holds, where God has designs on our witness and work. But so long as we are faithful in the field he has given us, he will in time lead us to new pastures: or he may want us to stay where we are for many more years. Wherever it is, if it's his will, we'll be given ample opportunity to fulfil our ambassadorial status.

Suggested hymns

Blessed city, heavenly Salem; I come with joy to meet my Lord; In heavenly love abiding; Like a mighty river flowing.

St John of the Cross, Poet, Teacher of the Faith
1591   14 December   **A Ready Writer**
S. of Sol. 2.8–17; Ps. 121; 1 Cor. 2.1–10; John 14.18–23

'Yet among the mature we do speak wisdom, though it is not a wisdom of this age or of the rulers of this age, who are doomed to perish. But we speak God's wisdom, secret and hidden, which God decreed before the ages for our glory.' 1 Corinthians 2.6–7

Destined for glory?
Born in Avila in 1542, Juan de Yepes was to have a short but eventful and blessed life. He studied under the Jesuits, and was admitted into the Carmelite Order in 1563, graduated from Salamanca University, and was ordained in 1567. He met Teresa of Avila, and defended her cause among the Discalced Carmelites – a stand that enraged the grandees of the Calced. After a time in prison, during which he wrote some of his best works, on his release tension flared up again among the Spanish Carmelites; and the political machinations were such that John was exiled, this time by the General of the Discalced, the rigours of his banishment contributing to his death at the early age of 49, on 14 December 1591.

Trials and tribulations
Teresa impressed John considerably, not least by her brave stand against the evils of the time, and her writings were frequently linked to his own works.

> The height of contemplation is a height most sublime, trodden by few, and upon the road to it the devil is wont to conceal himself, and put on a mask in order to deceive those whom he cannot deceive with his own countenance. The experiences concerned are acts of our souls, very much loftier than anything related to sense; they are difficult to understand, and are frequently uncomprehended by the very person to whom they belong. Therefore it is not surprising if the doctrine which treats of them appears new, extraordinary and difficult, and if in the past it has been subjected to calumnies like that of *The Ascent of Mount Sion* and that of the holy Mother Teresa of Jesus ... Let us here set down the words of the holy Mother in her *Conceptions of the Love of God* (f.377, p.2): 'Not like certain learned

men who, not having been led in this way of prayer by the Lord, and not having the beginnings of spirituality, try so hard to reduce everything to reason, and to measure everything by their own understanding, that it looks as if all their learning is going to enable them to succeed in comprehending all the wonders of God.' If only they would learn something from the most holy Virgin!

> Reply of R.P.M. Fray Basilio Ponce de Leon, Prima
> Professa of Theology, University of Salamanca, to the
> Notes and Objections which were made concerning certain
> propositions taken from the book of our Father Fray John
> of the Cross, 11 July, 1622.

Speaking wisdom
'We speak wisdom,' Paul told his friends at Corinth – and there stands a line nearly two millennia long of Christians like Paul, Teresa and John of the Cross, right down to our own day, who have struggled under God to put wisdom into words.

What words shall we leave, for those who are yet to come?

Suggested hymns
A new commandment I give unto you; And can it be; Take my hands; Take my life, and let is be.

St Stephen, Deacon, First Martyr
26 December (or transferred to 29 Dec.)
Spirited Witness   2 Chron. 24.20–22; Ps. 119.161–168; Acts 7.51–60; Matt. 23.34–39

'You stiff-necked people, uncircumcised in heart and ears, you are for ever opposing the Holy Spirit, just as your ancestors used to do. Which of the prophets did your ancestors not persecute? They killed those who foretold the coming of the Righteous One, and now you have become his betrayers and murderers.' Acts 7.51–52

First of many
Stephen was the first of many martyrs for Jesus; but he went to glory fighting in spirited, fearless defence. Called to be a waiter

of tables, he didn't stop at merely serving food in the 'daily distribution' (Acts 6.1), but 'improved his talent with due care', speaking up and out with fervour for his Lord. We may be engaged in very menial work, or perhaps we are so busy we don't know how to take a break. Whatever our occupation, Stephen's example today begs attention. We can always find or make time for God. Stephen's life may not have been long, but he made it count.

Not only a first-century malady

'Stiff-necks' were not only a first-century malady; they're still with us, making extra problems in a life that is complicated enough. Usually, pigheadedness sits atop them, which makes them extra-weird – but weird or not, they are dangerous, as Stephen discovered only too forcefully.

In the natural world, the people afflicted with this malady will rarely listen to logic, common sense or reason, which is probably also why they find faith such a problem. Jesus, like Stephen, didn't mince his words when dealing with stiff-necks: 'Why do you not understand what I say? It is because you cannot accept my word. You are from your father the devil, and you choose to do your father's desires' (John 8.43–44).

Those out-and-out Satanists, who foul society and the Internet with grimey faces and hideous blood-smirched skin, can easily be recognized. More sinister are those who hide under a cloak of respectability (too often, religious respectability). Yet 'by their fruits' we shall know them. Stephen didn't worry too much about identifying individuals in the murder-seeking crowd; he ventilated his castigation of evil for evil to make its own identification.

At Christmas time

Coming as it does right in the middle of our Christmas celebrations, Stephen's day sounds a sombre yet triumphant note. We thrill with awe as we read of Jesus, *on his feet* in glory, waiting to welcome home the Church's first martyr. Just fancy, a table-waiter gaining such a victory that the Lord could not remain seated, but got to his feet in joy (Acts 8.56)! Will Jesus, in equal joy for how we have witnessed, be on his feet to give us a welcome, too? Will there be any stars in our crowns when 'the other side' is reached?

I am thinking today of that beautiful land
I shall reach when the sun goeth down;
When through wonderful grace by my Saviour I stand,
Will there be any stars in my crown?
Will there be any stars, any stars in my crown,
When at evening the sun goeth down,
When I wake with the blest, in the mansions of rest,
Will there be any stars in my crown?

E. E. Hewitt

For the present, to encourage us at every step of the way, God has given us stars in our spirit – nine of them: 'love, joy, peace, patience, kindness, generosity, faithfulness, gentleness and self-control' (Gal. 5.22–23). Nine stars, fruits of the Spirit, with the potential to shine out from every Christian as light to the world.

The brightness with which these stars shine out, depends on how well we put this gift of God to work.

Suggested hymns
Can you count the stars that brightly; Give me oil in my lamp; Shine, Jesus, shine; The light of the world in the darkness.

St John, Apostle and Evangelist
27 December Writer and Thinker Ex. 33.7–11a; Ps. 117; 1 John 1; John 21.19b–25

'This is the disciple who is testifying to these things and has written them, and we know that his testimony is true.' John 21.24

The 'different' Gospel
We call the first three Gospels – those of Matthew, Mark and Luke – the 'Synoptics', because they share so much material in common and follow broadly the same pattern in their recording of Jesus' life and ministry. But John's Gospel is very different; it's more the product of a thinker than a recorder. John quotes the Old Testament much more than the other evangelists. He's saying, in effect: 'Look, check it out, whatever I am telling you about Jesus. I'm not

writing in a vacuum, but of prophecy fulfilled.' Past, present and future come together in this Gospel; strange though it may seem, we can even say that the Old Testament was written because of Jesus, and that he came because it had been written. It's just one way in which God seems to make a nonsense of 'time', time as we presently understand it.

John's 'theological' writing shows the author's attempts to search also behind the ministry of Jesus, to the meaning of what he did and said. The Parousia had not come quickly after Pentecost, and by the time that John wrote questions were being asked. When will Jesus come? What are we to do in the meantime? What is the reason for it all – this life, and the next? The apostles had mainly left Jerusalem, James had been killed, Rome had convincingly sacked the city. John saw the need for a Gospel that grounded Jesus' ministry on earth and glorified him in heaven; a Gospel for the mature believer and the enquirer alike; a Gospel that would inform as well as encourage – but also a Gospel that freely admitted to being but a fraction of the whole story (John 21.25).

Today's Johns
Today's Johns continue the work. We still know only a tiny fraction of the whole story; but week by week, day by day, we seek to bring what we do know to others. As modern-day Johns, we preach, teach, baptize, heal and encourage. By our words, our understanding and interpretation of God and his way, please God others may be led to a knowledge and love of the Saviour, and a commitment to his will.

God's word
Jesus is God's word: that is the central point of John's Gospel. He must know he is tangling at the limit of comprehension; we can cope with an earthly Jesus, but how can we see the man as the word? 'I know it's difficult, but try it, all the same,' John is saying. And his Prologue, where this advanced teaching is concentrated, forms our main Gospel reading of Christmas morning, and invariably the last and major reading of a carol service. Partially anaesthetized with the euphoria of the season, we tend not to think too deeply about the words, though we know them so well that any variation in their reading is quickly noticed. 'To *all* who received' this word (= light = Jesus), and 'believed in his name, he gave power to become children of God', John tells us

(John 1.12). This is why he is setting out his Gospel, for *all* who will read and receive and acknowledge Jesus.

In the midst of our Christmas busyness, this deeply moved and deeply moving apostle is saying, 'Think, now – Jesus *is* God's word, here in your hearts. What does this mean to you?'

He is asking to mean everything to us.

Suggested hymns
Jesus is Lord, creation's voice proclaims it; Thine for ever, God of love; When all thy mercies, O my God; When came in flesh the incarnate word.

Holy Innocents 28 December Obeying the King Jer. 31.15–17; Ps. 124; 1 Cor. 1.26–29; Matt. 2.8–13

'Then [Herod] sent them to Bethlehem, saying, "Go and search diligently for the child; and when you have found him, bring me word so that I may also go and pay him homage . . ." Now after they had left, an angel of the Lord appeared to Joseph in a dream and said, "Get up, take the child and his mother, and flee to Egypt, and remain there until I tell you; for Herod is about to search for the child, to destroy him." ' Matthew 2.8, 13

Only one king to obey
Here we have two kings: Herod and God. Both are giving orders, Herod to the Magi, and God (through his angel) to Joseph. One king, eaten up by paranoia and hatred, fearful of his position and suspicious of anyone whom he sees as a threat, gives orders which are countermanded by God (v. 12). The other tells a village carpenter to trek 250 miles south-west with his family to a foreign land away from an unseen threat (which may or may not materialize) – and he, not understanding but simply trusting, obeys.

Caught up in the middle of these conflicting monarchs and commands are innocent children, to whom, with the best of intentions, we find it difficult to do justice, in the middle of the Christmas celebrations.

Who were they? How many of them were there? And what may they have become, had their young lives been spared? Surely God need not have allowed the disgraceful massacre, so soon after giving us the joy of Jesus' birth? However illogical, useless or even selfish, these questions have been asked by successive generations of Christians over two thousand years. Why, God, why?

Sin's tragedy

It's part of the tragedy of any sin that it involves others – often innocent parties – as well as the sinner. Think of the millions who suffered – and who are still suffering, if not personally, then their families – as a result of Hitler's sin. And so the little ones of Bethlehem and their families suffered, because of Herod.

What are we to say? 'If only the Magi hadn't come in search of Jesus . . . ?' Or, to take a modern example: 'If only I hadn't stopped to run that errand for the housebound neighbour, I'd have been in time to see mother before she died . . .' There is always an 'if only', with hindsight or wishful thinking. It had been foretold that a tragedy of this sort would take place (Jer. 31.15), and Herod's paranoia invited it to happen then.

Some die young

Life would, paradoxically, be chaotic if everyone was programmed to die on his or her seventieth birthday. Where would be the challenge of faith? Wouldn't there be millions of death-bed conversions? Wouldn't the crime rate rocket? Before, and after, Jesus came, some people have died young and some have been spared to live a long life. We don't know for certain what we shall be doing in glory (though the Bible gives us innumerable hints that we'll be engaged in exciting work for God), but it's obviously God's plan that it's an 'all-age' programme. Although they were apparently taken so young, the little people of Bethlehem had fulfilled their purpose, otherwise God would not have allowed them to be taken.

We may reverently believe that in glory a special place was reserved for them.

Suggested hymns

Children of the heavenly King; In vain the cruel Herod's fear; Unto us a Boy is born; When wounded sore, the stricken heart.

Naming and Circumcision of Jesus
1 January   The Importance of a Name
Num. 6.22–27; Ps. 8; Gal. 4.4–7; Luke 2.15–21

'And because you are children, God has sent the Spirit of his Son into our hearts, crying, "Abba! Father!" So you are no longer a slave but a child, and if a child then also an heir, through God.' Galatians 4.6–7

His name is Jesus

There was to be no doubt about the naming of Mary's child; that had been made clear – doubly clear – when Gabriel had announced the news of his conception to Mary (Luke 1.3), and also when Joseph had been informed (Matt. 1.21). So now, Paul tells the Galatians, it also matters to God what we are called (not slaves, but children), and what we, in turn, are to call God (Abba, Father). Only a beautifully loving God would care about such things.

He was to be born and brought up according to the law, with ritual duly observed. But from the beginning, his name was to reflect his mission. Jesus means 'saviour', and that is what he would be. God would be 'Abba' to Christians, who were privileged to be so intimately related to him as a child who trustingly, confidingly calls his father 'Dad'. It's a real 'Dad' who takes an interest in everything his children do, and a real 'Dad' with whom they, in turn, feel they can run to in times of joy, fun, trouble and need.

Names today

Sometimes the names our parents and godparents choose for us seem strange, and not always to our liking as we grow older. Yet, since these names in practice are used more by others than ourselves, more often than not we accept them. At confirmation, some take a 'chosen' name, and can choose whether they subsequently wish this to be the one by which they are to be known. Often these chosen names are of saints, and reflect the impact the particular saint has had on our lives, or qualities of the saint which we, or others, have noticed in our lives.

A circumcised Child

As part of the formal ritual, Jesus was also circumcised, in accordance with the laws governing every male Jewish child. But by the time Paul was writing to the Galatian church, the question of circumcision for Gentile Christians had been resolved: non-Jewish

Christians were not obliged to undergo this operation, but were to see it in spiritual terms, as a circumscribing of the heart (i.e. observing the commands of Jesus, and drawing a line against anything that was not in accordance with his teaching).

Ritual circumcision, simply put, *had not worked* for the Jews. It had, admittedly, set them apart from non-Jews, but it had not made them better, more God-fearing people. The ministry of Jesus drew a line under their formal observances. People could not accuse him of being an unorthodox Jew: he had, for thirty years or so, observed everything his 'nationality' demanded. 'But, now . . .', he could declare, as he preached and taught and ministered. 'This has been from ancient time – but now, *I* tell you . . .' He had not come to give them a new Torah in total, still less a cumbersome Mishnah or Gemara, but a new covenant, which looked for faithfulness from the heart rather than reliance on ritual or animal offerings in lieu of repentance for sin and love for God.

It was all very new, even revolutionary, for many Jews to take on board; but when, as a nation, you have been doing something for thousands of years, it can be hard to change – especially if you cannot see the Saviour in your midst.

Suggested hymns
At the name of Jesus; Jesus, the name high over all; Name of all majesty; There is a name I love to hear.

Epiphany   6 January   Treasure for a King
Isa. 60.1–6; Ps. 72; Eph. 3.1–12; Matt. 2.1–12

'On entering the house, they saw the child with Mary his mother, and they knelt down and paid him homage. Then, opening their treasure-chests, they offered him gifts of gold, frankincense and myrrh.' Matthew 2.10–11

The rich bring gold
These were influential, perhaps royal, guests, whose learning and wisdom had encouraged them to recognize the star as the sign of the King of the Jews. Were these the only foreigners who came? Who else did they tell? Lord, we're grateful for Matthew's

257

inclusion of this visit, but we would like to know so much more!

Perhaps, had it not been for these Magi and their visit to Herod, there would have been no massacre of the innocent children? Yet this had been foretold, and would probably have happened anyway. Herod was so suspicious, he would have heard of Jesus sooner or later.

Precious gifts

They brought the best gifts they could find. It doesn't matter what price the world puts on our service and gifts for God, so long as they are the best we can bring – the 'first-fruits', to use a beautiful word that has largely dropped out of parlance: not to calculate how much food, petrol and clothing we need, and then to bring God (some of) what's left – but to make him a love-offering first, whether of money, time or talents.

Money

Money is important, insofar as it can be used to further God's work and word in the world. The Jews were obliged by the Torah to give God a tithe of their income – and some, including the Pharisee in Jesus' parable, were inordinately proud of being so observant. Jesus in the Gospels seems not to have placed such emphasis on monetary giving. He apparently carried no money himself (Judas Iscariot was the less-than-honest treasurer of the mission team), sending Peter on one occasion to fish for the tribute money; and having to ask for a coin to be shown him when he dealt with the question of what should be paid to Caesar. He praised a poor woman for her self-sacrificing offering, contrasting her generosity with the ostentatious giving of the wealthy – and he could turn water into first-class wine, and feed thousands with a schoolboy's lunch, without any money changing hands. When a man came to him, admitting a strict observance of the Torah (which would include tithing), Jesus told him it wasn't enough: he must give away everything he had.

So, perhaps understandably, Christians have never seen tithing in quite the same way as the Jews. Certainly, if it's seen as a means of 'insurance', with eternity as the pay-off, the value has gone. God's favour cannot be bought. The Magi's gift was not brought as a bribe, or a down-payment, but out of love and respect.

Talents
Artwork, craftwork, engineering, writing, cooking, gardening . . .
the list of what we can do beautifully and best, grows longer as
history advances, even though some crafts die out and are replaced
by others. Giving these in God's service is the very highest use
that we can put them to. Using them as a means to bring others
to God, we are practically working out our gratitude to him for
the gifts that he has worked into us. It may be designing a stained-
glass window, building a church in a remote part of Africa, cutting a bunch of homegrown roses to take to a sick neighbour,
inviting new members of the church for coffee and a chat. The
Magi's myrrh was brought as a gift of love, for sweet-smelling
appreciation.

Time
God gives us all the time we need, to do his will. If we squander
it on other pursuits, we cannot blame him if we find ourselves
short of time. Time for others, in God's name, is time well spent;
many people have been 'helped round the corner', out of worry
or grief, by having 'a listening ear'. We don't always need to talk:
listening with patience and sympathy can often speak louder than
words. The Magi's gift of frankincense proclaimed Jesus a King,
mute though it was.

Suggested hymns
As with gladness men of old; O, worship the Lord in the beauty
of holiness; The wise may bring their learning; We three kings.

St Agnes, Child-Martyr at Rome 304
21 January   **Meek as a Lamb**   Ecclus. 51.1–3;
Ps. 45; Rev. 7.13–17; Matt. 18.1–7

*'Then one of the elders addressed me, saying, "Who are these, robed in
white, and where have they come from?" I said to him, "Sir, you are
the one that knows." Then he said to me, "These are they who have come
out of the great ordeal; they have washed their robes and made them
white in the blood of the Lamb."' Revelation 7.13–14*

Youth, wealth and beauty

Youth, wealth and beauty were all on the side of the fourth-century Roman girl, Agnese. Although barely 13 years old, suitors were lining up to seek her favours. But she calmly declared that she belonged to Jesus; he, as her bridegroom, had the first and only call on her affections.

Her words inflamed a passion of hatred rather than love in the local governor. This was a time when the persecution of Christians under the emperor Diocletian was at its height, and Agnes was threatened with death if she did not recant and marry a pagan. She refused to deny her Lord, and as an interim measure the governor committed her to a brothel. Her sweetness and humility charmed even the hardened sinners who frequented the place, and Agnes retained her virginity. Finally, she was killed – according to one legend, being stabbed in the throat, and to another being beheaded.

A tender lamb

She is usually depicted with a lamb as her emblem. In a particularly beautiful window at Christ Church, King Sterndale, Derbyshire, she is shown in glory holding a lamb, over a cameo depicting her on the way to glory offering her neck to the executioner.

She was buried on the Via Nomentana, near Rome, and the church erected over her grave, Chiesa Sant' Agnese Fuori le Mura, though much altered, can be seen there today. Her fame had so spread by the time of the emperor Constantine, that he had his daughter baptized near the saint's grave.

A martyr's crown

Our lives, by comparison with those of Agnes and the white-robed martyrs of John's vision, can seem quite ordinary; but no life created by God can ever be ordinary. Each of us has a purpose that no one else can fulfil: how can anyone who is so unique be ordinary? And, life and death being in God's hands, he has decreed that not every Christian shares with Agnes the martyr's way to eternity via execution. Yet in a way we are all called to be martyrs – to lay our lives on the line for Jesus. That may involve a violent death, like our saint's, or it may be a quiet dedication that simply puts God before ourselves and our desires. St Antony of Egypt lived to be over a hundred and underwent severe temptations in the desert. The Little Flower of Lisieux, Thérèse, lived only a few years more than Agnes, and was ill for much of the time. Some have sought martyrdom, and some have had it violently thrust upon them. It is not for us to question God's dealings with anyone else, but to resolve to do our best for him, to preserve integrity and Christian consistency – and to leave the outcome in his hands.

Suggested hymns
Blessed city, heavenly Salem; In heavenly love abiding; Let saints on earth in concert sing; The head that once was crowned with thorns.

Conversion of Paul   25 January   Good from Bad
Jer. 1.4–10; Ps. 67; Acts 9.1–22; Matt. 19.27–30

'All who heard [Paul] were amazed and said, "Is not this the man who made havoc in Jerusalem among those who invoked this name? And has he not come here for the purpose of bringing them bound before the chief priests?"' Acts 9.21

Letters of intent
Of course he had: that had been Paul's reason for riding to Damascus. He'd had the incriminating letters in his pocket when Jesus struck him down on the road – though by this time the letters had probably been burned. But folk had not forgotten his zeal against the Church, and Paul was going to need great fervour and charity to convince the Damascene Jews and Christians of the genuineness of his conversion. It was going to be even more difficult when he returned to Jerusalem, but there Barnabas would support him (Acts 9.27).

A generous spirit
We, too, need a generosity of spirit, to see the best in people about whom we may have reservations. Are they proclaiming Jesus? Do they believe that he is the Son of God, risen from the dead and alive for ever? Then, why are we remembering the past? Why are we perpetuating sins for which they tell us they have repented and been forgiven? If God has been generous enough to forgive, why should we harbour a spirit of unforgiveness? Yes, we may think it's taking a big risk, to say we believe their conversion is

genuine, but how blessed were those who took that same risk with Paul! There are times when God does call us to live as dangerously as this: and who knows what blessings may be ours (and the other person's) when we step out in faith and accept that someone else besides ourselves can receive the grace of God.

Paul's courage
On this festival of his conversion, may we also pay tribute to the courage of Paul, who could turn from persecuting to preaching – knowing that his past would rankle in the minds of his listeners, yet determined to show his gratitude to the Lord who had gone to no little trouble to meet and ask for his conversion. It had taken rank determination to arraign Christians and to get them tortured, but now courage had to be added to that determination, courage to overcome scepticism and predictable vindictiveness against what many would see as a 'turncoat'.

Our courage
It takes courage of a similar kind today, to stand up and stand out for Christ – whether we have painted the town red in a pre-conversion period, or have grown up from being 'cradle-Christians'. We shall probably not have come near to Paul's extent of persecution, so our listeners will not have torture and death to remember, but the world will always find something to criticize. Make no mistake: twenty-first century Christians do need courage, in good measure.

Success!
In Damascus, Paul was successful in the defence of his conversion. It was a big stepping-stone along the way to mission; and on the strength of this he felt able to go to Jerusalem. We need our courage, not merely for one great event, but for all the little opportunities and challenges of every day. And the more we stand out for Jesus, the ... easier it becomes? Not necessarily, but we get more used to doing it!

Suggested hymns
Captains of the saintly band; Fight the good fight; Soldiers of Christ, arise; We sing the praise of him who died.

Presentation of Christ in the Temple
(Candlemas)   2 February   **A Light for Revelation**
Mal. 3.1–5; Ps. 24; Heb. 2.14–18; Luke 2.22–40

'"My eyes have seen your salvation, which you have prepared in the presence of all peoples; a light for revelation to the Gentiles, and for glory to your people Israel."' Luke 2.30–32

More than light
Jesus came as light – not merely *a* light, but as light that illumines the mind, revealing not sight but knowledge; shining not only on what can be seen, but also known. If we see Jesus only as a wonderful person who died for the world's salvation (marvellous though this is, and absolutely true as it is), we are missing some of the purpose of his coming – for he lived, died and rose again to teach us how to live, to give us his gospel, to reveal to us who we are in him, and what his mission is for us; that we are not given life here only to save our soul by believing for eternity, but to work out the revealing light that God has worked into us, to bring others to a revelation whereby they may accept Christ (himself, as well as what he gives) for themselves.

It was to prove a strange irony, that God's chosen people, the Jews, would reject the revelation, and would have one of their number betraying Jesus, while the priests themselves would howl for his crucifixion; yet the Gentiles would make the leap from pagan religions and cults to accepting the light on offer. But the acceptance would not be universal: from both the Jewish and Gentile world, many would be called, but few would be chosen. Many would choose to stumble along in the darkness of spiritual unknowing.

In times of testing
The revelations continue, as God shows us more and more of himself, in situations and experiences that take us further into his purpose. We may not see the next step ahead, but we can have confidence that he is there: that he not only knows the experience ahead, but how its outcome will prepare us for the next . . . and the next.

As our experience-in-God deepens, and we focus increasingly on him, so (it may seem strange, or perfectly logical) our perception of the present is enriched. We can become so preoccupied with present circumstances that they blot out any future hope and expectation; that is not how Jesus operated, and nor is it how God is asking us to live.

'Revelation' is not confined to the present – that is its power and beauty. It brings together past, present and future into a coalescing of time, and gives us a glimpse of the divine scheme of things. God works in time, and yet beyond time's limits. Simeon, as he held the baby Jesus in his arms that day, rejoiced in the present honour of cradling the Saviour – yet looked forward as he saw in spirit the Saviour's light as a revelation to Gentiles as well as to Jews: revelation on a worldwide scale.

If Candlemas does not inspire and encourage us to broaden our Christian horizons, we may question how much of the Saviour's light we have accepted.

Suggested hymns
Christ is the world's true light; I sing the Lord God's praises; Light's abode, celestial Salem; Shine, Jesus, shine!

SS Cyril and Methodius, Missionaries to the Slavs 869 and 885   14 February   Spreading the Word   Isa. 49.1–6; Ps. 24; Rom. 10.11–15; Luke 9.1–6

'Listen to me, O coastlands; pay attention, you peoples from far away! The Lord called me before I was born, while I was in my mother's womb he named me.' Isaiah 49.1

Brother monks
Born in the ninth century in Thessalonica, Cyril and Methodius gave up high positions to become monks in a monastery on the Bosphorus. But the brothers' linguistic aptitude encouraged the emperor to send them into deepest Russia where they converted the Khazars. Returning to the monastery, they were almost immediately despatched by the Patriarch of Constantinople to preach to the Moravians. The mission was difficult, but the brothers persevered, and were recalled eventually to Rome where Pope Nicholas I wanted to meet them.

By the time they reached Rome, the pope had died, but his

successor determined to consecrate them bishops. Before the ceremony, however, Cyril died. For some time, Methodius laboured
on alone, but was resented by the German bishops for the work
he had done among the Moravians. In the end, he returned to
Constantinople, where he completed a translation of the Bible in
Slavonic, which he had begun with Cyril.

Peoples from far away

'Peoples from far away' are still travelling long distances with
God's word. In some areas the wheel of history has made a complete revolution, as missionaries from countries to whom Britain
took the gospel are coming to preach and evangelize here. And
in other places there are many who seek to break new ground,
taking the gospel into places where no Christian has yet been.

From before birth

God knows us while we are still in the womb, before we have
been born. How much of our life is predestined, or how much
'freedom of choice' we really have, has never yet been determined.
But we, who have been alerted by God, surprised by the divine,
are under an obligation to respond by giving him our best time,
talents and devotion.

And that means sharing the gospel, whether on the home front
or in some corner of a foreign field. Christians fired up by the
Holy Spirit to white-hot heat for mission can make the difference
between eternal life and eternal death for a large number of people.
If this prospect rates a low score on our priorities, we are certainly
far below white heat.

New ground

In breaking new ground, Cyril and Methodius ran up against
stiff opposition. If we are experiencing little opposition in our
own mission field, we could well question whether we are in the
right place, or witnessing in the best way. Perhaps a sea-change
is indicated. A congregation faced with considerable repair and
maintenance bills for their old church, launched out in faith and
demolished the building. In its place, they built the largest modern
church they could afford, seating 300 people. Within a few weeks
of its opening, they were getting more than 250 to every service.

Some of the (older) members had been unhappy with the new building – but they had to admit the venture's success.

What is our own exciting adventure rating on our local priority chart?

Suggested hymns
Like a mighty river flowing; O Jesus, I have promised; The Church's one foundation; Thy kingdom come, O God.

George Herbert, Priest and Poet 1633
27 February   **A Busy Life**   Mal. 2.5–7; Ps. 1; Rev. 19.5–9; Matt. 11.25–30

'And the angel said to me, "Write this: Blessed are those who are invited to the marriage supper of the Lamb." And he said to me, "These are the true words of God." ' Revelation 19.9

Short and sweet
Born in 1593, of an aristocratic Pembroke family, Herbert gained honours at Trinity, Cambridge, and later ran successfully for Parliament. His friendship with Nicholas Ferrar at Little Gidding persuaded him to seek orders, and in 1626 he was ordained deacon. From 1630 until his death three years later, he served as rector in the little country parish of Bemerton, near Salisbury. He proved a conscientious parish priest, yet also found time for much writing; and hymns such as those listed below are still firm favourites today. His was a short life, but a sweet one, and its fragrance has spread far beyond the rural retreat of Bemerton.

The banquet
As we read of the heavenly marriage supper of the Lamb revealed to John, let us also share Herbert's lines on 'The Banquet':

> Welcome sweet and sacred cheer,
> Welcome dear;
> With me, in me, live and dwell;
> For thy neatness passeth sight,
> Thy delight
> Passeth tongue to taste or tell.

O what sweetness from the bowl
Fills my soul,
Such as is, and makes divine!
Is some star (fled from the sphere)
Melted there,
As we sugar melt in wine?

Or hath sweetness in the bread
Made a head
To subdue the smell of sin;
Flowers, and gums, and powders giving
All their living,
Lest the enemy should win?

Doubtless, neither star nor flower
Hath the power,
Such a sweetness to impart;
Only God, who gives perfumes,
Flesh assumes,
And with it perfumes my heart . . .

When I had forgot my birth,
And on earth
In delights of earth was drowned;
Good took blood, and needs would be
Spilt with me,
And so found me on the ground.

Having raised me to look up,
In a cup
Sweetly he doth meet my taste,
But I still being low and short,
Far from court,
Wine becomes a wing at last!

Multum in parvo

We need not think of Herbert's early death as a waste, a tragedy
– any more than the early death of John the Baptist, or even Jesus.
'Mission accomplished', in the sight of God, can come at any time.
We are so programmed to schedules, timetables and prolonging
our time on earth that we often allow quantity to superimpose on

quality. Doing all we can while we can is surely preferable to planning what we might not be able to do.

Suggested hymns (all Herbert's)
Come, my Way, my Truth, my Life; King of glory, King of peace; Let all the world in every corner sing; Teach me, my God and King; The God of love my Shepherd is.

St David, Bishop of Menevia, Patron of Wales
c. 601   1 March   **Pleasing to God**   Ecclus. 15.1–6; Ps. 16; 1 Thess. 2.2–12; Matt. 16.24–27

'But though we had already suffered and been shamefully maltreated at Philippi, as you know, we had courage in our God to declare to you the gospel of God . . . not to please mortals, but to please God who tests our hearts.' I Thessalonians 2.2, 4

The Holy Spirit's help
David (Dewi) was born at Henfynyw, Cardigan, the son of a Prince, Sant, and a Saint, Non. Several legends tell of how the Holy Spirit guided the boy in his study of the Scriptures, in the form of a dove hovering near his lips.

At Ty Gwyn, David's teacher was St Paulinus, who encouraged his monastic vocation. David eventually became abbot at Ty Gwyn, founding 12 other monasteries also, and setting up a community at Mynyw.

Holy boldness
At the Synod of Brefi, David waxed so eloquent against the Pelagian heresy that the Primate of Wales, St Dubricius, resigned in his favour. David immediately moved his See from Carleon to Mynyw, where he was to stay until his death.

He found time to win a great victory over the Saxons, on the battlefield, having ordered the Welsh soldiers to wear a leek in their helmets, so that friend and foe could be easily distinguished.

On his deathbed, David's last words to his friends are said to have been: 'Rejoice. Hold fast to the faith. And remember to fulfil those small tasks that you have learned while you were with me.'

Small things well

If we do little things well, the big tasks will take care of themselves; but a casual attitude to the simple things will mean the greater challenges will suffer. Follow Paul's advice, and set out to please God; that's all that matters. Doing many small things well now is better than waiting for a world-shattering opportunity that may never come. We need to make decisions where we are, not where we are not.

God's cardiac testing

God 'tests our hearts' by first giving us the strength, and then the opportunities for using it. The world dangles a carrot before us, demands great effort to win it, and then often tweaks it further out of our reach. The wonder is that so many people seem to prefer the world's underhand methods to the gracious unmerited favour of God. How can the world be made to get its act into better perspective? For many, realization will come too late.

Were we to run a spiritual heart-test of our own, we would probably be either too harsh or too lenient with ourselves. But certainly each of us has hidden talents, untapped resources, unused strengths. Why is this? Because we have the Holy Spirit, who is limitless.

Had David lived longer, he would surely have done more. But God had plans for his hidden talents, untapped resources and unused strength, in eternity.

Suggested hymns

A sovereign Protector I have; Guide me, O thou great Redeemer; Lead, kindly light; Like a mighty river flowing.

St Patrick, Bishop, Missionary, Patron of Ireland c. 460   17 March   The Shamrock Saint
Isa. 51.1–11; Ps. 96; Rev. 22.1–5; Matt. 10.16–23

'Then the angel showed me the river of the water of life, bright as crystal, flowing from the throne of God and of the Lamb through the middle of the street of the city. On either side of the river is the tree of life with its twelve kinds of fruit, producing its fruit each month; and the leaves of the tree are for the healing of the nations.' Revelation 22.1–2

An English saint

It comes as something of a surprise to many to learn that the saint synonymous with the Emerald Isle was actually born in England, of Roman stock. He was 14 when traders kidnapped him and took him to Ireland, where for some time he tended sheep near Ballymena, Co. Antrim, before escaping to France on a dog-trading boat.

He had learned to pray while shepherding in Ireland, and in Gaul became a student under St Germanus of Auxerre, being tutored also at the monastery of Lerins. Yet his heart was in the land of his shepherding; and, after being consecrated bishop by Germanus, Patrick returned to Ireland, where he spent the rest of his life as Bishop of Armagh, travelling long distances to preach and teach the gospel. Having seen the established parochial system successfully operating in Gaul, he tried to replicate it – but Ireland was not ready for it at this time. Patrick died at Saul, on Strangford Lough, Downpatrick, in or around the year 461, having laid the foundations of the Church in Ireland that continue to undergird it today.

O Patrick, hail, who once the wandering race
Didst win to be God's faithful resting-place,
And Ireland's love to soothe his wounded face.
Alleluia! Alleluia!

In dreams thou heardest thy distant children cry
To bid thee, holy one of God, draw nigh,
Lest all the Gaelic clans but live to die.
Alleluia! Alleluia!

Christ was thy sword, thy breastplate and thy shield,
And Christ the living strength, that helped thee wield
A sacred spell o'er hill and lake and field.
Alleluia! Alleluia!

Christ was thine eye, and Christ thine ear and tongue,
And Christ the peerless song thy brave lips sung,
And Christ thy challenge to the Druids flung.
Alleluia! Alleluia!

O lonely strife no man can ever tell,
The years thou barest cross and staff and bell,
To war with all the powers and hate of hell.
Alleluia! Alleluia!

Yet Ulster's plain thou choosest for thine own,
Armagh thou madest be thy royal throne,
To holy Down thou lef'st thy burying-stone.
Alleluia! Alleluia!

Shane Leslie

Healing of the nations

Patrick's is an earthly, practical example of the heavenly tree of life in John's vision: returning to the land of his slavery, to lighten it with the gospel. The healing of the nations begins with the healing of strife, ignorance or apathy in the heart – in the family, among neighbours, between communities – and only then, across national boundaries. Are we trying to win the decathlon before we've laced up our running shoes?

Suggested hymns

Father of all those far-scattered sheep of Christ (*WH*); For all the saints; Hail, glorious Saint Patrick (*WH*); I bind unto myself today (St Patrick's Breastplate); O Patrick, hail (*WH*). (*WH = Westminster Hymnal*)

St Joseph of Nazareth   19 March   'With Chisel, Saw and Plane'   2 Sam. 7.4–16; Ps. 89.27–36; Rom. 4.13–18; Matt. 1.18–25

'[Mary's] husband Joseph, being a righteous man and unwilling to expose her to public disgrace, planned to dismiss her quietly. But just when he had resolved to do this, an angel of the Lord appeared to him in a dream, and said, "Joseph, son of David, do not be afraid to take Mary as your wife, for the child conceived in her is from the Holy Spirit." ' Matthew 1.19–20

Why the silence?

Was Joseph really the strong, silent type that the Gospels – who record no word from him – would indicate? Or did Mary (if, as

271

is supposed, she provided the data for the birth stories) consider that Joseph's 'fatherhood' was so unusual, that her Son, as *Son of God*, did not need Joseph's words to be recorded? We do not know – but certainly Joseph was a good man, who was obedient to God's word as conveyed by angels, and took the greatest care of Mary both before the nativity and afterwards. We presume that Joseph died at some point between when Jesus at the age of twelve was taken to the Temple (Luke 2.41ff.) and when at thirty or so years old he began his public ministry.

Joseph the parent

St John Chrysostom saw in Joseph's care for Mary and Jesus the pattern for all fathers. Unquestionably, Joseph must have pondered long and deeply about what God was doing in his life – not least, what Mary's Child would turn out to be. Is it possible that God took Joseph before Jesus began his ministry, so that there would be less confusion about him as 'Son of God'? Yet the people of his home town Nazareth remembered Joseph, and were quick to cry out: 'Isn't this the carpenter's son?'

The challenge

Joseph met the challenge of being a surrogate father to Jesus with dignity and courage. He had been chosen for a task unparalleled in history, and proved a worthy 'husband' to Mary. The startling announcement of the angel, followed by the excitement of John the Baptist's birth, the traumatic hunt for a bed in census-packed Bethlehem, and then the 250-mile trek to safety in Egypt, must surely have persuaded Joseph that life as a village carpenter was not God's only plan for him. Yet on the Holy Family's return to Nazareth, he seems to have settled down once again to the routine of carpentering with equanimity and dedication.

Without fully understanding, Joseph surely realized that the boy born of Mary was special; and that he, Joseph, had been uniquely blessed in being chosen for the fathering of him. Joseph is a pattern for all fathers – of patience, trust and quiet love – and on this day we should remember all those who are called to this work.

Not single-handed

We should note, with gratitude and awe, that God did not leave Joseph to care single-handed for Mary and Jesus. The visits of angels, before and soon after Jesus' birth, are recorded: perhaps there were more. Indeed, if necessary, there would surely be other visitations and revelations, as God guided Joseph through the care and upbringing of his Son. Our own missions may seem far simpler than Joseph's, but still we can have confidence that when help is needed it will be given. No one has yet made it to glory without divine help – and no one will ever need to.

Suggested hymns
Come, sing with holy gladness; Guide me, O thou great Redeemer; Lead, kindly light; Put thou thy trust in God.

Annunciation of our Lord to the Blessed Virgin Mary 4 April (transferred from 25 March) **Gift of Power** Isa. 7.10–14; Ps. 40.5–10; Heb. 10.4–10; Luke 1.26–38

'The angel said to her, "The Holy Spirit will come upon you, and the power of the Most High will overshadow you; therefore the child to be born will be holy; he shall be called Son of God."' Luke 1.35

God's gift
Mary had been specially chosen to be *Theotokos*, 'Mother of God', but for the divine to be implanted in her womb, she needed power, the overshadowing of the Most High – and this powerful gift would enable the Son of God to be born in her. It's impossible to understand *how* it happened, but at least we know *why*: so that the world could be saved. One frail little woman would birth the world's Saviour. Who but God could have conceived such a plan out of such powerful love?

And who but Mary would have been trusting and brave enough to give her 'fiat' to the plan? Who had taught her such trust? What quiet courage enabled her to cope with the angel's visit? Was she really trembling inside? We do not know. It's enough, that she gave her consent, for we also do not know if God had any 'Plan B' in reserve.

Into the unknown
We step into the unknown every day when we awake, and usually we manage without making a drama of it. But, faced with a crisis,

do we turn first to God, or try to meet the challenge by ourselves? Doesn't it help our ego-building if we can persuade God that he is obsolete? Of course, we don't phrase it so baldly, but that's the impression we surely give. If only we were less self-confident, and more trustful of the Lord, we should save ourselves much angst.

> Mary Immaculate, Star of the morning,
> Chosen before the creation began,
> Chosen to bring, for thy bridal adorning,
> Woe to the serpent, and rescue to man.
>
> Here in an orbit of shadow and sadness,
> Veiling thy splendour, thy course thou hast run;
> Now thou art throned in all glory and gladness,
> Crowned by the hand of thy Saviour and Son.
>
> Sinners, we worship thy sinless perfection,
> Fallen and weak, for thy pity we plead;
> Grant us the shield of thy sovereign protection,
> Measure thine aid by the depth of our need.
>
> Frail is our nature, and strict our probation,
> Watchful the foe that would lure us to wrong;
> Succour our souls in the hour of temptation,
> Mary Immaculate, tender and strong . . .
>
> Bend from thy throne at the voice of our crying;
> Bend to this earth which thy footsteps have trod;
> Stretch out thine arms to us, living and dying,
> Mary Immaculate, Mother of God.
>
> F. W. Weatherell

Today's angels

Today's angels are still busy (if we are to believe in full employment in heaven). Gabriel will never have to bring news of a saviour to a virgin of 2005 – but in millions of other ways God is intervening in lives who would otherwise not make it to glory. How and why he does it may only become apparent long after the event; but if we pray for an open heart to be aware of his presence, he will go to work on us as he went to work on Mary.

Suggested hymns

The angel Gabriel from God; For Mary, Mother of our Lord; I'll sing a hymn to Mary (*WH*); Virgin wholly marvellous (*WH*). (*WH = Westminster Hymnal*)

St George, Martyr, Patron of England *c.* 304

23 April **A Christian Fighter** 1 Macc. 2.59–64 or Rev. 12.7–12; Ps. 126; 2 Tim. 2.3–13; John 15.18–21

'Therefore I endure everything for the sake of the elect, so that they may also obtain the salvation that is in Christ Jesus, with eternal glory. The saying is sure: If we have died with him, we shall also live with him; if we endure, we will also reign with him; if we deny him, he will also deny us; if we are faithless, he remains faithful – for he cannot deny himself.' 2 Timothy 2.10–13

Knight of Cappadocia?

George was not born in England, as may be supposed, but is thought to have been a knight of Cappadocia. Legend has it that he was riding one day through Libya, when he came to the city of Sylene, where there was great trouble. A marauding dragon had caused havoc among the flocks of sheep. These having been exhausted, he was now being fed human flesh; and when George arrived on the scene, the King of Sylene was about to sarifice his daughter to the beast. The knight undertook to fight the dragon, on condition that the fifteen thousand or so inhabitants of the city became Christians. The king agreed to these terms, and George successfully despatched the beast.

Roman soldier?

Another legend has George in the imperial Roman army. Once, when the emperor was addressing his officers, certain priests that were present attempted to foretell the outcome of an engagement by reading the entrails of animals. Some Christians among the officers made the sign of the cross, and the enraged emperor ordered them to be beaten and deprived of their rank. He followed this up by an edict demanding that all Christian clergy should sacrifice to pagan gods. George, coming on a copy of this edict nailed to the door of the emperor's palace, ripped it off and was tortured to death as a punishment.

Which is true?
We do not know which, if either, legend is true – only that England's patron saint, whoever, wherever he was, was a Christian man of courage.

> Leader now on earth no longer,
> Soldier of the eternal King,
> Victor in the fight for heaven,
> We thy loving praises sing.
> Great Saint George, our patron, help us,
> In the conflict, be thou nigh;
> Help us in that daily battle,
> Where each one must live or die.
>
> Praise him who in daily battle
> Never shrank from foeman's sword,
> Proof against all earthly weapon,
> Gave his life for Christ the Lord.
> Who, when earthly war was over,
> Fought, but not for earth's renown,
> Fought, and won a nobler glory –
> Won the martyr's purple crown.
>
> Help us when temptation presses;
> We have still our crown to win;
> Help us when our soul is weary,
> Fighting with the powers of sin.
> Clothe us in thy shining armour,
> Place thy good sword in our hand;
> Teach us how to wield it, fighting
> Onward towards the heavenly land.
>
> *J. W. Reeks, 1849–1900*

Suggested hymns
Fight the good fight; Mine eyes have seen the glory; Soldiers of Christ, arise; We are marching in the light of God.

St Mark the Evangelist   25 April   This Must
Take Place   Prov. 15.28–33 or Acts 15.35–41;
Ps. 119.9–16; Eph. 4.7–16; Mark 13.5–13

'When you hear of wars and rumours of wars, do not be alarmed; this must take place, but the end is still to come.' Mark 13.7

St Peter's stenographer

Papias, Bishop of Hierapolis, tells us that Mark was Peter's interpreter and wrote down the apostle's remembrances of the life and ministry of Jesus. If these remembrances form the Gospel of Mark, they tell us that Mark was an able writer and arguably the first to pen a 'Gospel' as we know it. Peter calls him affectionately 'my son Mark' (1 Peter 5.13), but he could also have been the Mark who worked as a missionary for some time with Paul and Barnabas – and whose seeming defection from the mission was the cause of a rift between the two older men, Paul choosing Silas as his new companion, while Barnabas took Mark on another mission.

In Gethsemane

It's thought that Mark slips a bit of autobiography into his Gospel, when he describes the young man in Gethsemane on the night of Jesus' arrest; grabbed by one of the soldiers, he wriggles free and races off into the darkness, leaving his loincloth in his would-be captor's hands (Mark 14.51–52). Perhaps this episode contributed to Mark's giving such prominence in his Gospel to the Passion, and to the sayings of Jesus relating to the End of the world. His writing moves quickly, urgently: obviously he wrote at the behest of a man who knew he was near the end of his life, but who wanted his message recorded to help those who had not had the privilege of being with Jesus. We can almost hear the aged Peter, in constant danger of martyrdom at Rome, saying: 'Mark, my son, write quickly, but be accurate; this is exactly what happened, and what the Lord said. People must know, when I am no longer here to tell them.'

Our record

It would be good if those who write diaries and (auto)biographies about lives not lived for Christ spent as much or more energy in sharing the gospel. There has only been one life lived that has the capacity to save the world – and this is the life we should be publishing. Our personal record is written in heaven, by the Almighty, and he stands in no need of copyright infringement. It's Christ's record that matters. Mark has given us the one we need; it is of no account that his autobiography is not available. We are all here to promote Christ, not ourselves – and Mark gives us valuable material for that promotion. His is a Jesus who is also on an urgent mission: to seek and to save the lost. So Mark (and Peter) go to no pains to give us the birth stories, but begin with the preaching of John and the start of Jesus' own mission.

Mark's is simple, unsophisticated Greek, and he writes for those with little or no knowledge of his subject. His writing ends abruptly, as the resurrection has become a reality, in the middle of a sentence (Mark 16.8). Did Peter die at this point? Or was he arrested? Did Mark write more, and if so was the ending lost, or destroyed? It is one of the unsolved mysteries of history.

But enough of the Gospel survives to help us and others to glory.

Suggested hymns
Christ is the world's true light; For the might of thine arm, we bless thee; Lord, thy word abideth; Meekness and majesty.

SS Philip and James, Apostles   2 May
(transferred from 1 May)   'We Will Be Satisfied Then'   Isa. 30.15–21; Ps. 119.1–8; Eph. 1.3–10; John 14.1–14

'Philip said to [Jesus], "Lord, show us the Father, and we will be satisfied." Jesus said to him, "Have I been with you all this time, Philip, and you still do not know me? Whoever has seen me has seen the Father. How can you say, 'Show us the Father'?"' John 14.8–9

An earnest enquirer
Philip was a native of Bethsaida, who is mentioned in John's Gospel as bringing the somewhat sceptical Nathanael (Bartholomew) to meet Jesus and thereafter to join his mission team. Willing to ask questions on his own or others' behalf, Philip's enquiries were used by Jesus to increase faith at the feeding of the multitude, and

also in today's reading, where almost certainly Philip voices a question which the other disciples had been discussing. Thereafter, we know nothing more of this Philip, though a deacon of the same name surfaces in Acts, where he converts the Ethiopian chancellor of Candace's court (Acts 8).

James the Less
Called 'the Less' to distinguish him from the brother of John, this James was a relative of Jesus, while the other led the early Church in Jerusalem, suffering martyrdom under Herod in or around the year 62. The son of Alphaeus, James the Less may also be 'James the younger', whose mother Mary was at the cross on Good Friday (Mark 15.40).

Christian satisfaction
Philip had sought 'satisfaction', cast-iron assurance of what God had promised and Jesus had taught. Yet his question earned a gentle rebuke, for Jesus told him it was obsolete: Philip was asking for what had already been revealed to him.

With two thousand or more years of Christian history behind us, we are still good at asking God questions, some of the answers to which have already been revealed – in Scripture, or by experience or personal revelation. It may be natural to seek more assurance, more satisfaction, yet God still reserves much of what we desire, until glory.

> When by his grace I shall look on his face,
> I shall be satisfied then.
>
> Ed Nathan

Shall we? Or by that time shall we want to know more, see more, do more, in glory? If we have not looked on the face of Christ – in the needy, the sick, the destitute – on earth, shall we see him in heaven? What is Christian satisfaction, but the knowledge that our Lord loves us enough to die for us? God at work in Christ's Holy Spirit is the 'satisfaction' that stands between the world and eternity.

Our varied mission
Philip's mission may have taken him far from Jerusalem. James' may have been more localized. Whether our own mission spans

the globe or is concentrated on the home-front, may God give us the spiritual energy to keep asking, to keep seeking more and more satisfaction. When we have stopped asking, we shall (spiritually speaking) have stopped living. If we cannot be enthusiastic for more revelations, more enabling, more divine encouragement, we shall be like those Laodiceans of the first century who were so lukewarm as to be ordinary (Rev. 3.16).

Suggested hymns
Give me oil in my lamp; In full and glad surrender; Make me a channel of your peace; Seek ye first the kingdom of God.

St Matthias the Apostle 14 May **If**
Isa. 22.15–25; Ps. 15; Acts 1.15–26; John 15.9–17

'[Jesus said] "If you keep my commandments, you will abide in my love, just as I have kept my Father's commandments and abide in his love."'
John 15.10

That two-letter word
That little two-letter word 'If' stands between what we do and don't do, what happens and doesn't happen. If the lot had not fallen on Matthias, what then? Would we have not kept his feast? If no lot had been cast, would the Church have been different even though there were eleven instead of twelve at the helm? In any case, James' martyrdom in or near AD 62 left the Twelve incomplete. But the lot was cast, and it fell on Matthias. We don't know any more about him, other than that he had been a disciple of Jesus, and that a Gospel bearing his name circulated for a time before dropping into history.

Ecclasiastical formalities
Archbishops, bishops, archdeacons and the rest of the Church's hierarchy, are replaced today as they die or retire – for we have built up a formal establishment over the centuries, which is seen in its perpetuation to give stability to the Church. Whether lots are cast, advertisements answered, shortlists shortened, or invitations sent out, with each appointment one person is chosen and others are not. However much the word 'rejection' is avoided, there is

often still disappointment and sometimes a real sense of unfulfilled vocation among those not chosen for certain positions. But today we focus on Matthias, the 'winner', who would certainly feel blessed at having been chosen. God's power at work could be seen in the method used for election, rather than human beings being seen to show partiality and preference.

Selection
'If I'd been selected . . .' And the inference today is sometimes: 'I felt God was calling me to serve him in such-and-such a post. If he was, why wasn't I chosen? Perhaps he didn't want me to have the job? So whose voice did I hear?' And the two-letter word has, before we know it, sparked off all sorts of doubts and heart-searchings.

Before the negativity takes root, we'd do well to remember our Lord's own use of this same infuriating, intriguing and surprisingly innocent little word: 'If you love me, keep my commandments.' He tied it into his laws, in a way that diffuses the angst and frustration that so often accompany the world's use of 'if'. *If* we've been (or think we've been) unfairly treated, remember how much more Jesus suffered, and how he was big enough to pray for his enemies. *If* we're looking for an excuse not to do some work for God, remember how hard Jesus worked, for us.

If, if, if – such a *silly* word! Yet it wraps itself around every challenge of every moment. 'If you love me . . .', Jesus whispers, 'you'll do this, that, or whatever . . . because, *if* you don't, it means you don't love me!'

Wow!

The biggest 'if'
From Jesus' teaching in Matthew 24.14 and Mark 13.10, we can infer the biggest 'if' of all: IF we don't get the gospel published in every nation, will the End of the world be delayed? Will Satan have more time to cause havoc?

Before the questions go any further, hadn't we better press on with publishing the gospel? IF not . . .

Suggested hymns
A charge to keep I have; I heard the voice of Jesus say; In full and glad surrender; Jesus, still lead on.

St Augustine, First Archbishop of Canterbury
605   26 May   **No Turning Back**   Isa. 49.22–25;
Ps. 98; 1 Thess. 2.2b–8; Matt. 13.31–33

*'[Jesus said] "The kingdom of heaven is like yeast that a woman took
and mixed in with three measures of flour until all of it was leavened."'*
Matthew 13.33

Setting out
In 596, Pope Gregory the Great, eager to evangelize the British,
sent Augustine, Prior of St Andrew's monastery in Rome, with 40
monks to England. But as they journeyed through France, they
were so disheartened by stories of the appalling religious situation
in England that the monks despatched Augustine back to Rome
to ask the Pope to abort the mission. Gregory, however, brushed
Augustine's plea aside, declaring: 'Better not to set out on a mission, than to give up before that mission is accomplished!' Duly
chastened, Augustine returned to France and rejoined his monks,
who were at least somewhat cheered that Gregory had persuaded
in the meantime a group of French priests to swell the mission
team.

The arrival
They sailed across the Channel, arriving in Kent in 597. Augustine
was welcomed by King Ethelbert who was still a pagan although
married to Bertha, the Christian daughter of the King of Paris.
Within a short while, Ethelbert was baptized, and Augustine was
consecrated Archbishop of the English. He set up his See at Canterbury, later founding two more Sees, London and Rochester.

He laboured for seven years in England, but at his death in 605
much of the land was still pagan, and some of the bishops in Wales
and the south-west were refusing to alter their Celtic practices.

Little return
The seeds had been sown, and Augustine's successors would see
the great benefits that his labours had initiated. But he himself
may have considered there was little visible return before his death
– as can happen today. If we are battling in our Christian witness,
we need not assume that we are in the wrong place. Augustine
had very convincingly been sent to England. He knew he was in
the place where God wanted him to be – the right man in the

right area at the right time. Others would build on the foundations he laid; just as others will build on ours. The scale of the returns we see in our lifetime is not as important as the knowledge that we are where God has chosen.

Keeping on
It's tempting, when we run up against problems, to turn back or take another direction, even to persuade ourselves that God is pointing us to another task. Had Augustine resumed his duties as Prior of St Andrews (assuming that Gregory had not appointed a successor immediately), no doubt he would have done a good work. But an even greater work was waiting for him at Canterbury. The devil knew that, and thus tried to prevent his continuing the journey to England. Very often a setback is the prelude to a success, as the devil pulls out all the stops in an effort to prevent us from doing God's work. 'Beware when all men speak well of you!' warned Jesus at one point. When everything is going swimmingly, we may in fact pause to consider why Satan is not interested in rocking the boat!

Suggested hymns
For I'm building a people of power; Oft in danger, oft in woe; Put thou thy trust in God; Spirit of God, as strong as the wind.

Visit of the Blessed Virgin Mary to Elizabeth
31 May   **Loving Help**   Zeph. 3.14–18; Ps. 113; Rom. 12.9–16; Luke 1.39–49 [50–56]

'In those days Mary set out and went with haste to a Judaean town in the hill country, where she entered the house of Zechariah and greeted Elizabeth.' Luke 1.39–40

Mother-talk
Mary and Elizabeth were neither the first nor the last expectant mothers to get together to share their joys and hopes. There is something very precious about being the holder of a growing life – and the two women, though years apart in age, would have much to share. But primarily they would share the wonderful ways in which God was working in their lives: two women, two

miracles, two babies. Elizabeth was well past child-bearing age, while Mary was a virgin. Both boys, as yet unborn, had already been named by the angels. And both (though their mothers did not as yet know this) would grow up to be known the world over.

As Mary greeted her cousin, Elizabeth felt John spring for joy in her womb. What an opening to the visit! And Mary stayed for three months, until John was born – by which time her own pregnancy would be well advanced. The extra pair of hands, as well as the companionship, would be valuable to Elizabeth, and Mary would see at first hand what an exciting time were the last three months of pregnancy.

Sharing joy
We are sometimes much more ready to share our sorrows than our joys. It has been said that one tells one's friends a sorrow, but only one's *best* friend a joy. What a shame to be so chary of spreading good news!

Since the angel had told Mary about Elizabeth's condition, the inference is that the older woman had not then told Mary. Was Elizabeth nervous that it could be a dream, a 'phantom pregnancy'? Was she afraid that people would laugh, or sneer, at her claiming pregnancy at her age? Mary's visit, acknowledged at the outset by the unborn John, would do much to give Elizabeth confidence. And Mary stayed to give her all the help she could, which tells us a lot about the woman whom God had chosen to be the mother of his Son.

Motherhood
The mission of motherhood has altered relatively little, although, in the so-called sophisticated West, births can be more traumatic than in far less affluent countries. Expectant mothers today may be hedged around with medical and social services; but these are no excuse for not visiting with the carriers of new life. The sheer tension of waiting and expecting can make nine months seem much longer. Every mother will empathize with Mary's state and feelings by the time she came to the night of Jesus' birth; yet, but for her time spent with Elizabeth, it could have been even more traumatic.

Ministry to the expectant
Every Christian, in a way, is expectant – of glory, of seeing Jesus, of moving on in eternity to greater things – and Bible groups,

worship and praise are no doubt already geared for this. But how, as a parish, do we witness and minister to our expectant mums?

Today, with its special focus, is also a good time to focus on mums – not half a world away, but on the home front.

Suggested hymns
Angelus ad virginem; For Mary, mother of the Lord; Maiden, yet a mother (*WH*); O Mother blest, whom God bestows (*WH*). (*WH* = Westminster Hymnal)

Thomas Ken, Bishop of Bath and Wells, Hymn-writer 1711   8 June   Fisher of Men
Jer. 9.23–24; Ps. 15; 2 Cor. 4.1–10; Matt. 24.42–46

'[Jesus said] "Who then is the faithful and wise slave, whom his master has put in charge of his household, to give the other slaves their allowance of food at the proper time? Blessed is that slave whom his master will find at work when he arrives." ' Matthew 24.45–46

Early associations
Ken was born in 1637, at Little Berkhamstead, but lost his parents when still quite young and went to live with his sister, Anne, who was married to the 'compleat angler' author, Isaac Walton. While Isaac pursued writing and fishing, Ken's interests were directed into the Church, taking holy orders after Oxford and being appointed chaplain to Bishop Morley at Winchester.

He tutored generations of students at Winchester College, where he composed many hymns, two of which continue to be favourites, 'Glory to thee, my God, this night' and 'Awake, my soul, and with the sun'. He sang the doxology of these at least three times a day for the rest of his life.

Baptismal healing
While chaplain at Winchester, Ken baptized a five-year-old boy at the church of St John-in-the-Stoke. The boy had been deaf for several years, was paralysed, and was also prone to epileptic fits. After his baptism, he spoke clearly for the first time in his life: 'My name is Matthew. Dr Ken baptized me.' Ever afterwards, he could walk and talk normally and never suffered another fit.

Fishing for souls

While his uncle mused on the banks of Derbyshire's River Dove, Thomas Ken beavered away, fishing for souls first at Winchester and then as Bishop of Bath and Wells: quietly, conscientiously, able to relate to young and old alike, and determined that no soul should be denied a knowledge of Jesus for any lack of zeal on Ken's part.

His example is surely an inspiration to today's Christians to hone their fishing skills, as 'faithful and wise slaves' working out Christ's commission, giving others 'their allowance of food at the proper time'. The 'food' here is the word of God, the 'time' every minute that God allows us on earth. We are where we are, because he has placed us here; we are what we are, because he has called and chosen us. We may long to be somewhere else: if it's his will, he will make this possible; if not, we are to accept our present situation. We may look at others and wish we were more like them; perhaps, if we knew everything about them, we'd see why God has made us different. Our mission is unique. Let us value this singularity, and make it the best mission we can. If we fall down on any part of it, God will find someone else to do it – but they won't accomplish it in quite the way we could, because God designed it for us, with loving care to bring out what he knows is in us.

'Does God think I can do such-and-such?' we may ask, incredulously, as new challenges come to meet us. No, God doesn't *think*; he *knows* we can do it, in Christ's strength. So, where's the point in arguing otherwise?

Suggested hymns

Awake, my soul, and with the sun; Forth in thy name, O Lord, I go; Glory to thee my God this night; Like a mighty river flowing.

St Columba, Abbot of Iona, Missionary 597
9 June   Lighting the Lamp   Isa. 61.1–3; Ps. 34; 1 Thess. 2.2–12; Luke 12.32–37

'[Jesus said] "Be dressed for action, and have your lamps lit; be like those who are waiting for their master to return from the wedding

banquet, so that they may open the door for him as soon as he comes and knocks." ' Luke 12.35–36

Spreading the word
Born in Co. Donegal, Columba grew up with a love of the Scriptures, and for 15 years after ordination preached to his countrymen and founded many monasteries including those of Derry, Kells and Durrow. Hour after hour was spent in copying the Gospels, much of the Pauline corpus and the Psalms. Copyright laws were not as strict as today, but Columba's work provoked a dispute between rival clans, and he deemed it expedient in 563 to sail to Scotland, where on the Isle of Iona he founded the monastery still visited today by many pilgrims.

The Iona base
Iona became the centre of Celtic Christianity, and daughter-houses were founded on the Scottish mainland as well as in England. Still Columba travelled widely, from house to house, and yet he made time for continuing his copying of the Scriptures. On 8 June 597, working on his beloved psalter, he came to the verse, 'Those who seek the Lord lack no good thing' (Ps. 34.10). Feeling suddenly tired, he laid down his pen and told his cousin Baithin to finish the work. He died in his sleep the following day.

Ready and waiting
Filling each day with work for God, completing each task as best we can, committing the future to God's care, and living the present to the full, keeps us in 'ready-and-waiting' alertness for his directions, his guidance – and perhaps his coming before we go to glory. The method of his coming may surprise us: the fact of it should not. Suppose he came today? Would he find us about his business? Or tonight? Would we be sleeping the deep sleep of weariness, the broken sleep of worry, or the peaceful rest of a day's work well done?

Would we greet him with apprehension, or joy? Or would we think it was someone or something else?

Are we looking for completely new employment hereafter, or a continuing of our present work? Or a blissful (but perhaps rather boring) rest? Oh, Lord, surprise us with joy!

Perhaps there will be a new gospel to preach, new worlds to

evangelize, new methods to learn, new beings to meet ... Oh, Lord, surprise us with joy!

Thrilling with anticipation
Since there will be 'new heavens and a new earth', we shall not see our present world replicated in eternity. With such a new prospect, God is inviting us to thrill with anticipation. We shall probably meet St Columba: will he be evangelizing? founding new congregations? We may even be helping him – and perhaps we shall remember this day, back on earth, when we focused on his early ministry in Ireland, and then on Iona and the British mainland.

Suggested hymns
I bind unto myself today; I cannot tell why he whom angels worship; Inspired by love and anger; Spirit of God, as strong as the wind.

St Barnabas the Apostle   11 June
The Encourager   Job. 29.11–16; Ps. 112; Acts 11.19–30; John 15.12–17

'News of this came to the ears of the church in Jerusalem, and they sent Barnabas to Antioch. When he came and saw the grace of God, he rejoiced, and he exhorted them all to remain faithful to the Lord with steadfast devotion; for he was a good man, full of the Holy Spirit and of faith. And a great many people were brought to the Lord.' Acts 11.22–24

'I believe in him'
Had Barnabas not spoken up for Paul, at the outset of his ministry, Peter and the others may have taken more convincing of the genuineness of Paul's conversion (Acts 9.27). This is our introduction to this man of encouragement. Then in today's reading, Barnabas is at it again, bolstering the faith of the folk in Antioch. Thank God that the Jerusalem Church had been guided to send such an affirming and strengthening disciple! 'Take my word for it, Paul is a changed man!' – and the disciples, taking the word of Barnabas, had realized that in the future when an encourager was needed, he was the man; history has shown how wise they were.

Barnabas the Cypriot

Barnabas was a Levite, from Cyprus; and in later days, when he and Paul went their separate ways after the dispute over John Mark (whom Barnabas again defended, giving encouragement to the younger man) Barnabas went back 'home' again to Cyprus with Mark (Acts 15.39). Today a little church with a pretty cupola stands on the island over the grave where tradition has it that Barnabas is buried.

'Christian' Antioch

Syrian Antioch, where Barnabas so encouraged the believers, was where the disciples were first called 'Christians' (Acts 11.26): a tribute to our saint's dedicated work there. Rather than be called 'Disciples of Barnabas' – which would have been perfectly natural, cf., e.g., Matt. 9.14) – they took (or were bidden to take) the name of their Lord.

Would our lives stand up to us walking about with the placard, 'I am a Christian'? The implication is there, for example, when we march in the Procession of Witness on Palm Sunday or Good Friday – yet some Christians are even too shy to join in these processions. May we remember Barnabas and the first 'Christians' of Antioch, and never be slow in standing up and out for Jesus.

Affirming others

May we also, on 'Barnaby Bright', as this day (in the old calendar, the longest of the year) used to be called, resolve to 'do a Barnabas', and affirm and encourage others in their ministry. This in itself is a valuable ministry, and may make the difference between a person's staying the course or giving up in despair. Can't each of us recall some words of encouragement that made a mountain of difference for us? They may have come from a trusted friend, or a stranger – or, heaping coals of fire on our heads, from someone whom either we had wronged, or who had a grudge against us, yet who was big enough to bridge the gap and cheer us on.

The disciples at Antioch were going great guns, but that was no reason for withholding encouragement; we are never so self-sufficient as to stand in need of 'encouragement-deprivation': affirmation is as vital when life is going well as in the bad patches. Remember when the first disciples returned from their initial mission; elated with the work's success, they clustered round Jesus, bursting with news of exorcisms, healings and the like. And Jesus

crowned their euphoria with a tremendous helping of encouragement: 'I watched Satan fall from heaven like a flash of lightning,'
he told them (Luke 10.18).

Would that our Lord could encourage us in such a way!

Suggested hymns
Courage, brother, do not stumble; Happy are they, they that love
God; Help us to help each other, Lord; When I needed a neighbour.

St Alban, First Martyr of Britain *c.* 250
22 June   A Life for a Life   Wisd. 3.1–3; Ps. 63;
2 Tim. 2.3–7; John 12.24–26

'[Jesus said] *"Those who love their life lose it, and those who hate their*
life in this world will keep it for eternal life. Whoever serves me must
follow me, and where I am, there will my servant be also. Whoever serves
me, the Father will honour." ' *John 12.25–26*

A brave man
Alban was a soldier in the Roman city of Verulamium (now
St Albans, Hertfordshire) around the middle of the third century.
One day, a Christian priest sought sanctuary from persecution in
his house. Alban took him in and fed him. Meanwhile, the priest
made such a good job of teaching him the faith that Alban was
converted. When eventually soldiers came in search of the priest,
Alban exchanged clothes with him and let himself be arrested,
while the priest escaped. The saint was tortured before being martyred, and today many pilgrims still visit his shrine in the cathedral
at St Albans.

Laying down one's life
Greater love has no one than to lay down one's life for a friend,
Jesus taught, and Alban paid the highest possible price of love, in
facilitating the escape of the priest. One inevitably thinks of a
similar sacrifice, some seventeen centuries later, when Maximilian
Kolbe – a priest himself – gave his life for that of a fellow prisoner,
Francis Gajowniczek, in Auschwitz concentration camp. Our own
struggles may seem minor by comparison, but if we can give glory
through them to God, they are worth every second. The trial may

cost us time, position, wealth, health, but it probably won't go so far as to make a martyr out of us. God is not looking for heroics, but steadfast, calm stickability. The world today has to a large extent refined its torture into ridicule and indifference. Both of these, if long continued, threaten to sap a Christian's strength and enthusiasm: the little niggles and heartaches wear the spirit just a little every day. That is why we need to keep our prayer-lines open to God, to seek his grace and his strength at the first sign of trouble; to put him between us and the foe; to draw strength from his love. Only thus shall we keep our spiritual equilibrium. Otherwise, the niggles will grow into worries, and the worries into full-blown fear.

A healthy mind

Especially when we are sick, niggles grow out of all proportion with the speed of lightning – which is why it's important constantly to tap into God's healing power. We need to pray for grace to keep sickness and disease from our bodies. God is not unmindful of such prayers; though he may respond in a way other than that for which we are looking. If in fact he allows the sickness to persist, we can be assured that prayer will bring the grace necessary to fight the devil. Prayer, at its simplest, simply means we are not fighting alone.

Those whom we help

In return for all the help God freely gives to us, we must freely give to others – not seeking to know how they use it, but trusting God to build on his love-investment, through us and then through them. Alban's priest may have converted many more, with his hard-won freedom; but even if he died before any further ministry, our saint's conversion and sacrifice would have been worthwhile.

Suggested hymns

A new commandment I give unto you; Come, let us sing of a wonderful love; Love divine, all loves excelling; Love is his word.

Birth of John the Baptist   24 June   Strong in Spirit

Isa. 40.1–11; Ps. 85.7–13; Acts 13.14b–26 or Gal. 3.23–29; Luke 1.57–66, 80

'The child grew and became strong in spirit, and he was in the wilderness until the day he appeared publicly to Israel.' Luke 1.80

Gaining strength

'Each trial will make you the stronger,' runs the old gospel hymn – and we understand this perfectly, as life advances and the Lord helps us through one test after another. Looking back, we may wonder how ever we came through: we didn't, in our strength; it was God-in-us, kicking the 'im' out of 'impossible'.

But John had become spiritually strong from an early age. By the time he was thirty or so, he was at the peak of his ministry. It had to be so, for his life would be short, yet long enough to accomplish the work God had willed. We don't know the details of John's wilderness preparation – perhaps it was as devil-ridden as that of Jesus himself. Perhaps, since Elizabeth and Zechariah had been old by the time John was born, his parents had died long before the start of his ministry. Had God led the boy/young man into the wilderness into seclusion or to rigorous testing? We can be sure that with such a unique vocation as the forerunner of the Lord, God would have John's preparation worked out with divine precision and forethought.

Our vocation

With no less precision and forethought, God is also preparing us for our vocation and mission. Most of us will have a longer preparation than John, because we shall live longer. Day after day, the Lord by challenges and trials is working on the strengthening of our spirits. We may feel the testing is too rigorous. Or we may think we should be more involved, more committed, more challenged. We can let God be the judge of what we need at any time. But once we are convinced that he is calling us to further mission, then we should go for it in faith. There would come a day in the wilderness when God made it known to John that the time for public ministry had come – and it would be of little use the Baptist protesting that he wasn't ready, or that he'd 'never done it before', or that he wouldn't know what to say. God would continually prod until John got up and got busy with his preaching.

Our tasks, as our strength
It's similarly no use our telling God that we need more spiritual stamina before we'll do whatever he is prodding us to do. Procrastination is, in such a case, sinful. When God calls, he gives the grace and the strength for whatever task he is calling. The fact that we 'feel' unready or inadequate is irrelevant. God is ready, and he is absolutely adequate for the job. If we spent less time in getting physical tests for this, that or the other undertaking or ailment, and more time in trusting God to give us the strength we need, we'd save the NHS a lot of time and ourselves a lot of angst.

John's obedience
Whether he 'felt' adequate or not, John answered God's call; and from the relatively few details we have, we can believe that John didn't spend much time in sitting down and brooding about his 'feelings'. Eating simply, dressing simply, living simply, he simply said 'Yes' to God, and found himself haranguing Pharisees, soldiers and lordly Sadducees, as well as the crowds in general, declaring that 'The time is fulfilled, and the kingdom of God has come near; repent, and believe in the good news' (Mark 1.15).

Suggested hymns
Bright the vision that delighted; Oh, the love of my Lord is the essence; On Jordan's bank the Baptist's cry; The great forerunner of the Lord.

St Irenaeus, Bishop of Lyons, Teacher of the Faith c. 200 28 June Defender of the Faith
Wisd. 7.7–10, 15–16; Ps. 34.2 Peter 1.16–21;
Luke 11.33–36
'First of all you must understand this, that no prophecy of scripture is a matter of one's own interpretation, because no prophecy ever came by human will, but men and women moved by the Holy Spirit spoke from God.' 2 Peter 1.20–21

Third-generation believer
Irenaeus was Christianly proud of the fact that he had known Bishop Polycarp of Smyrna (d. 155), who in turn had known

St John. 'The things we learned in childhood are part of our soul,' he once wrote; and he was a staunch defender of the faith as given in the four canonical Gospels. (This was a time when 'apocryphal' Gospels were being ventilated, and new believers were at times confused with the increased literature purporting to be 'Lives of Christ' or 'Memories of the Apostles'.)

In 177, the 90-year-old Bishop Pothinus of Lyons was martyred, and Irenaeus was elected in his place. It was a relatively peaceful episcopate, though Irenaeus was often in argument against the Gnostics, who sought knowledge for knowledge's sake. In reply, the Bishop explained the 'Rule of Faith':

For the Church, though dispersed throughout the whole world, even to the ends of the earth, has received from the apostles and disciples this faith: in one God, the Father Almighty, who made the heaven and the earth and the seas and all things that are in them; and in one Christ Jesus, the Son of God, who became incarnate for our salvation; and in the Holy Spirit, who proclaimed through the prophets the dispensations and the advents, and the birth from a virgin, and the passion, and the resurrection from the dead, and the incarnate ascension into heaven of the beloved Christ Jesus, our Lord, and his future manifestation from heaven in the glory of the Father, to sum up all things, and to raise up anew all flesh of the whole human race, in order that to Christ Jesus, our Lord and God and Saviour and King, according to the will of the invisible Father, every knee should bow, of things in heaven, and things in earth, and things under the earth, and that every tongue should confess to him, and that he should execute just judgement towards all; that he may send spiritual wickednesses, and the angels who transgressed and came into a state of rebellion together with the ungodly, and unrighteous, and wicked, and profane among men, into the everlasting fire; but may, as an act of grace, confer immortality on the righteous and holy, and those who have kept his commandments, and have persevered in his love, some from the beginning and others from their repentance, and may surround them with everlasting glory.

Irenaeus, Against the Heresies, *I.10.1*

Our defence
Our defence of the faith today may be couched in less formal terms. Many are 'turned off' by traditional rhetoric, and ask, 'But what does Jesus mean to *you*?' – a question not so far removed from Jesus' to Peter and the other disciples: 'But who do *you* say I am?' (Matt. 16.15).

We may not have Bishop Irenaeus at our side when we answer such a question, but we surely have the same four Gospels that he used – and, even more importantly, the same Holy Spirit of Jesus in us.

Suggested hymns
I heard the voice of Jesus say; Lord Jesus, think on me; Lord, speak to me, that I may speak; Tell out, my soul, the greatness of the Lord.

SS Peter and Paul, Apostles   29 June
God's Breaking-in   Zech. 4.1–6a, 10b–14; Ps. 125; Acts 12.1–11; Matt. 16.13–19

'[Jesus] said to them, "But who do you say that I am?" Simon Peter answered, "You are the Messiah, the Son of the living God." And Jesus answered him, "Blessed are you, Simon son of Jonah! For flesh and blood has not revealed this to you, but my Father in heaven."' Matthew 16.15–17

From faith to faith
Peter had faith. Of that there was no doubt. Called from the local fishing fleet at Galilee, he was *primus inter pares* of the Twelve, and specially inspired to come out with this awesome declaration of the messiahship of Jesus. With the temporary default of the Passion denials behind him, he would go from faith to (more) faith; taking the gospel to the Gentiles, until – as tradition has it – as Rome's first bishop, he was martyred.

Paul's conversion, on the road to Damascus, saw the end of his time of persecuting the Church, and the beginning of what proved to be the most energetic and wide-ranging mission yet – ending, as Peter's, with martyrdom at Rome.

Today, we honour both of these giants of the faith, in comparison with whom our own mission may seem far less exciting. But it is ours, not theirs. And every mission has the potential to be even more exciting and far wider-ranging than Peter's or Paul's. Our lives are what we make them, albeit within the parameters set by God. Peter could have stayed in the Galilean fishing fleet. Paul could have continued his chosen path of persecution. The New Testament would probably have looked much slimmer, but the Church would have carried on. Yet, because both apostles answered the call of Christ, God used them beyond their greatest dreams, making extraordinary Christians out of them both.

According to tradition, each apostle met death bravely, in the strength of Christ. Peter's martyrdom, in keeping with his life as recorded in the Gospels, where he alternately faltered and recovered, came after an extraordinary encounter. Persecution of Christians having been stepped up, he was advised by his friends to seek for a while the comparative safety of the countryside; but as he travelled out through the suburbs of Rome, he met a man walking towards the city. '*Quo vadis*? (Where are you going?)' he asked the stranger (inquisitive as ever!). 'I am going to Rome, to be crucified – again,' was the quiet reply – and, overcome with shame, Peter retraced his steps into the city, where he bravely met martyrdom.

Paul, though his Roman citizenship entitled him to the more speedy death by beheading, nevertheless chose to be crucified like his Master. The ministry of both apostles was tremendous, but they had their differences: such as over the question of Gentile admission to the faith (Gal. 2.11). We too may disagree with aspects of another's ministry; do we ignore the divergence and walk away in a huff; or sit down together and argue it out (cf. Isa. 1.18)? Remember when the disciples complained to Jesus that another man was performing exorcisms in Jesus' name. 'We tried to stop him', John reported, 'because he was not following us' (Mark 9.38). But Jesus would not negate a ministry being performed in his name.

As we celebrate the lives and varied ministries of Peter and Paul, we may reflect on how wide our own parameters are set.

Suggested hymns

Come and see the shining hope; For the might of thine arm, we bless thee; Jesus, stand among us; Jesus, where'er thy people meet.

296

St Thomas the Apostle   3 July (or transferred to 4 July)   **Apostle to India**   Hab. 2.1–4; Ps. 31.1–6; Eph. 2.19–22; John 20.24–29

'But Thomas (who was called the Twin), one of the twelve, was not with them when Jesus came. So the other disciples told him, "We have seen the Lord."' John 20.24–25a

The empty chair

Thomas was 'one of the twelve', and as such had responsibilities and obligations – and surely one of these was to have kept company with the others on such a dramatic day as that of the resurrection. He may have had other business, or a family commitment; for whatever reason, his seat was empty that evening when the others met: and look what he missed! We may think the odd meeting now and then doesn't matter; yet if it's a meeting which we are entitled to attend, there will be something in it for us and we shall be the poorer for not being there. Thomas had a whole week to regret his absence, before he learnt his lesson. He was duly with the others on the following 'Sunday', when the forgiving Jesus convincingly answered his disbelief.

The missionary

According to tradition, Thomas took the gospel to India, where he suffered martyrdom and is thought to be buried at Mylapore, where Christians still call themselves 'Christians of St Thomas'. In the New Testament Apocrypha, there is a Gospel bearing Thomas' name. Discovered near Chenoboskian in Upper Egypt in 1945, it comprises over 100 logia ascribed to Jesus. It begins:

> These are the secret words which the living Jesus spake, and Didymus Judas Thomas wrote them down.
> (1) And he said: He who shall find the interpretation of these words shall not taste of death.
> (2) Jesus said: He who seeks, let him not cease seeking until he finds; and when he finds he will be troubled, and if he is troubled he will be amazed, and he will reign over the All.
> (3) Jesus said: If those who lead you say unto you: Behold, the Kingdom is in heaven, then the birds of the heaven will be before you. If they say unto you: It is in the sea, then the fish will be before you. But the Kingdom is within you, and it is

outside of you. When you know yourselves, then shall you be known, and you shall know that you are the sons of the living Father. But if you do not know yourselves, then you are in poverty, and you are poverty.

(4) Jesus said: The man aged in his days will not hesitate to ask a little child of seven days about the place of life, and he shall live. For there are many first who shall be last, and they shall become a single one.

(5) Jesus said: Know what is before thy face, and what is hidden from thee shall be revealed unto thee; for there is nothing hidden which shall not be made manifest.

(6) His disciples asked him: Wilt thou that we fast? And how shall we pray? Shall we give alms? And what rules shall we observe in eating? Jesus said: Do not lie; and that which you hate, do not do. For all things are revealed before heaven. For there is nothing hidden which shall not be manifest, and there is nothing covered which shall remain without being uncovered.

Our Christian duty
May we ever be mindful of our Christian duty, as we celebrate Thomas' feast today. 'We have seen the Lord' is a wonderful thing to hear from someone else; it's even more wonderful when we can declare it ourselves.

Suggested hymns
Colours of day; Come, ye faithful, raise the strain; Jesus, these eyes have never seen; Like a mighty river flowing.

St Benedict of Nursia, Abbot of Monte Cassino, Father of Western Monasticism
c. 550   11 July   **Master Builder**   Prov. 2.1–6; Ps. 119.57–64; 1 Cor. 3.10–11; Luke 18.18–22

'According to the grace of God given to me, like a skilled master builder I laid a foundation, and someone else is building on it. Each builder must choose with care how to build on it. For no one can lay any foundation other than the one that has been laid; that foundation is Jesus Christ.' 1 Corinthians 3.10–11

The cave monks

Born in Nursia, Umbria, around the year 480, Benedict was sent to Rome for a formal education, but when he was 20 he retreated to a cave in the Subiaco mountains and lived a hermit's life. However, men flocked out to join him, and within a short time he had founded 12 mountain communities each consisting of 12 monks.

In 529, Benedict and a small group of monks moved from Subiaco to Monte Cassino, mid-way between Rome and Naples. On the mountain's summit, he found a temple dedicated to the worship of Apollo. Benedict razed it to the ground and built a monastery in its place, which was to become world famous. Here at Monte Cassino he formulated house laws which, as the Benedictine Rule, was to be taken up by many monastic communities, and noted as much for its practicality as for its spirituality.

Around 550, Benedict died at his beloved Monte Cassino. His Rule continues to be valued by many religious communities today.

In winter, that is from 1 November until Easter, as far as possible the brethren must get up at the eighth hour of the night, so that they rest for a little over half the night, and rise when they have had a good sleep. But the time that remains after 'Vigils' shall be spent in study . . .

As the prophet says, 'Seven times in the day do I praise thee.' We will complete this sacred number seven, if, at lauds, at the first, third, sixth, ninth hours, at vesper time and at compline, we carry out the duties of our service . . .

Idleness is the enemy of the soul. Therefore, at fixed times, the brothers should be busy with manual work, and at other times in holy reading . . .

A mattress, woollen blanket, woollen under-blanket and a pillow, shall be enough bedding. Beds are to be searched frequently by the abbot for private belongings. And, if anyone is found to possess anything he did not receive from the abbot, he shall be very severely disciplined . . .

From the Rule *of Benedict, chs 8, 16, 48, 53*

Taking pains

It was a model Rule, prepared by a man who had also taken great pains in the building of his large monastery: an imposing house, yet simply constructed to facilitate the simple twofold Rule of worship and work.

A hard act to follow? Thousands have managed it.

Suggested hymns
And can it be; Awake, my soul, and with the sun; I need thee every hour; Take my life, and let it be.

St Mary Magdalene   22 July   For Whom Much Is Forgiven   S. of Sol. 3.1–4; Ps. 42.1–7; 2 Cor. 5.14–17; John 20.1–2, 11–18

'But Mary stood weeping outside the tomb. As she wept, she bent over to look into the tomb, and she saw two angels in white, sitting where the body of Jesus had been lying, one at the head and the other at the feet. They said to her, "Woman, why are you weeping?"' John 20.11–13a

More tears?
Well, didn't Mary know how to weep? Having lived the grim existence of a prostitute, the butt of scorn and sarcasm, she would be no stranger to tears. Then Jesus had met her, and had healed her from her addiction to sex; and she would have known the bittersweet taste of tears of joy and release from sin. And then her Lord – for whom she would die – had been crucified, and once more the bottom had dropped out of her world. Yet the gloom had been pierced by a glimmer of light: she could perform one last act of love for him, in coming to the tomb to anoint his body.

And finally, as that last glimmer was darkened, in the discovery of the opened, *empty* tomb – Mary broke down. She was beyond terror; she didn't run from the angels. She just wept, for her world had crashed around her.

In the depths
For us, who know what joy that first Easter Day brought, it is difficult to replicate Mary's utter despair and grief. And why should we? For even hers was soon to be turned to joy ... and then to frustration, when the disciples didn't believe her ... and

then confirmed . . . and doubly confirmed when Pentecost arrived. Mary's life, although we know relatively little from the Gospels, was a series of deep lows and high joys.

Yes, rather like our own lives, though perhaps our highs and lows are not so far apart.

All forgiven
But on this feast day of the Magdalen, we focus on Jesus' complete forgiveness of her purple past: so complete that he gave to Mary as her crowning joy the privilege of being the first person to see him resurrected. If that wasn't convincing evidence that her sins – which had been many – were all forgiven, what was? It tells us that our own sins – big, little, black, white, forgotten and remembered – are dealt with by God: convincingly, completely and absolutely. Why do we need to worry over confessed and forgiven sins, when God has blotted them out of his remembrance? Mary could have chosen not to part with her past – to worry over forgiven sin, for all the world as if she didn't trust Jesus. Had she done anything so stupid, it's certain that she'd have been any-where but at the tomb that morning.

Our gratitude
So, how are we showing our gratitude to God for his forgiveness? Or have we started worrying over something else already?

Suggested hymns
Dear Lord and Father of mankind; Magdalene, thy grief and glad-ness; Thy kingdom come, O God; We sing the praise of him who died.

St James the Apostle 25 July The Able Apostle
Jer. 45.1–5; Ps. 126; Acts 11.27—12.2; Matt. 20.20–28

'But Jesus answered, "You do not know what you are asking. Are you able to drink the cup that I am about to drink?" They said to him, "We are able." He said to them, "You will indeed drink my cup . . ."' Matthew 20.22–23a

A leading question

Neither James nor his brother John would ever have dreamt that their request would become worldwide news. Don't we all hope that at the Great Assize embarrassing words and actions will have been wiped off our slate, by a Father who is merciful and loving? But till kingdom come, people will remember that James and John sought preferential treatment in glory.

It has always been so: humankind has a much worse 'forgettery' for these matters than God. We can reverently believe that Jesus loved James and his brother too much for their misguided words to spoil the friendship. But did he see – with divine foresight – the early martyrdom of James (Acts 12.1ff.), as he replied gently and considerately to the disciples' request?

Ah, James, you're already thinking of glory – soon, so soon, you will be there!

Did Jesus think something of the sort? Oh, surely he knew. But he would not kill his friend before the time by telling James what was in store.

The first apostle to suffer martyrdom

James was the first of the apostles to be martyred, and his death must have been a severe blow to the young Jerusalem church. It would only be natural for the Christians to value as their leader one who had been with Jesus. Called from the fishing fleet at Galilee, James had been one of the 'inner circle', with Peter, Andrew and his own brother John – closer than anyone else (Mary excepted) to Jesus for the duration of his earthly ministry. We can imagine how people would ask him, time and again, for reminiscences of that period.

But someone had to be the leader, in every church that was planted, and Jerusalem was such an important foundation that its leader would have an extra-high profile. James would assume the office, knowing only too well the dangers involved.

A turn-off?

Today, when called to high or prominent office do we assess first the pros and cons? And if the cons are many, do they turn us off accepting the position? How much are we prepared to sacrifice, in the interest of peace and security? Or are we prepared to 'recklessly abandon' to God (as Oswald Chambers, one-time principal of the London Bible College, used to say)? Such reckless abandonment doesn't involve necessarily dramatic heroics, but a confidence and trust in God, that he will see us through, come what may.

There would be no great panoply, no parading in the tasselled robes of the Jewish religious hierarchy, for James as head of the Church in Jerusalem. The Christian Church had yet to elaborate its vestments and liturgy.

Yet James afforded a martyr's crown.

Suggested hymns
Disposer supreme; For all the saints who from their labours rest; For all thy saints, a noble throng; Let saints on earth in concert sing.

SS Anne and Joachim, Parents of the Blessed Virgin Mary 26 July A Quiet Couple
Zeph. 4.14–17; Ps. 127; Rom. 8.28–30; Matt. 13.16–17
'Unless the Lord builds the house, those who build it labour in vain . . . It is in vain that you rise up early and go late to rest, eating the bread of anxious toil; for he gives sleep to his beloved.' Psalm 127.1a, 2

Childlessness
Tradition has it that Joachim lived at Nazareth, and quite early in life fell in love with Anne whom he married. But they had no children, and as time went on they became the butt of scorn and ridicule. In anguish, Joachim went into the wilderness, where he fasted for 40 days as he sought God's will for their marriage.

Anne had also been born in Nazareth, her father Akar having brought his wife there for their daughter's birth. She, like Joachim, was devastated at having no child of their own; but one day, while Joachim was in the wilderness, Anne was praying under a hazel tree, when an angel appeared to her and promised a girl-child.

Anne was around forty when Mary was born. 'She will be known the world over,' the angel had promised Anne. And so it was. According to tradition, Joachim and Anne lived to see Mary give birth to Jesus, though Joachim died soon after the Presentation of Christ in the Temple (Candlemas), (Luke 2.22ff.).

Simple trust

Even at Christmas it's easy to overlook this quiet couple who had nurtured the blessed Virgin, had parented she who was to become *Theotokos* (Mother of God), and who with dignity and trust placed themselves in the will of God, content for others to take the limelight. Such self-effacement, in the parents of Mary, is exquisitely beautiful, and an indication (if we needed it) of Mary's own nature.

Trust in God

The psalmist had this same trust, in abundance, looking to God for the undergirding of any enterprise – whether a simple act such as going to bed or getting up, or a major work like building a house or guarding a city. Do we trust God on such a wide scale, or only for the mega-miracles we believe are beyond us anyway? We trust him with our lives – but do we trust him to heal our toothache, start the car, find a missing hanky? Do we limit the Lord's help and guidance to the stuff of which sermons are made, while we struggle to Bible study with a migraine, for all the world as if we think God couldn't fix something so unimportant?

When will we learn that the Lord is unlimited? He's not the head of the Holy and Undivided Trinity *plc* – God's 'plc' stands for 'pure loving concern'. Can we, again and again, tell ourselves (and anyone else who will listen): God is limitless. Anne and Joachim believed the angel – and Mary was born. Zechariah and Elizabeth believed – and John the Baptist was born. Mary and Joseph believed – and who doesn't know the result of *their* trust?

May each and all of these miracles increase our own faith.

Suggested hymns

A safe stronghold our God is still; Give me the faith that can remove; I feel the winds of God today; My faith it is an oaken staff.

Mary, Martha and Lazarus, Companions of our Lord 29 July **Good Friends** Isa. 25.6–9; Ps. 49.5–10; Heb. 2.10–15; John 12.1–8

'Six days before the Passover Jesus came to Bethany, the home of Lazarus whom he had raised from the dead. There they gave a dinner for him.

Martha served, and Lazarus was one of those at the table with him.'
John 12.1–2

The value of friendship

They had shared joy and sadness, this little family, with Jesus – and the friendship was deep and lasting. We are blessed with our friends, though often we only truly realize this at their funerals. May God give us the grace to show and tell our appreciation while we still have our friends here with us.

Friendship is a gift from God, immeasurable in value and limit-less in worth. Ever since God looked at creation, and decided that it was 'not good that man should be alone' (Gen. 2.18), we have felt the need of someone to share our lives. Friendships come between all types of people, in all sorts of situations and from all kinds of reasons.

In the Old Testament, one of the most beautiful friendships was that between David and Jonathan. Although Jonathan stood in direct natural line of succession, and could thus have felt aggrieved that David and not he would be king after Saul, he did not admit jealousy into his mind, and actually proved a buffer between David and Saul, which helped the stability of Israel as well as facilitating an uneasy peace between the two men until Saul finally overstepped the mark and descended to consulting a medium.

The mission team

Jesus, at the head of his mission team, valued the companionship and loyalty of his disciples: yet it was essentially a 'teacher – pupil' relationship, even though he called them 'friends'. So often they needed to be taught the fuller meaning of the sermons he preached to the crowds; so often, too, they must have tried his patience, when they seemed not to grasp even simple teaching.

But with the family at Bethany, he would be able to relax, in a home environment, perhaps reminding him of the home where he had grown up in Nazareth. He loved all three of the household: Lazarus, with whom he could talk, as man to man; Mary, who was prepared to listen to his every word, quietly, reverently and thoughtfully; and Martha, eager to make the most of her kitchen skills in turning out the best meals in town. Jesus would surely have appreciated the love that went into her cooking – though on one occasion Martha's kitchen-sinkery overflowed into a complaint about Mary's lack of help, and earned her a rebuke (albeit so gentle) from Jesus.

At a time of tension
When tension was mounting, in the week leading up to his Passion, Jesus sought refuge in the evening with the precious little family in Bethany (Matt. 21.17). Did he prepare his friends for what was about to happen? Perhaps.

For today, let us simply give thanks that these friends were there for Jesus when he needed them.

Suggested hymns
Brother, sister, let me serve you; Help us to help each other, Lord; What a Friend we have in Jesus; When I needed a neighbour.

Transfiguration of our Lord   6 August
Glory Revealed   Dan. 7.9–10, 13–14; Ps. 97; 2 Peter 1.16–19; Luke 9.28–36

'Now about eight days after these sayings, Jesus took with him Peter and John and James, and went up on the mountain to pray. And while he was praying, the appearance of his face changed, and his clothes became dazzling white.' Luke 9.28–29

In communion with God
Even if we don't see a 'glory' round the person, it's nevertheless beautiful to see someone at prayer. Somehow, there is an other-worldliness, as the pray-er, detached from his or her surroundings, concentrates on God. Why don't we pray more? Because the world is ever-ready to distract us.

It's noteworthy, for *Luke*, that Jesus was praying when he was transfigured. Neither Matthew nor Mark mentions this. How did Luke get his information? We do not know. It may have been in one of his written sources, or verbally from Mary or one of the disciples. There are times when we are praying when we lose track of time, or when words run out and we simply rest in God's presence, or when we are consciously listening out for what he may be saying. Perhaps, at those times, were anyone to see us, we too may look different – not transfigured with the radiance of

Jesus, but ... different. Yet perhaps it's part of the mystery of prayer that usually only God sees us at these times.

We are not told whether the disciples were also at prayer. Whatever they were about, the *shekinah*-glory would rivet their attention. Luke implies that they had all but nodded off to sleep before the glory. Perhaps it was a hot day – or it may have been night-time, when the glory would seem even brighter.

From 'the other side'
And from 'the other side' came Moses and Elijah, also brilliant with glory. Luke, again, uses his unique source, in telling us that the three – Jesus, Moses and Elijah – were discussing the coming events (i.e. the Passion) in Jerusalem. It would appear that this was the reason for their coming. We may reverently believe that all of heaven was getting ready to oversee these events, the reason for Jesus' incarnation. It would be totally understandable for God to supplement Jesus' prayers by sending these two Old Testament prophets to encourage him before the ordeal.

But the disciples could not understand. The discussion on a Passion, coming on top of the brilliant glory and two resurrections, was too much for them to take in.

Our 'shocking' God
God is still, in many ways, a 'shocking' God – surprising, jolting us into situations where we so often feel unable to cope. And yet he is *expecting* us to cope; he expected Peter and John and James to benefit from the transfiguration, to accept with joy the fact that the 'dead' in the Lord are not dead; that the hereafter is brilliance and light; that Jesus was soon going to accomplish his mission. God was preparing them for future events on earth and in heaven.

But they couldn't take it in. How do we fare, in the daily challenges God sends?

Suggested hymns
From glory to glory advancing; In days of old on Sinai; There's a light upon the mountains; 'Tis good, Lord, to be here.

St Clare of Assisi, Founder of the Minoresses (Poor Clares) 1253   11 August   True Riches

Hos. 2.14–15, 19–20; Ps. 62; 2 Cor. 4.6–10; John 15.4–10

'For it is the God who said, "Let light shine out of darkness," who has shone in our hearts to give the light of the knowledge of the glory of God in the face of Jesus Christ.' 2 Corinthians 4.6

Taking the veil

Clare Offreduccio was born in 1193, in Assisi, and it was inevitable that she would learn early of the life and work of the local boy turned monk, Francis. His example so inspired her that she thought of leaving home and her considerable fortune for the life of poverty. She was in the church for the Palm Sunday liturgy, when suddenly she felt unable to go forward to receive her palm from the bishop – whereupon the bishop came down from the altar to present it to her. Taking this as a sign, Clare ran away from home, to Francis.

At that time, Francis had not founded a women's convent, and so he sent Clare to live with the Benedictine nuns at Bastia. But in 1215 he established a house for women religious, and appointed Clare as its first abbess. She was to hold the position until her death in 1253. Today, the order she founded, the Poor Clares, has spread to many countries, and continues the work of prayer and service she began, in a world which still needs both.

Family opposition

Clare's family could not understand their daughter's rejection of all that wealth could buy – still less when Clare's sister followed her into the convent. Clare was adamant that little luxuries which could have been accommodated in the convent were forbidden, and was constantly urging her followers towards stricter mortifications. She herself wore a hair shirt and in Lent fasted on bread and water.

In an age when so many luxuries are classed as 'basics' or 'essentials', Clare's example may today seem excessively harsh. We have only to see a disruption in transport services to discover the 'basics' of real life today; bread and toilet rolls are the first to be stockpiled.

The light of God

When we've stopped deciding what is or is not essential, can we evaluate the light of God that we are giving to others? Not hoarding as an essential, for it's not for selfish use, but using it, sharing it, to make others' lives brighter. The vast coffers of the Offreduccio's made that one family's life brighter, no doubt, but the light of Clare's self-abnegating poverty shone far brighter and far longer. Are others' troubles lightened because of what we do and say? If it's a question that's not easy to answer, perhaps we need to get serious with God to discover why.

Making a point for God

Clare's conversion from wealth to poverty, was, even by modern standards, quite dramatic. Whether our own lives make the point as clearly lies with us.

Suggested hymns

All for Jesus, all for Jesus; Be thou my vision; My times are in thy hands; Take my life, and let it be.

The Blessed Virgin Mary (Feast of the Assumption)   15 August   Taken to Glory

Isa. 61.10–11 or Rev. 11.19—12.6, 10; Ps. 45.10–17;
Gal. 4.4–7; Luke 1.46–53

'Then I heard a loud voice in heaven, proclaiming, "Now have come the salvation and the power and the kingdom of our God and the authority of his Messiah, for the accuser of our comrades has been thrown down, who accuses them day and night before our God."' Revelation 12.10

Mother of God

Mary, *Theotokos* (Mother of God), lived to see the resurrection of her Son, and the founding of the Christian Church in Jerusalem. Taken into the care of John the beloved disciple at Calvary, we don't know how long she lived. In the Eastern Orthodox Church her *Dormition* (Falling Asleep) is observed, while the Western (Catholic) Church celebrates her bodily assumption into heaven, although this was only promulgated formally by the Vatican a century or so ago.

There are those who aver that Jesus in life loved his mother so much he would be unlikely to allow her body to see a natural death: therefore Mary's bodily assumption would not only account for the absence of a known grave, but would also be consistent with what we know of her relationship with Jesus from the Gospels.

But whether we subscribe to her assumption or not, we may surely believe that she is presently with Jesus, and loved in glory no less than when she was on earth.

God's mother-love

In Mary, we see the tenderness, purity and sweetness of mother-love that God must also have – for could he create anything unknown to himself? He could have saved the world through Jesus, without involving Mary; but he placed such a high value on the love of a mother, that Jesus was blessed for the whole time he was here with Mary's loyalty, care and devotion.

It's a thousand pities that the fraught time of the Reformation saw many Protestants confusing Mariology (devotion to Mary) with Mariolatry (worship of Mary) – and the Church in the West (Catholic *and* Protestant) is only slowly returning to the simple Marian acknowledgement that the early Church accorded the Mother of our Lord. Jesus loved Mary so tenderly: can we not love her, too, in simple, unconditional affection?

> Shall we not love thee, Mother dear,
> Whom Jesus loves so well?
> And to his glory year by year
> Thy joy and honour tell? . . .
>
> Joy to be Mother of the Lord,
> And thine the truer bliss,
> In every thought and deed and word
> To be for ever his.
>
> And as he loves thee, Mother dear,
> We too will love thee well;
> And to his glory year by year
> Thy joy and honour tell.
>
> Sir H. W. Baker

For Mary, Mother of our Lord; I'll sing a hymn to Mary; O purest
of creatures, sweet Mother, sweet Maid; This is the image of the
Queen.

St Bartholomew the Apostle   24 August
Faithful Follower   Isa. 43.8–13; Ps. 145.1–7;
Acts 5.12–16; Luke 22.24–30

*'[Jesus said] "You are those who have stood by me in my trials; and I
confer on you, just as my Father has conferred on me, a kingdom, so
that you may eat and drink at my table in my kingdom, and you will
sit on thrones judging the twelve tribes of Israel."'* Luke 22.28–30

Standing by
It's believed that Bartholomew is the Nathanael of John's Gospel
(John 1.44f.), whom Philip introduced to Jesus. At the outset cyni-
cal of anyone hailing from Nazareth, Bartholomew was won over
by Jesus' recognition, and became one of the Twelve. Tradition has
it that he suffered martyrdom under King Astyages of Armenia, by
being beheaded; he is often portrayed with a butcher's knife as
his emblem. From a doubtful beginning, Bartholomew had stood
by Jesus, and had made good. We may regret knowing so little
of him, but perhaps one day the years of silence will speak in
glory.

Bartholomew's Gospel
There are several apocryphal writings carrying Bartholomew's
name, the best known of which is the *Gospel of Bartholomew*. The
Venerable Bede acknowledged that this work had been known to
Jerome (fourth century): 'We learn from Heinrich von Herford
that Ludwig the Bavarian was acquainted with the Gospel of
Bartholomew.' In the Gospel, Bartholomew asks Jesus where he
went from the cross, and Jesus replies:

> When I descended with my angels to the underworld, in order
> to dash in pieces the iron bars and shatter the portals of the
> underworld, Hades said to the devil, I perceive that God has
> come down upon the earth. And the angels cried to the mighty

ones: Open your gates, you princes, for the King of glory has come down to the underworld. Hades asked: Who is the King of glory who has come down to us? And when I had descended five hundred steps, Hades began to tremble violently, and said: I believe that God has come down. His strong breath goes before him. I cannot bear it. But the devil said to him: Do not submit, but make yourself strong. God has not come down. But when I had descended five hundred steps more, the strong angels cried out: Open, doors of your prince! Swing open, you gates! . . . Beelzebub replied: It is a prophet, and you think it is God. The prophet has made himself like God . . . But the devil perceived that the Word of the Father had come . . . Hades said: Where shall we hide ourselves from the face of God? . . . And I went in and smote him with a hundred blows and bound him with fetters that cannot be loosed.

Gospel of Bartholomew I.9–20

Jesus' triumph
Whether Bartholomew's Gospel preserves the actual words of Jesus or not, we have Paul's word for it that Jesus did triumph over principalities and powers (e.g. Col. 2.15) – New Testament 'speak' for Satan and his underworld. Alleluia!

Suggested hymns
A charge to keep I have; Christian, seek not yet repose; Judge eternal, throned in splendour; The head that once was crowned with thorns.

St Gregory the Great, Bishop of Rome, Teacher of the Faith 604   3 September
Mission to the Angles   Ecclus. 47.8–11; Ps. 100; 1 Thess. 2.3–8; Mark 10.42–45

'[Jesus said] "For the Son of Man came not to be served, but to serve, and to give his life a ransom for many."' Mark 10.45

Public service
Gregory had a formal education in Rome, and then trained as a civil administrator, before being ordained by Pelagius II and

becoming one of the seven papal deacons. He was despatched to the Court of Constantinople, as the Pope's agent, from 579 to 585, which was an eye-opening experience for the Italian, as he found that the problems and life of the Italian church made little or no impression even on the Patriarch of Constantinople.

A retiring life?

Returning to Rome, Gregory became abbot of the monastery he had earlier converted from his dwelling-house; but his was not to be a secluded life; for one day walking through the city he saw some slaves in the market. They were Saxons, from England. 'Angles,' they replied, when Gregory asked what nationality they were. 'I think you are not Angles, but angels,' he told them – and the desire to evangelize the English was born in his mind.

Eventually, he set out for England, but was almost immediately recalled to Rome, to help in the prayer offensive against the plague. Many fell victim to the disease, including the Pope; and Gregory was elected in his place; so the mission to the English was delegated by Gregory to Augustine.

An energetic pope

As pope, Gregory was tireless, and showed also a charitableness that endeared him even more to the people. He abolished the fees for Christian burial (which had become a burden for the poorer classes that many could not afford). An accomplished musician, Gregory revised the liturgy and wrote many hymns. The Gregorian plainsong chant is still loved today.

Servus servorum

He was able to make a Roman peace with the marauding Lombards, and also to redeem their prisoners, his earlier experience in Constantinople warning him to steer clear of any alliance or co-operation from that quarter. And it was Gregory too, who, in unfeigned humility, coined the phrase that the Bishop of Rome was 'the servant of the servants of God'.

His was a busy life, with far-reaching consequences – not least for England, where Gregory's sending of Augustine saw a See founded at Canterbury, and two more at London and Rochester; and the foundations laid for the Church in England as we know it today.

Small wonder that this energetic and beloved pope carries the title of 'great'.

Suggested hymns
And can it be; And did those feet; Father, hear the prayer we offer; Tell out, my soul, the greatness of the Lord.

Holy Cross Day   14 September   Mystery of the Cross   Num. 21.4–9; Ps. 22.23–28; Phil. 2.6–11; John 3.13–17

'He humbled himself and became obedient to the point of death – even death on a cross.' Philippians 2.8

Stumbling block

To the Greeks it was a mystery, to the Jews a stumbling block. Yet God in his wisdom had the Saviour of the world die in this shockingly shameful way, at the hands of an alien power, in his 'own' country and at the insistence of his 'own' people.

Small wonder that the cross has teased the imagination of so many out of thought. From the apocryphal *Acts of John* (second/third century), we have the 'Revelation of the Mystery of the Cross':

And [my Lord] showed me a Cross of Light firmly fixed, and around the Cross a great crowd, which had no single form; and in it (the Cross) was one form and the same likeness. And I saw the Lord himself above the Cross, having no shape but only a kind of voice; yet not that voice which we know, but one that was sweet and gentle and truly (the voice) of God, which said to me, 'John, there must be one man to hear these things from me; for I need one who is ready to hear.' This Cross of Light is sometimes called Logos by me for your sakes, sometimes mine, sometimes Jesus . . . Christ, a door, a way, bread, seed, salvation, resurrection, Son, Father, Spirit, life, truth, faith, grace, and so it is called for men's sake . . .

The Cross then is that which has united all things by the word and which has separated off what is transitory and inferior, which has also compacted all things into one. But this is not that wooden Cross which you shall see when you go down from here, nor am I the man who is on the Cross . . .

The multitude around the Cross that is not of one form is the inferior nature. And those whom you saw in the Cross – even if they have not yet one form – not every member of him who has come down has yet been gathered together. But when human nature is taken up, and the race that comes to me and obeys my voice, then he who now hears me shall be united with this race and shall no longer be what he now is, but shall be above them as I am now . . .

When he had said these things to me . . . he was taken up without any of the multitude seeing him. And going down I laughed at them all since he had told me what they had said about him, and I held this one thing fast in my mind, that the Lord had performed everything as a symbol and a dispensation for the conversion and salvation of man.

Acts of John 98–100, 102

One day, please God, the true mystery of the Cross will be revealed.

Suggested hymns
Cross of Jesus, Cross of sorrow; On a hill far away; There is a green hill far away; When I survey the wondrous cross.

St Matthew, Apostle and Evangelist
21 September   **Calling All Sinners**   Prov. 3.13–18; Ps. 119.65–72; 2 Cor. 4.1–6; Matt. 9.9–13

'[Jesus] said, "Those who are well have no need of a physician, but those who are sick. Go and learn what this means, 'I desire mercy, not sacrifice.' For I have come not to call the righteous, but sinners." ' Matthew 9.12–13

Matthew's introduction
One wonders how Matthew may have felt at such an introduction to the faith. It had been wonderful to receive and answer the call of Jesus; but how many of us would have wished our sinfulness to be talked about so openly? Don't we spend much of our time in hiding our faults and failings from others? Matthew was

learning early that being with Jesus meant being open. For many, this lesson takes a lifetime to learn.

Gospel-writer

Many believe that Matthew the tax-collector was also the writer of the Gospel that bears his name. He was a Jew from Capernaum, and he wrote for his fellow countrymen – yet he of all the evangelists gives us the story of the first Gentile visitors to Jesus, the Magi.

It's arguably the most 'structured' of the Gospels, which suggests that Matthew was competent with his pen, and determined to present a Gospel that could form the basis of teaching in the Church. A large collection of Jesus' sayings is brought together to form the 'Sermon on the Mount'. (In Luke, by comparison, much of this material is replicated, suggesting that both Matthew and Luke were using a common source which scholars call 'Q' (*Quelle*) but Luke has scattered his material hither and yon in his Gospel.) Matthew also emphasizes Jesus' teaching on bringing back recalcitrants to the faith – again, seemingly targetted at the organization and operation of the early Church congregations. In chapter 25, Matthew gives us the only gospel record of Jesus' parable of the sheep and the goats: teaching on our twofold mission and ministry, to our Lord and to each other.

Next to nothing is known of Matthew following the ascension of Jesus, though one tradition has it that he suffered martyrdom in Ethiopia.

Early testimony

Matthew is mentioned in several apocryphal writings, including the *Gospel of the Ebionites*, the *Sophia Jesu Christi* and the *Books of Jeu*. In his mammoth *Historia Ecclesiastica*, Eusebius of Caesarea mentions that 'Matthew composed in the Hebrew tongue' the Gospel which has been consigned to him from early times and without objection being raised (*HE* III.39.16); and Irenaeus, Bishop of Lyons, declared that Matthew wrote as the first of the evangelists – a view which the Church later took up so enthusiastically that until Vatican II the Roman Catholic Church adhered to.

The call

Matthew's call gives us much hope and encouragement, that God meets us where we are, not where we are not. He doesn't wait for us to be perfect (he would be waiting for a long time), but

316

calls us to help us attain perfection in his good time. Some people declare: 'I'm not good enough to . . . become a Christian . . . take office in the Church . . . teach others the gospel . . .' God is saying: 'Don't worry, I *know* you're not good enough – but if you're willing to accept *my* goodness, let's see what we can make of you, together!'

Suggested hymns
I heard the voice of Jesus say; Make me a channel of your peace; Take my hands, and make them all thine own; Take my life, and let it be.

St Michael and All Angels   29 September
Holy War   Gen. 28.10–17; Ps. 103.19–22; Rev. 12.7–12; John 1.47–51

'And war broke out in heaven; Michael and his angels fought against the dragon. The dragon and his angels fought back, but they were defeated, and there was no longer any place for them in heaven.' Revelation 12.7–8

Between the worlds
We find Michael in the book of Daniel, assisting in the lives of God's chosen people; and here in Revelation (as well as in the little book of Jude) victorious in heavenly warfare. In the apocryphal writings, such as in these extracts from the *Apocalypse of Paul*, Michael is seen as assisting souls between the human and spiritual worlds:

> And the voice of God came and said: As this soul has not grieved me, so I shall not grieve it; as it has had compassion, so I shall have compassion on it. Let it therefore be handed over to Michael, the angel of the covenant, and let him lead it into the paradise of jubilation, that it may be there until the day of resurrection and become also a fellow-heir with all the saints . . .
>
> Again he led me where the river of milk was; and there I saw in that place all the infants whom King Herod had slain for the name of Christ, and they greeted me. And the angel said to me: All who preserve their chastity and purity, when they come forth from their bodies, are handed over to Michael after they

317

have worshipped the Lord God, and they are brought to the children, and they greet them, saying: 'You are our brothers and friends and associates.' Among them they will inherit the promises of God . . .

All those who have given hospitality to strangers, when they come forth from the world, first worship the Lord God and are handed over to Michael and by this route are led into the city, and all the righteous greet them as sons and brothers and say to them: 'Because you have kept humanity and hospitality for strangers, come, receive an inheritance in the city of our God.' . . .

And after that I saw heaven opened and the archangel Michael coming down from heaven, and with him the whole host of angels, and they came to those who were placed in the punishments. And seeing him they cried out again with tears, and said: 'Have mercy on us, archangel Michael have mercy us and on the human race, for because of your prayers the earth continues. We have now seen the judgement and known the Son of God.' . . .

And Michael answered and said: 'Listen when Michael speaks: It is I who stand in the Presence of God every hour [Dan. 12.1]. As the Lord lives, in whose presence I stand, for one day or one night I do not cease from praying continually for the human race, and I pray for those who are (still) on earth . . . and I continue to pray until the earth bring forth its fruit; and I say that if anyone has done even only a little good I will strive for him and protect him until he escapes the judgement of punishments. Where are your prayers? Where is your repentance?'

Apocalypse of Paul 14, 26, 27, 43

It's a measure of the careful forward planning of the Almighty, that he has provided – as our introduction to paradise – an archangel mighty enough to conquer the dragon in heaven, yet gentle and loving enough to welcome a soul who has come through the rigours of Christian life on earth – not perfectly, but having done his or her best.

Suggested hymns

Angel-voices, ever singing; Jerusalem, my happy home; O what their joy and their glory must be; Ye holy angels bright.

St Francis of Assisi, Friar, Deacon, Founder of the Friars Minor 1226   4 October
What Is Good   Micah 6.6–8; Ps. 100; Gal. 6.14–18; Luke 12.22–34

'He has told you, O mortal, what is good; and what does the Lord require of you but to do justice, and to love kindness, and to walk humbly with your God?' Micah 6.8

Early wild oats
Born in Assisi in 1181, what did Francis want to do as a young man but to have a good time? His father, Pietro di Bernadone, was a successful cloth merchant, and gave his son the means to hold his own with the 'wild set' of Assisi; the favourite pastime of the young men being to ride out to skirmishes with like-minded men of rival towns. After one such engagement, Francis found himself in prison at Perugia, where he had time to reflect that there was surely more to life than fighting and being caught.

Chiesa San Damiano
Soon after his release, he was praying in the woebegone Church of San Damiano, when the crucifix over the altar seemed to say, 'Francis, rebuild my church!' Fired with enthusiasm, Francis raced home, extracted a bale of fine scarlet cloth from his father's stock, sold it and ran back to give the priest of San Damiano the money for church repairs. An enraged Pietro took his son to court, where the presiding bishop ordered Francis to repay his father. 'From today, my only Father is God,' cried Francis – and embraced the lady he was to court for the rest of his life, Lady Poverty.

For love of his Lord
In a rough brown robe, Francis returned the money to Pietro, and set about rebuilding San Damiano with his bare hands. Each evening he would go down to Assisi to beg his food – and soon other men began to join him. They lived on the mountain in absolute poverty, Francis maintaining that to have a house would mean needing furniture, and furniture meant books, and books meant possessions . . .

Mission to the East

Fired with a desire to evangelize the Muslims, Francis journeyed to the Holy Land. The Crusades were at this time in full swing, and the little man in the brown robe stood out among the colourful knights, and – more out of curiosity than anything else – was granted an audience with the Sultan Malek al-Kamil at Damietta in Egypt. The meeting was friendly: Francis was treated with kindly respect throughout his mission, but conversions were hard to come by.

Friars Minor

Back home in Italy, the Pope had officially sanctioned Francis' Order of Friars Minor. Soon, however, as the numbers increased, so did the modifications to Francis' original austerities, and he eventually relinquished the leadership at what he saw as a compromise of ideals. All his life he remained a loyal member of the brotherhood, and died on the evening of 3 October 1226, in the arms of Brother Bruno. Only when the brothers were preparing his body for burial did they discover his stigmata, which Francis had done his best to conceal for the previous two years.

A dedicated life, and one whose work is continued today, of 'the little poor man' (*Il poverello*), who, loving poverty, made many rich.

Suggested hymns

All creatures of our God and King; All things bright and beautiful; Be thou my vision; Make me a channel of your peace.

St Luke the Evangelist   18 October

Only Luke   Isa. 35.3–6 or Acts 16.6–12a; Ps. 147.1–7; 2 Tim. 4.5–17; Luke 10.1–9

'Do your best to come to me soon, for Demas, in love with this present world, has deserted me and gone to Thessalonica; Crescens has gone to Galatia, Titus to Dalmatia. Only Luke is with me. Get Mark and bring him with you, for he is useful in my ministry.' 2 Timothy 4.9–11

Just the two of us

This is Paul at his most human, practical and down-to-earth: Timothy, look who's left me – all going on missions (except

Demas), doing great work – but there's just the two of us left to carry on here: *only Luke is with me.*

Good for Luke! He was the right sort of friend to have, who would not desert the aged Paul. They'd been through fire and water together, and a good pal does not walk out on his friend.

The doctor on the team

Luke, the Greek physician, seems to have joined the mission team in Troas, around the time of the *cri de coeur* from Macedonia (Acts 16.9f.), when the 'we passages' in Acts begin. Within the past deade, our knowledge of this staunch ally has been dramatically increased, with the discovery in 1998 of a lead casket inscribed 'S.L.Evang.', in the Santa Giustina basilica, Padua. A search had been instituted, following a request from the Metropolitan Archbishop Hieronymos, of Ephesus, to Mgr Antoni Mattiazzo of Padua, for the return of 'some of the holy relics of St Luke, which we believe are at Padua, so that we can re-consecrate them in the land of his birth'. The Vatican entered into the spirit of the thing, by also arranging the transfer of a skull in St Vitus's Cathedral, Prague – which had long been venerated as being that of Luke. A detailed examination by pathologists at Padua University found that 'the skull brought from Prague ... matches ... the skeleton exactly' (*The Times*, 3 February 1999).

Physiology of Luke

From the relics, the scientists posited that Luke was small of stature, stockily built with a well-formed, long face and cranial structure. It's likely that he died in his eighties, of natural causes including pulmonary emphysema – and also that he suffered from arthritis and a bad back: complaints worsened if not induced by his travels on Paul's mission team.

Writer/recorder

Whether or not 'Theophilus', to whom Luke addresses his Gospel and Acts, was a real person, Luke comes over as a methodical writer/ recorder, determined to get the news of Christ and the early Church set down accurately. He is keen for his writings to be checked out, grounding them in verifiable places and during the time of verifiable officials and rulers, all of which gives us confidence in his work. He is dealing with amazing people and amazing happenings. But his message is: this is *what* happened, and *why* it happened. I don't know *how* some of it happened – but believe it, anyway!

And surely no doctor's report has ever been more wonderful to receive and believe!

Suggested hymns
Christ, who once amongst us; Tell out, my soul, the greatness of the Lord; Thine arm, O Lord, in days of old; We have a gospel to proclaim.

SS Simon and Jude, Apostles   28 October
Each for All   Isa. 28.14–16; Ps. 119.89–96;
Eph. 2.19–22; John 15.17–27

'So then you are . . . citizens with the saints and also members of the household of God . . . with Christ Jesus himself as the cornerstone . . . in whom you also are built together spiritually into a dwelling-place for God.' Ephesians 2.19–22

Members of the Twelve
Nearing the end of the Church's year, is the commemoration of these two relatively unknown members of the Twelve: Simon the Canaanite zealot and Jude who was a relative of Jesus and probably the author of the little New Testament letter that bears his name. One legend has it that Simon died a natural death in Edessa, others that both were martyred in Persia (Iran). A church in Rome, having acquired their relics in the seventh century, was dedicated to them both on 28 October, since when their festival has been celebrated on this day.

Quiet witness
They may, for all we know, have had long, successful and vibrant ministries, converting many to the faith. But if history recorded these, we have yet to discover the record. Citizenship 'with the saints' doesn't depend, however, on the world's recording, but on God's; and the Almighty keeps accurate records. It doesn't matter whether our work is recognized or remembered on earth. God has his tally, and that is enough. In the great structure of Christ's Church, we all work for Christ, and each shares in God's gifts to

322

all. There is room, by the grace of God, for individuality and the exercise of unique gifts – but the benefits are for God, and to him be the glory every time. We can safely aver, with the parable of the workers in the vineyard in mind, that the mission of Simon and Jude would be as valuable in God's sight as that of Peter and Paul. God does not pay at piece-work rates, but for life's work – every piece of work we do, counts with him.

Drops of water, grains of sand?
Are we, then, like drops of water, together making little streams, bigger rivers, greater seas and oceans? Or grains of sand, swirled in their millions by the waves, and eventually compacted together into massive rocks, only for the dissecting process to begin all over again?

Most certainly not! Water drops and sand grains lose their individuality. There is nothing in the Bible to suggest a like fate for us, but everything to show that we continue in the next world to be the people we have been in this. Although Saul sinned, in asking the Witch of Endor to recall Samuel, when the prophet came he was still Samuel. On the Mount of the Transfiguration, Jesus talked with a very recognizable Moses and Elijah.

God has not taken infinite pains to create us as individuals for that beautiful creativity to last only for a few years. He works with eternity in view. If it's not in our view, it should be for, whether we like it or not, that's where we are heading – with Simon and Jude, and countless millions more.

Suggested hymns
Around the throne of God a band; For I'm building a people of power; I think when I read that sweet story of old; Jesus, stand among us.

All Saints' Day   1 November   Who from Their Labours Rest?   Rev. 7.9–17; Ps. 34.1–10; 1 John 3.1–3; Matt. 5.1–12

'They are before the throne of God, and worship him day and night within the temple, and the one who is seated on the throne will shelter them. They will hunger no more, and thirst no more; the sun will not

strike them, nor any scorching heat; for the Lamb at the centre of the throne will be their shepherd, and he will guide them to springs of the water of life, and God will wipe away every tear from their eyes.' Revelation 7.15–17

Constant worship
According to this vision of John, the saints in glory exchanged earthly labours for round-the-clock worship of God: a magnificently unfair deal! These are the saints whose example encourages us to keep on keeping on; they have overcome great trials, the like of which we may never have to face. But even more important have been their *little* victories, over *little* matters, the daily *little* challenges that can either make us spiritually stronger, or break us down in despair and grief.

Every day, depending on which calendar we are following, we commemorate one or more of these saints; but there are thousands, millions, whose names have not been recorded. Yet the God who can know everything about every saint is also concerned enough about us, to thrill with joy when we honour their memory.

No more tears
They – like us – have shed many tears during their time on earth. They have cried more than most people, loved more than many, and lived more than all. But in glory God 'will wipe away every tear from their eyes'. That is not wishful thinking, but a solemn, contractual promise from the Almighty. There won't be anything to cry about – because Satan will not be around.

Austerities
Some saints have performed feats of auterity that take one's breath away: sleeping on beds of nails; living on grass, or a meagre diet of bread and water; going without shoes in the severest of winters; immuring themselves into caves or cells for many years, or living exposed to the elements on tall pillars. With the suppression or withdrawal of bodily comforts, the spirit has grown stronger. Are we to feel guilty if such rigours don't apply to our own lives? No – remember that individual created by God, and given your name, your vocation, your mission, and your talents and opportunities. We are who we are, and not someone else. We have the gifts we've been given, and not someone else's.

But the responsibility to use our gifts to the full in God's service is our responsibility and not someone else's. Each of the saints we remember today was answerable to God for particular, individual gifts – and not someone else's.

Standing alongside
If the thought that in glory we may be standing alongside giants of the faith such as Peter, Paul, Francis or Thérèse of the Child Jesus, doesn't spur us on to show God we love him even more than to date we have been loving, what will it take?

Suggested hymns
Around the throne of God a band; For all the saints who from their labours rest; For all thy saints, a noble throng; Ten thousand times ten thousand.

Commemoration of the Faithful Departed (All Souls' Day)   2 November   These We Have Known   Lam. 3.17–26, 31–33 or Wisd. 3.1–9; Ps. 23 or 27.1–6, 16–17; Rom. 5.5–11 or 1 Peter 1.3–9; John 5.19–25 or John 6.37–40

'[Jesus said] "And this is the will of him who sent me, that I should lose nothing of all that he has given me, but raise it up on the last day. This is indeed the will of my Father, that all who see the Son and believe in him may have eternal life, and I will raise them up on the last day." '
John 6.39–40

Not of the martyrologies
These souls are not recorded in the great martyrologies. They are the saints we have known and loved in our families and our circle of friends: the saints who taught us first of Christ; who took us to church; helped us to grasp the essentials of the faith. They showed us by the example of their lives, that Jesus was their Saviour. We are the better for having known them; each day we remember them in our hearts, but today gives us the opportunity to share their memories, as in churches up and down the land their names are read out and we rejoice with the faithful militant

here on earth, that the faithful triumphant in heaven are not forgotten. We are all a year closer to reunion, and eternity is a long time to look forward to.

Treasure from the past
It's a day for remembering, and the past is always waiting, waiting to help us in the recollection: to assure us that there have been bad times, but – often with the help of those now in glory – we have been brought through every trial. There have also been joys – joys shared with our loved ones. Let us remember as many of the good times as the others. God has given us memories to link us with our loved ones, into his purposes. Often these memories have themselves given us courage to carry on – for Christ's sake, for *their* sakes.

Our legacy
And today reminds us also that, on All Souls' Days to come, others may remember us, if we have given them cause. The way we live our lives today has in some measure been shaped by those whose memories we are honouring; they, in a sense, have contributed to the memories our own lives will one day leave. The closer we draw to God, in communion with these souls, the more Christlike will our lives become. It's the divine alchemy at work – the invisible rays of glory spanning the Divide on days such as this.

But in our remembering, we cross that Divide: we see, through vast expanses of ether that seem nothing at all, the faces that never grow older, the eyes that smile into ours with the light of Christ. And why should we dim this light? These souls are not dead, but very much alive; they are the friends we know. They have not changed into other people. The only difference is that they are totally with God, while we are still on the road that leads to heaven.

Suggested hymns
A few more years shall roll; Days and moments quickly flying; In heavenly love abiding; Let saints on earth in concert sing.

A Sermon for Harvest Thanksgiving

Harvest of life   Ex. 23.16–21; Ps. 65; Rom. 8.18–25;
Matt. 6.25–34

*'[Jesus said] "Therefore I tell you, do not worry about your life, what
you will eat or what you will drink, or about your body, what you will
wear. Is not life more than food, and the body more than clothing?"*
Matthew 6.25

The visible harvest
The familiar sights and scents of harvest are a balm in themselves:
ripe apples and oranges blend with onions and cabbages, chrysan-
themums and Michaelmas daisies. May those of us fortunate
enough to worship at a 'traditional' Harvest Thanksgiving spare
a thought for those worshipping today in places where no such
beauty and bounty is to be seen. We usually forget that Harvest
Thanksgiving as we know it has only been operative for a little
more than a century-and-a-half, since the Revd Hawker of
Morwenstow, Cornwall, instituted it in 1843. It quickly became
one of the most popular services of the year – and long may it
continue.

The invisible harvest
But there is also the invisible harvest that is always being accumu-
lated; and that is much more important than the flowers, fruit and
vegetables. It's the harvest about which Jesus was teaching: the
harvest of the soul – LIFE. At times we stand in danger of putting
what we term the 'essentials' of life (food, drink, clothing) before
life itself. And while it's right that at Harvest Thanksgiving we
do give thanks to God for our material harvest, the Lord is eager
to know how we are bringing in the harvest of our lives. Are we
giving him the first fruits (i.e. the best) of our time and our talents?
Are we using his gifts in his service? If not, what are we wasting
them on? (Oh, Lord, my favourite harvest hymn is coming up in
a minute or two. I don't want to think about 'waste'!)

Why not? A third of the world is enjoying a wonderful material
harvest, while the other two-thirds is struggling to be fed, watered
and clothed. Isn't that wasting God's natural harvest gifts? If we
could get the balance right, if we could use God's spiritual gifts
as he wants us to use them and as he has planned for them to
be used, wouldn't the spiritual answer also solve the natural

problem? This topsy-turvy world is the way it is because it has got itself out of synch with God. We spend millions in sending more ironmongery into space to learn more about uninhabited worlds, while some of the inhabitants of planet earth are starving.

Double starvation
They are doubly deprived – of food, water and clothing, but also of the gospel of Christ. Christ is the bread of heaven. He can supply their food. He has the living water. He can supply their drink. And he is the Word of God. He can clothe us with a suit of armour resplendent and capable enough to confound Satan and every weapon the devil possesses.

The Lord of the harvest
We pray and sing to the 'Lord of the harvest', but, unless we make him Lord of the harvest of our lives, as well as our gardens, *next* year's Harvest Thanksgiving will still find two-thirds of the world struggling to know what we're talking about.

Suggested Hymns
Fair waved the golden corn; Lord of our life and God of our salvation; The sower went forth sowing; To thee, O Lord, our hearts we raise.

A Sermon for Remembrance Day
11 November (or transferred to 6 Nov.)
The Stand against Satan   Ezek. 37.1–14; Ps. 46;
Eph. 6.10–17; Mark 13.1–10
'Be strong in the Lord and in the strength of his power. Put on the whole armour of God, so that you may be able to stand against the wiles of the devil.' Ephesians 6.10–11

Our defence
Remembrance Day brings its tears, inevitably. And God gave us the ability to cry in this life, to release tension, but also to show how we care. A person who doesn't cry, doesn't care much about anything or anyone. In the next life, God will wipe all tears from

our eyes, because there will be no reason to cry: no war, no injuries or pain, no bereavement. There will be no Remembrance Day services either.

But as we remember today those who have fallen in war, let us also remember that this recollection is in itself a stand against Satan. The devil doesn't want us to remember: he wants the dead to be forgotten; for, in remembering, we are perpetuating love, courage, selflessness and a longing for peace. Every time we remember – every Remembrance Day service we attend – is a stand against war, and one step closer to peace. To stay away – to show we didn't care – would be to play into Satan's hands.

November comes round each year, as a defence against war and all the agony it brings. Each year, the remembrance in recalling the past is in itself a pledge to work with renewed vigour for future peace. And therefore it is good that each year the millions of poppies are bought and worn well in advance of today, as well as for some time afterwards. It is good that the wreaths remain at cenotaphs and memorials for weeks, even months, afterwards – to remind us again and again of the reason for today's remembrance. For who can look at a poppy and not remember? And who can remember, without a stiffening of the resolve to do *something* about changing war to peace?

Every little helps!
That 'something' may be as simple as turning away from a cenotaph to smile at a complete stranger. Or it may be as tremendous as getting involved in a national or international peace process. We can all do something, to see that peace takes over from war: in our hearts, our homes, our parishes, our countries, our world. If everyone put on the armour of God, as outlined in today's New Testament reading, we'd make *such a difference* – yes, even in the topsy-turvy world of today. *Our* work for peace is the best remembrance we can offer to the Lord who is the Prince of peace: the best tribute we can give, to those who we are remembering today.

Crying for the world
The fallen are helping us, with the memories of who they were, what they gave and why they did what they did. They are there, in glory now, urging us on in spirit to work for peace – really to work for it, as well as wish for it. But there is something that

they cannot do, because God will not allow it: *they can cry no longer.*

So, *we* must cry for the world: we must see the anguish, and cry for it, shed tears for it – tears which are not an end in themselves, but by the grace of God the means to a lasting peace.

How? God will show us how, if we really, really want to know.

Suggested hymns
Let there be peace on earth; O God, our help in ages past; O valiant hearts, who to your glory came; Thy kingdom come, O God.

Scripture Index

Book	Ch	v	page		Ch	v	page		Ch	v	page
Gen.	22	2	158		16	27–28	193			13	36	12
Num.	21	5	66		17	6–8	51			14	9–10	184
Josh.	1	9	70		18	18–20	197			16	10	188
Judg.	7	19	235		18	21–22	201			17	18, 29	192
1 Sam.	18	14–16	148		20	13–15	205			18	9–11	195
	21	6	152		21	32	209			19	11, 19–20	199
	24	11	156		21	43–46	213			20	32	203
	28	6–7	160		22	7–9	217			26	24–25	207
2 Sam.	2	4–5	164		22	18, 21	220	Rom.	5	2b–5	68
	7	20–21	168		24	12–14	229		5	18–19	59
	23	3–4	243		24	44	1		7	19–20	162
1 Kings	10	1	180		25	11–13	233		8	1–2	166
	18	21	7		25	40	240	1 Cor.	3	12–13	109
Ps.	50	14–15	61		26	14–15	80		11	23–24	89
Isa.	1	17	57		27	59	95	2 Cor.	5	21	55
	2	5	1		28	1–2	97	Gal.	1	11–12	41
	5	3–4	82		28	19–20	133	Eph.	1	17–18	127
	6	4–5	135	Luke	1	72	18		2	17–18	113
	42	4	35		2	20	20		5	8b–9	74
	52	9	3		8	15	144		6	19–20	70
	55	10–11	227		9	13	140	Phil.	2	1–2	29
	65	24	25		24	32	107		2	5	25
Lam.	3	21–23	78	John	1	12–13	22	Col.	1	11–12a	33
Ezek.	3	4	41		1	18	31		1	22–23	93
Dan.	6	10	105		1	35–36	39		3	15–16	72
	7	13–14	231		2	11	47		3	15–17	224
Ecclus.	48	4a, 9	53		2	30–31	102	1 Thess.	4	16	233
Matt.	1	20	14		3	17	63		5	4–6	237
	2	14–15	27		6	57–58	137	Philemon		6–7	49
	3	12	5		10	4–5	111	Heb.	1	3	37
	3	16	35		11	14–15	76		9	13–14	84
	4	16–17	43		12	20–21	85		12	1–2a	87
	7	24–25	142		14	10–11	115	1 Peter	1	8–9	45
	9	21–22	146		14	21	119	1 John	2	7–8	215
	10	8	150		17	3	125		2	22–23	211
	10	26–31	154		19	28–30	92		3	11	219
	11	4–5	10		19	41	95		4	2, 4	223
	13	24, 38–39	170		20	15, 17	99	Rev.	1	9–10a	239
	13	52	174	Acts	1	7–8	123		1	13–14, 17–18	101
	14	13–14	178		2	3–4	129		21	9–10	117
	14	31–33	182		2	19–21	131		22	2	121
	15	27–28	186		4	13	172		22	16	16
	16	16–17	189		12	5, 12	176				
					13	12	180				

Notes

....
....
....
....
....
....
....
....
....
....
....
....
....
....
....
....
....
....
....
....
....
....
....
....
....
....
....
....

Subject Index

Absolution 166
Agreement 198
Angels 17–18, 27, 61, 274
Austerity 324
Baptism 19, 36, 99, 134–5
Baptist, John 5, 10–11, 35, 39–40
Beauty 121
Bereavement 95–6, 123, 178–9, 300
Betrayal 80, 115
Blame 64
Choice, freedom of 111
Christ, divinity of 30,49
    teaching of 11
    flock of 112
    light of 44–5, 74–5, 155, 216
    love of 21
    the Gate 212
    the King 241
    the heartwarmer 108
Christian(s), character 68
    challenge of 163
    life 51
    satisfaction 279
    title of 11
    uncommon 106, 185
Christlikeness 65
Circumcision 256
Commandment, new 120
Consistency 85
Courage 172, 262, 275–6, 290
Cross, the 56, 93, 314
Differences, religious 113–15
Discernment 223
Disunity 30. 118
Encouragement 3–5, 25, 29, 33–4, 39, 42, 50–2, 71, 76–7, 88–9, 100, 288
Endurance 144, 158, 229

Enlightenment	127–9
Enthusiasm	42, 137
Eternity	138
Eucharist	
(see also Last Supper)	140–1
Expectation	1, 124
Expediency, divine	217
Faith	8–9, 20, 27, 37, 43, 45, 71, 77, 79, 84, 125, 158, 167–8, 172, 184, 221, 295, 311
versus fear	120
Fear / Fear not	33, 34, 52–3, 70–1, 120, 154, 161, 213, 219
Forgiveness	202–3, 301
Foundations	142–3
Friendship	149, 305
Gifts, diversity of	129
precious	258–9
Glory	48, 52, 54, 62, 101, 116, 235, 306
God, as master of time	7
as security	222
covenant of	19, 32, 119
dealings of	103
generosity of	206
in Christ	115
inventiveness of	231
light of	1–2, 128, 189, 243
love of	10, 23, 26, 32, 46
memory of	18
mother-love of	310
our helper	63
provision of	47–8
purpose of	13
Son of	15, 31
strength of	33
tears of	82
the Music-Maker	5
will of	147
Gospel, our	41–3
today's	173
Grace	55, 73, 204
Gratitude	62, 66–7, 72, 169
Harvest	327

Healing   146, 150, 184, 271, 285–6
Heartburn, spiritual   107
Heaven   44, 174–5
Holistic ministry   25, 59
Holy Spirit   14–15, 29, 30, 32, 41, 52, 110, 84,
                                            132, 268
        power of   130
        fire of   131
Hope   50, 69
Humility   260
Investment, God's   136
        our   136, 194
Joseph, father of Jesus   27, 28, 271–3
Joy   3, 20, 22, 33, 46, 72, 130, 144–5, 229, 284
Judas(es)   80
Justice   35–6, 64
Last Supper   89–90, 139, 140
Life, eternal   125
Light, inner   127
Love   83, 119
Loyalty   164–6
Marriage   49
Mary, mother of Jesus   15, 47, 48, 273–4, 309
Mercy   214
Miracles   200
Mission   4, 8, 14, 21, 23, 25, 33, 35, 51, 76–7, 105, 108, 151,
              188, 196–7, 225, 236, 245, 264, 287, 207
        parochial   104
Monasticism   299, 308, 319
Mother Church   72–3
Motherhood   186, 284
Naming   256
Occult   161, 200
Peacemaking   156
Persecution   82–3
Perseverance   88, 283
Poverty   11
Prayer   42, 105, 117, 169, 176–7, 187, 191
        of Jesus   167
Planning   122
Pride   180–2

Priorities	105, 109
Proclamation	171
Readiness	237
Reconciliation	115, 247
Reflection	2
Remembrance	133
Repentance	44
Repetition	155
Resurrection	46, 99, 103, 107, 192, 233
Revelation	41–3, 189–91, 263
Sabbath	239
observance	104, 152
Sacred, the	221
Sacrifice(s)	159–60
Salvation	45, 64
Satan	2, 5, 6, 9, 26, 30, 40, 41, 52, 56–7, 60, 64, 69, 89, 115, 120, 128, 148, 157, 161, 170, 208, 223, 329
Scripture(s)	28, 38, 42, 107, 215, 252, 316, 321
Secular, the	221
Seed-sowing	6–7, 171
Selection	281
Sensitivity	148
Sermons	133, 192
Sin	44–5, 56, 255
Sleep	79
Social gospel	59–9
Speaking out (for God)	39–40
Stiff-necks	251
Strangers	112
Suffering	68
Sun of Righteousness	98, 124
Teaching	134–5
Testing	76–7, 292
Transfiguration	54–5
Trust	38, 62–3, 85, 227–8, 304
Truth	92, 125–6
sober	208
Unexpected, the	210
Unity	119
Way, the	211
Wisdom	127, 250

Woe   135
Women   187
Worship   153

Notes

Notes

....
....
....
....
....
....
....
....
....
....
....
....
....
....
....
....
....
....
....
....
....
....
....
....
....
....
....

Notes

....
....
....
....
....
....
....
....
....
....
....
....
....
....
....
....
....
....
....
....
....
....
....
....
....
....
....
....
....
....
....

Notes

Notes

Notes

....
....
....
....
....
....
....
....
....
....
....
....
....
....
....
....
....
....
....
....
....
....
....
....
....

Notes